The Masters
and the
Spiritual Path

CLIMB THE HIGHEST MOUNTAIN SERIES

The Masters
and the
Spiritual Path

Mark L. Prophet · Elizabeth Clare Prophet

SUMMIT UNIVERSITY PRESS®
Corwin Springs, Montana

THE MASTERS AND THE SPIRITUAL PATH
by Mark L. Prophet and Elizabeth Clare Prophet
Copyright © 2001 by Summit University Press
All rights reserved

Parts of chapter 3, "Ascended and Unascended Masters,"
were published in Mark L. Prophet and Elizabeth Clare Prophet,
Foundations of the Path (Corwin Springs, Mont.: Summit
University Press, 1999).

For information, contact Summit University Press,
PO Box 5000, Corwin Springs, MT 59030-5000.
Telephone: 1-800-245-5445 or 406-848-9500.
Web site: www.summituniversitypress.com
E-mail: info@summituniversitypress.com

Library of Congress Catalog Card Number: 00-111767
ISBN: 0-922729-64-6

SUMMIT UNIVERSITY ❧ PRESS®

Cover: "Krishna—Spring in Kulu," a painting by Nicholas Roerich.
Nicholas Roerich Museum, New York, N.Y. Used by permission.

06   05   04   03   02   01   6   5   4   3   2   1

To all who look for salvation in this age,
to all who know that the hour is come
when the true worshipers shall worship
the Father-Mother God in Spirit and in Truth,
to all who would climb the highest mountain,
we dedicate this volume as the next step.

Contents

2 · The Ascension   79

4 · Hierarchy   177

Figures

Note: Because gender-neutral language can be cumbersome and at times confusing, we use the pronouns *he* and *him* to refer to God or to the individual and *man* or *mankind* to refer to people in general. We use these terms for readability and consistency, and they are not intended to exclude women or the feminine aspect of the Godhead. God is both masculine and feminine. We do, however, use the pronouns *she* and *her* to refer to the soul because each soul, whether housed in a male or a female body, is the feminine counterpart of the masculine Spirit.

Introduction

IN THE BEGINNING, GOD PROVIDED THE path of initiation for the soul's evolution in time and space. He intended the soul to return to Spirit and live forever in the consciousness of God as an individualization of the God Flame.

Mankind's failure to follow the Path has necessitated the coming of teachers, avatars, prophets and Messengers of the LORD. In East and West they have come, to deliver the message of salvation (self-elevation) and self-realization. They have outlined the methods whereby each individual by free will could choose once again to be and to become the Real Self.

In this volume of the *Climb the Highest Mountain* series, we examine teachings of the Masters of the Great White Brotherhood,* both ascended and unascended. These teachings

---

*The Great White Brotherhood is a spiritual order of saints and adepts of every race, culture and religion. These Masters have transcended the cycles of karma and rebirth and reunited with the Spirit of the living God. The word "white" refers to the aura or halo of white light that surrounds them. For definitions of terms, see the glossary.

provide the opportunity for man and woman to return to the state of grace, to reenter the path of initiation, and to know the Masters as the very personal Gurus who will reintroduce the soul to her own Real Self, the Christ Self.

This Christ Self then becomes the teacher, the initiator, the integrator, the interpreter of the I AM THAT I AM, the individualized God Flame, the sphere of cosmic consciousness containing the All of the Spirit/Matter cosmos for and on behalf of the microcosm, man.

In the East four types of yoga have been evolved for the redemption of the four lower bodies and the mastery of the four elements. In the West the fourteen stations of the cross (balancing the seven rays in Spirit and in Matter) are the counterpart of the Eightfold Path of the Buddha—the Buddha who came to illustrate the eighth ray as the law of integration, the harmonizing of the four elements through the seven rays.

The paths that have been evolved in East and West are for the selfsame purpose of placing the hand of the soul in the hand of the Christ Self. For only thus can the Way be illumined by right knowledge, right aspiration, right speech, right behavior, right livelihood, right effort, right mindfulness and right absorption.

Chapter 1 of this volume, "The Highest Yoga," is concerned with you and God—and how the you that you are can become the God that you are. It illustrates the paths of soul reunion and soul liberation out of East and West. These paths have been evolved by the ascended and unascended masters of the Great White Brotherhood, in order that man and woman might overcome their wrong choices.

Once the soul has left behind the many paths of self-expression for the one Path above the many—the union of the self with the Self that is God—she* is ready to fulfill the highest

---

*The soul is the feminine counterpart of the masculine Spirit, and thus is referred to as "she."

yoga through the initiations of the sacred fire. Now she is ready to come under the tutelage of the Ascended Masters of the Great White Brotherhood, who have risen from the ranks of every religious discipline and merged with the Eternal One in the ritual of the ascension.

On the path of the ascension, the alchemical fires of the Holy Spirit draw all devotees of the flame to the goal of the One. Here all initiations converge in the one Guru, the Christ Self, in one Law, the I AM THAT I AM, in one Teaching, the science of Love that releases the soul to reunite with the one Source, the one Spirit.

In chapter 2, we discuss the ascension as the highest attainment on the highest path. It is the path that the disciple of East and West enters only when he or she has mastered the fundamentals of the laws of God taught by all of the world's great teachers.

The path of the ascension is a spiral that rises from the base of the pyramid of the Upanishads, the Vedas, the Gita, the oral transmission of the teachings of the great Indian sages, of Gautama Buddha, the Lord Shankarāchārya, the Lord Krishna, and the numberless nameless ones who have perpetuated the law of ancient Lemuria in Sanskrit mantras, mudras, meditations and modes of spiritual self-immolation.

The path of the ascension is built upon the Ten Commandments, the laws of Moses and Mohammed, of the prophets of Israel and the true priests of the sacred fire who have descended from the order of Melchizedek, king of Salem and priest of the most high God, and from Zarathustra.

The neophyte who would enter the Ascension Temple for intensive training may do so only when he has accepted his potential to become the Christ—rather than idolizing the Christ Jesus while sustaining his own sinful sense of sin. Jesus' example, his Sermon on the Mount, and his parables illustrate the essence of love and honor. Only when the science of love and honor as the basis of man's relationship with God and his fellowman is defined within the soul by the flame of the Holy Spirit are man and woman free to choose to enter the path of initiation that is the path of the ascension.

Chapter 3 is devoted to the ascended and unascended masters. Many souls there are among mankind who require a teacher in this age of cycles turning. And there is a specific Guru to meet the specific needs of the chela who is ready to be chela.

The ascended and unascended masters are the Gurus of the age. They are the living Masters. Each one confirms with Jesus the blessed bond of love that eternally ties the Master to his disciples, the Guru to the chela: "My sheep know my voice." Only the real Gurus of East and West, ascended and unascended, can declare unto their chelas:

> I am the door: by me if any man enter in, he shall be saved, and shall go in and out, and find pasture....
>
> I am the good shepherd, and know my sheep, and am known of mine....
>
> My sheep hear my voice, and I know them, and they follow me:
>
> And I give unto them eternal life; and they shall never perish, neither shall any man pluck them out of my hand.
>
> My Father, which gave them me, is greater than all; and no man is able to pluck them out of my Father's hand.[1]

For every Ascended Master Guru there are thousands of chelas scattered as seeds of self-awareness among mankind. If you number among them, you will know your Master's voice. You will not heed the voice of the stranger nor follow him. But when you hear your Master's voice call you, you will come and you will wait upon the Lord and upon the word of the Lord, understanding that the authority of the teacher lies in the fact that he has not only become the teaching but he ensouls it. He endows it with his life, his very personal, special individualization of the God Flame—making practical in the moments of time and space the teaching that has been preserved in written and unwritten form for thousands of years.

Thus both the Law and the Lawgiver are the necessary components of the path of initiation. You need the teaching but you also need the teacher to personify that teaching, to be the great example in your life, to be the point of contact with reality, to stand before you as the shining one who declares, "Lo, I AM. And because I AM, you—my son, my daughter—can also become all that I AM."

Chapter 4 contains a revelation of hierarchy that is as heaven-shattering as the discovery and splitting of the atom was earth-shattering. In fact they are one and the same mystery, for Matter is nothing less than the stepping-down of Spirit.

Energy moves in particles, particles of substance, and the atom is the simplest way to diagram that movement of energy in our present state of evolution. In this chapter, we derive many spiritual understandings from the study of the atom. If science evolves to the point where we see energy as an entirely different diagram, it won't make the diagram of the atom untrue. The principles are the same. There are sun centers because this is the pattern through all creation. There's a white fire core, the focal point of matter. And there is space.

Atoms become whole through uniting with other atoms into molecules. It comes right back to the brotherhood of man and the Fatherhood of God. God makes us incomplete so we have to learn the flow of love. And that flow of love between us all makes the one grand molecule of God's Body on earth.

The Masters and the Spiritual Path

As Saint Germain released this information, he said: "It is time that man should truly understand his environment, that through this knowledge, religion and science might become pillars in the temple of the golden-age civilization, equal in right and authority, one complementing the other, two halves of the spectrum of human knowledge, both receiving the inspiration of the Christ.

"For science comes down to man from the Mother aspect of God, and religion from the Father aspect. The Christ, as the Mediator between the two, brings forth those inspirations and revelations that lead men of empirical faith and intuitive reason onward in their quest for greater and greater knowledge of our expanding universe."

The scientific mind can be the most religious mind upon the planet, when it is imbued with the Holy Spirit. Without the awareness of the flame, the entire cosmos becomes a mechanical, a physical, a chemical manifestation devoid of meaning.

This chapter explains the relationship between the material and the spiritual universe. God is a single being with the infinite capacity to be himself or herself anywhere, any time. For many centuries, the object of mankind's worship has been one God, one universal Presence. Yet wherever God is in the universe, he individualizes himself for the purposes of creative expansion. For the very nature of the Infinite is to transcend itself.

Thus God has manifestations of himself throughout cosmos. We call these expressions of God "hierarchy."

Hierarchy is the Body of God throughout cosmos, the entire evolution of lifewaves ascended and unascended—Cosmic Beings, Elohim, Archangels, angels, spirits of nature, and the entire evolution of mankind.

You are a part of hierarchy. You are a link in the chain of Being that goes all the way back to the center of the cosmos, beyond our galaxy, beyond millions of galaxies to the very

Hub of Life. That chain, link by link, is forged of individualities whom God has created to externalize his Self-awareness in the plane of Matter. You depend upon those who are higher, who are above you in the arch of Being. And those who are below you depend upon you.

The message of the Great White Brotherhood is simply this: You are hierarchy. You count. You count as the supreme manifestation of God. You must count yourself not as a human being, but as a flame—for it is the individualization of that flame through your soul that makes you unique.

In this age of Aquarius, the torch is passed.
The torch is passed to you, if you will accept it.

Mark L. Prophet

Elizabeth Clare Prophet

MARK L. PROPHET AND ELIZABETH CLARE PROPHET
Messengers for the Great White Brotherhood

Chapter 1

The Highest Yoga: You and God

"I and my Father are one."

JESUS

The Highest Yoga: You and God

T HE SANSKRIT TERM *YOGA* MEANS "divine union," or the union of you and God—hence "yo-Ga." Many practices foreign to the Western world are entered into by the Eastern seeker for union with the Higher Self. Some of these practices demand stern disciplines; in fact, they may be considered austere by Westerners.

What many in the West think of as yoga is hatha yoga, which is a system of physical practices that allows the control of breath and bodily functions. This form of yoga is only one of many yogas taught in the East.

When practiced as an end in itself, hatha yoga can actually be a distraction from the path of God-realization, or union with God. But the Ascended Master Chananda, chief of the Indian Council, recommends hatha yoga as "an appropriate sequence of the exercise of the physical body for the interaction with the spiritual bodies and the chakras.... It is not a physical exercise for the exercise of the physical body. It is divine movement for the release of light that is even locked in your physical cells and atoms, in your very physical heart. Releasing that light transmutes toxins, fatigue and opposition to your victory. And therefore, not endless hours but a period of meditation and concentration combined with these yoga postures daily will reap much good. It will give you a surcease from the stress of bearing the burden of world karma and the burden of that certain type of chaotic energy which is uniquely Western in its vibration, emanating from the mass consciousness of uncontrolled feeling bodies and the wanton and reckless misuse of the mental body.

"This path is something that you can take up and yet not be deterred from your regular activity of service. We desire to see one-pointedness and discipline rise from the base of the physical pyramid and ascend to the crown. Many of you have pursued the discipline from spiritual levels, drawing forth the light of the Mighty I AM Presence down into the heart and into the lower vehicles. And this is as it should be, as the path of the Father is the descending light and the path of the Mother is the ascending light. Thus, we build from that foundation."[1]

Yoga is a method of freeing the light that is within us. The Ascended Masters call this light the sacred fire. This light, also called the Kundalini or the Goddess Kundalini, is coiled at the base of the spine. It stays there until we release it and allow it to flow up through the seven spiritual centers called chakras, located along the spine. According to Hindu tradition, when the light (the sacred fire) reaches the seventh or crown chakra, Atman becomes one with Brahman* and the soul attains enlightenment.

---

*Brahman is the eternal, absolute Being, absolute consciousness and absolute bliss. Brahman is the Self of all living beings. Brahman is the creator, the preserver, the destroyer or transformer, of all things.

In the Bhagavad Gita, Krishna says: "Brahman is that which is immutable, and independent of any cause but Itself. When we consider Brahman as lodged within the individual being, we call Him the Atman."[2]

Atman, as used in the Upanishads, means the divine spark or indwelling

There are indeed benefits to be conveyed to soul and body through the various systems of yoga that may be pursued under the direction of qualified instructors throughout the world. For all systems ultimately lead to what we have termed the highest yoga.

The practice of the highest yoga brings about the closest union that can take place between God and man. In the realization of this union, there is no longer any consciousness of the self being outside of God. Man finds himself so completely one with God that when he affirms "I AM that I AM," he makes the transition in consciousness from the awareness that "God in me is All-in-all" to the sublime recognition that "I AM All-in-all in God" ("I include all things in the allness of God that I AM").

In addition, the practice of the highest yoga can increase the power of transmutation in one's world. For as the essence of God is drawn into the being of man, it begins to transform man's very nature into the divine likeness. This takes place as the supplicant actively calls into manifestation those spiritual powers that are available to him through the divine seed that the Almighty has implanted within his consciousness.

"Take My Yoke upon You"

The word *yoga* has the same root as the English word "yoke." Thus yoga can be understood to be a method of spiritual union. Jesus said, "Take my yoke upon you and learn of me;...for my yoke is easy and my burden is light."[3] Perhaps he was really saying, "Take my yoga upon you." For Jesus had

God. It is the imperishable, undecaying core of man. *Atman* is a Sanskrit term meaning "breath." Most Western scholars translate Atman erroneously as "soul." It should really be translated as "Spirit," "God Self" or "the divine spark." Atman is identical with Brahman.

a yoga. He followed a specific discipline, in which he was trained in his travels in the East.

Tibetan manuscripts say that Jesus left Palestine for India at age thirteen, traveling with a merchant caravan.[4] There he studied under the white priests of Brahma, from whom he learned to teach the scriptures, heal the sick and cast out evil spirits. According to tradition, he went to Nepal, passed through Tibet and Afghanistan, and returned to Palestine at the age of twenty-nine to take up his mission there.

The fact that Jesus traveled in the East tells us that he is not confined to Christian doctrine and dogma. His teachings as recorded in the New Testament are compatible with karma, reincarnation and other Eastern concepts.[5]

The history of Jesus' travels also reminds us that he was a man like the rest of us. Even though he had been the Christ for long centuries, he had to learn and put on the fullness of his Christhood. As a teenager, he had to study and submit himself to the great gurus. In India he earned his doctorate and more. He came as a student, not a teacher—and yet he was welcomed in the East as the Enlightened One he was.

Those in the East who practice yoga may develop special powers called siddhis. These include many of the miraculous feats we have heard of in the West: knowledge of the past and future, knowledge of past lives, great strength, walking on water, flying, bilocation, mastery of the elements, the ability to surround oneself with a blaze of light, and the ability to choose the time of one's death. Some of these seemingly miraculous abilities were demonstrated by Jesus and by some modern Christian saints such as Padre Pio.

But the siddhis are not the goal. In fact, it is the supreme test of the yogi to give them up. Patanjali in his classic Yoga Sutras (written in the second century B.C.) refers to these supernatural powers as "obstacles to samadhi. . . . By giving up even these powers, the seed of evil is destroyed and liberation follows."[6] Jesus demonstrated this when he successfully passed the three tests of Satan in the wilderness.[7]

You can be a yogi whether or not you practice any kind of physical yoga. You are a yogi when you take upon yourself the yoke of Jesus Christ, which is light and which is easy. You are a yogi under the Ascended Masters, you are a yogi as you perfect the science of the spoken Word.

The Four Principal Yogas: Methods of Spiritual Union

In order to fully understand the highest yoga, we must be aware of the various forms of yoga as they have been practiced throughout the centuries by devotees of the Divine Mother.

There are four principal yogas: jnana yoga, the path of union with God through knowledge; bhakti yoga, the path of love and devotion; karma yoga, the path of selfless work; and raja yoga, the path of concentration and meditation. These four yogas can be placed in the four quadrants of the Cosmic Clock—jnana yoga in the mental quadrant, bhakti yoga in the emotional quadrant, karma yoga in the physical quadrant and raja yoga in the etheric quadrant.[8] (See figure 1.)

All four yogas require basic morality, including truthfulness, continence, cleanliness and harmlessness toward life. Different types of people are suited to different types of yoga, but that doesn't mean they must practice only one kind of yoga.

In fact, Hinduism encourages us to test all four of the yogas as alternate pathways to God. They are not mutually exclusive, because no person is solely reflective, emotional, active or experimental. Different occasions call for different responses. So you can test the four and take what suits your need.

FIGURE 1: The four principal yogas in the quadrants of the Cosmic Clock.

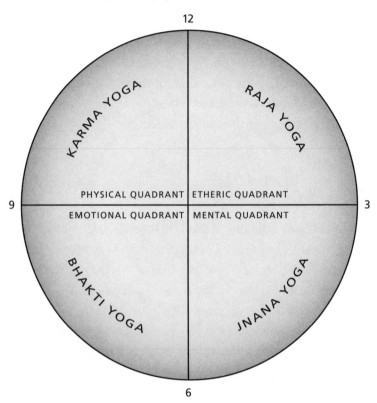

The First Principal Yoga:
Jnana Yoga

Jnana yoga is best suited to the contemplative or monastic person; it entails union with God through the dissolution of ignorance. Knowledge, of course, begins with self-knowledge. The jnana yogi seeks knowledge not only through study but through direct experience of God. Jnana yoga is also the path of discrimination between the real and the unreal. It falls in the second quadrant of the Cosmic Clock, the mental quadrant.

Shankara, the great ninth-century Hindu saint and scholar, writes in the voice of the guru advising the disciple: "It is through the touch of ignorance that you, who are the supreme self, find yourself under the bondage of the non-self, whence alone proceeds the round of births and deaths. The fire of knowledge, kindled by discrimination between the self and non-self, consumes ignorance with its effects."[9]

The guru first instructs his pupil in the four great Vedic statements.[10] The first is "Tat Tvam Asi" ("That thou art"), which means "Brahman thou art," "Thou art made in the image and likeness of Brahman." This statement can be placed in the etheric body, the first quadrant of the Cosmic Clock.

The second statement is "Aham Brahmāsmi" ("I AM Brahman"). This is the affirmation of the conscious identification with the Great God Self—Brahman. This statement belongs in the mental body, the second quadrant of the Clock.

The third affirmation is "Ayam Ātma Brahma" ("This Self is Brahman"). This Self is not the self of lesser desires. This Self is consumed by the all-consuming desire to be Brahman and to know the Self as Brahman. This desire is the spiritual fire that consumes all lesser desires, leaving the soul draped and drenched in only one desire, the desire to be Brahman. This statement is tied to the desire body, the third quadrant of the Clock.

The fourth statement is "Prajnānam Brahma" ("Consciousness is Brahman"). This mantra is the affirmation that all physical consciousness is Brahman. It delivers us from the agitation of the five senses, from the temptations of the flesh. It guards the temple of man as the temple of Brahman.

The fourth statement applies to the physical body, the fourth quadrant of the Clock. When the physical houses the LORD, then the desire body, the mental body and the etheric body follow. And the four sides of the pyramid mirror the flame of Brahman on the central altar of the King's Chamber.

After the pupil has learned these affirmations and embodied them, the guru instructs his pupil to meditate on his real nature. "That which is...devoid of name and form,...that which is infinite and indestructible; that which is supreme, eternal, and undying; that which is taintless—that Brahman art thou. Meditate on this in thy mind."[11]

Through this meditation, the disciple frees himself of the habits that bind him to the world. Piece by piece, he separates the real parts of himself from the unreal, like cream from milk.

"The student next devotes himself to meditation on Brahman... [until] there arises within him a mental state which makes him feel that he is Brahman.... With the deepening of meditation, the mind, which is a manifestation of ignorance and a form of matter, is destroyed, and... the Brahman reflected in the mind is absorbed in the Supreme Brahman.... This unity, indescribable in words, is known only to him who has experienced it."[12]

This mystical union does not mean that the yogi loses his capacity to think or to exist. "The mind is destroyed" means that the lower mind is gradually displaced because the mind of the yogi is one with the Mind of God, which is infinite in capacity. More and more of the Mind of God is in him, and less and less of the lesser mind.

Krishna has this to say about jnana yoga: "When wisdom is thine, Arjuna, never more shalt thou be in confusion; for thou shalt see all things in thy heart, and thou shalt see thy heart in me."[13]

The Second Principal Yoga: Bhakti Yoga

Bhakti yoga is the yoga of divine love. It falls on the six o'clock line of the Cosmic Clock, in the desire quadrant. It is considered to be the easiest of all yogas because it does not tell us to give up our passions, only to turn them toward God. "[The devotee] is asked to feel passionate desire to commune with God, to feel angry with himself for not making spiritual progress, to feel greedy for more spiritual experiences.... Bhakti-yoga does not say, 'Give [it] up'; it only says, 'Love; love the highest,' and anything that is lower will naturally drop away."[14]

Bhakti yogis practice devotion to God through devotional music, dance and constant repetition of his name. They often worship God in his incarnations. For example, Hindus believe that Vishnu has incarnated nine times as a God-man, an avatar. Worship of his incarnations as Krishna and Rama is very popular in India.

Bhakti yoga allows us to divert our desire for any human relationship into a relationship with God. And even when we have a human relationship, we are loving God through that person. We can choose the form that best suits our psychology and needs. We can worship God as father, mother, master, child, friend or lover.

Padma Sambhava, who in his final embodiment as a Tibetan master taught a form of yoga called guru yoga, says: "You can empower yourself by mirroring God within your soul. Entering into the path of bhakti yoga, the path of personal devotion to the Guru, is one way to do this. As you give your devotions, bow to your Gurus as they appear before you in your mind's eye."[15]

Bhakti yoga is a way of endearing yourself to God. As you form an attachment to God, God forms an attachment to you. And when he has tried and tested your soul and put you through the Refiner's fire, he in his good time extends to you his grace.

The Third Principal Yoga: Karma Yoga

Most people are not suited to a life of meditation and contemplation. They feel pulled to be active in the world, to pursue a career, raise a family, develop a skill or help others. Karma yoga falls on the nine o'clock line of the Cosmic Clock, the physical quadrant. It is the path to salvation for those who are suited to action.

The Sanskrit word *karma* is derived from the verb *kri,* meaning "to act." An action of any kind is karma, and every action is followed by a reaction.

Through his meditation and worship, the great bhakti yogi Ramakrishna achieved complete identification with the object of his devotion, the Divine Mother. He identified with her so completely that he would decorate his own body with flowers and sandalwood paste, instead of decorating her statue.

It is possible to reach great heights of spirituality (as did Ramakrishna) but leave undone the one thing that must be accomplished: the full balancing of karma. Through exercises and devotion, you can achieve exalted states of consciousness—it's like climbing a ladder. But by and by, you must climb down the ladder, take up the path of karma yoga, roll up your sleeves, go to work and balance your karma.

As Krishna explains in the Bhavagad Gita, "It is not right to leave undone the holy work which ought to be done. Such a surrender of action would be a delusion of darkness. And he who abandons his duty because he has fear of pain, his surrender is...impure, and in truth he has no reward.

"But he who does holy work, Arjuna, because it ought to be done, and surrenders selfishness and thought of reward [or praise], his work is pure, and is peace. This man sees and has no doubts: he surrenders, he is pure and has peace. Work, pleasant or painful, is for him joy.

"For there is no man on earth who can fully renounce living work, but he who renounces the reward of his work is in truth a man of renunciation. When work is done for a reward, the work brings pleasure, or pain, or both, in its time; but when a man does work in Eternity, then Eternity is his reward."[16]

If we work for personal gain and ego gratification, we are attaching ourselves to this world and to the fruits of our actions. If we work for the good of others or to the glory of God, we are liberating ourselves from past karmas.

It is a dangerous situation when people leave off the service of God and his work for meditation, contemplation and other spiritual activities. They have not learned that the work of the heart, head and hand is a chalice for true meditation, contemplation and contact with God.

The path of karma yoga shows us how to be in the world but not of the world. It shows how we can stop digging ourselves deeper into the mire of the human ego and instead work toward becoming a pure crystal through which the Atman can shine unobstructed.

Karma yogis must follow basic moral rules, never think evil thoughts, control their desires and passions, and never harm anyone mentally or physically. The karma yogi must never do work out of selfishness or feeling that he is making a sacrifice or a great effort. Krishna says that such work is impure. We must use the work to become detached from the world.

Salvation: By Works or by Grace?

Salvation is not automatic. We don't attain enlightenment simply by following the scriptures from A to Z. In the end, Hinduism teaches that salvation can be achieved only through grace. The grace of the Divine Lover is bestowed upon the lover. We can yearn for God but we can never attain him unless by his grace he gives us that contact.

Some people become truly angry at God because they do all the perfunctory things, all the ritualistic things demanded by an orthodox religion, and God does not come to them. Or they may become angry for a lifetime or more because God has taken a loved one in an untimely death. In succeeding lifetimes this anger against God is suppressed. It is so deep that they have no recollection or memory of it, and yet they carry this profound anger in the unconscious.

The Katha Upanishad says: "This Atman cannot be attained by the study of the Vedas, or by intelligence, or by much hearing of sacred books. It is attained by him alone whom It chooses."[17]

As Jesus said to his disciples, "Ye have not chosen me, but I have chosen you."[18] In the final analysis, God has to choose us. He has to choose to bend down and pick us up as little orphans on the side of the road and take us to his heart. When we wait on the LORD and love him and fulfill his requirements, he does ultimately extend us his grace. But he doesn't have to.

The Masters teach that we must work hard to work the works of God, but no matter how much work we do, we can never purchase our salvation. We can never really pay for or earn our ascension, because it's an incomparable gift. But in bestowing that gift, God measures our works. If our works are valid and fruitful and measure up to the standards of discipline, then God by his grace will give us our ascension. Then we realize that this ascension was not won by anything we did— but had we not done what we did, we would not have had that forcefield, that momentum whereby God could judge us worthy of his gift.

So the Ascended Master view of faith and works is that faith alone is not sufficient—you have to have the works. But we don't want to feel that our works are getting us to our ascension because then we will have spiritual pride. So, that fine attitude of humility (working the works of God but being nonattached) is where you step from selfishness to selflessness. It's something you have to feel in your heart.

The Fourth Principal Yoga: Raja Yoga

The fourth path to the goal, the royal road to integration, is through the white light in the etheric body. This path is the integration of all factors of the consciousness of the four lower bodies in the divine blueprint. It falls on the twelve o'clock line of the Cosmic Clock. It is raja yoga, the yoga of meditation and the control of the mind.

The Ascended Masters encourage our study of raja yoga. "We have need of those who see the path of Christhood as one of experiment," says Lady Master Leto, "experiment with the energies of self, as on the path of raja yoga, the path that is the integration of all of the yogas that mankind have known and all of the asanas, all of the meditations. It is the integration of the God Flame, the flame of Spirit within the crucible of Mater. . . .

"This is science. It is the science of the inner man becoming the manifestation of God. I desire that you should prove the way of the Christ and the Buddha scientifically, for it is Law. It can be demonstrated. It is physics. It is chemistry. It is psychology. It is beyond the senses and yet provable. It is intangible, yet tangible."[19]

Raja yoga has eight stages (also called parts or limbs). The first stage is abstention from evil-doing. There are five abstinences: non-violence, truthfulness, non-stealing, chastity and non-possession. This includes refraining from possessing whatever contributes to the enjoyment of the senses. The goal of the yogi is to obtain enlightenment through concentration. Distractions in the form of possessions take him away from that end.

The second stage of raja yoga is the five observances: purity, contentment, austerity, study of the scriptures, and the constant thought of divinity.

The third stage of raja yoga is the bodily postures, the asanas of hatha yoga. There are eighty-four postures, which help to strengthen the body and stabilize the mind. Thus hatha yoga has been called "the ladder to raja yoga."[20] According to Patanjali, "Posture becomes firm and relaxed through control of the natural tendencies of the body, and through meditation on the Infinite."[21]

The fourth stage of raja yoga is breath control, or pranayama. Patanjali describes pranayama as "stopping the motions of inhalation and exhalation. The breath may be stopped externally, or internally, or checked in mid-motion, and regulated according to place, time and a fixed number of moments, so that the stoppage is either protracted or brief."[22] The purpose of pranayama is to control the mind. It also purifies the body and promotes longevity.

The fifth stage of raja yoga is withdrawal of the senses from sense objects. The yogi who has faithfully practiced the first five stages should now be able to focus the mind.

But even raja yoga does not offer the violet flame. When you use the violet flame all the meandering and restlessness of the mind is transmuted, and you don't have to go on forever fighting distractions. You are gradually purifying the mental body. So the Mind of Christ is within that mental body, and there is a flow of concentration in contemplation.

The sixth stage of raja yoga is concentration on one object, and the seventh stage is meditation or contemplation: merging with the object. The yogi should first choose an object or form to contemplate, such as the image of a deity or his guru. Or he can fix the mind upon the inner light. Patanjali tells us that we can fix our minds upon "any divine form or symbol that appeals to [us] as good."[23] The yogi can move from contemplating this form to contemplating formlessness.

The eighth stage of raja yoga is identification or absorption in the Atman, the state called *samadhi*. Patanjali defines samadhi as follows: "Just as the pure crystal takes color from the object which is nearest to it, so the mind, when it is cleared of thought-waves, achieves sameness or identity with the object of its concentration.... This achievement of sameness or identity with the object of concentration is known as samadhi."[24]

There are lower and higher forms of samadhi. In the lower, the yogi attains identification with the spiritual teacher, guru or deity he has chosen to contemplate. In the highest form there is no separation between Atman and Brahman. As Shankara describes it: "There is no longer any identification of the Atman with its coverings."[25] This is the great mystery of the inner path of Hinduism.

You may also concentrate and focus your attention, as Saint Germain teaches, on your mighty I AM Presence, that focus of the I AM THAT I AM in the Chart of Your Divine Self. The painting will soon dissolve, and beyond it you will see the reality of your glorious Great God Self.

Focusing on the I AM THAT I AM polarizes your entire being to that level, which in Kabbalah is named Keter—the first sefirah to come forth out of Ein Sof. That is the point of sublime union. When you have idle moments, develop the habit of meditating on your mighty I AM Presence, pouring love to your mighty I AM Presence, exalting that Presence, thinking of all the wonderful attributes of the I AM Presence—and see how you become an electrode in the earth for drawing down the currents of that high state of consciousness into the planet.

In the East, the whole pattern is getting Matter up to Spirit, or getting the consciousness out of Matter, escaping Matter and going into Spirit. And that's why the word "OM" is used, because it cycles energies up into the Presence.

The emphasis in the West is bringing Spirit into Matter. We do that by the affirmation "I AM THAT I AM," which cycles energies from the Presence down to this plane.

That is our path. If we accept it, we can have the integration that we seek, which is the integration of the soul's reunion with the I AM Presence in the ascension. Raja yoga does not promise the ascension; the highest thing it promises is samadhi. But you come back from samadhi and you are still in this form; you are still carrying around your karma.

The Yoga That Leads to the Ascension: Agni Yoga

The highest yoga is agni yoga. This is the yoga of fire— sacred fire. It is beyond the four types of yoga that apply to the four lower bodies, because it leads to the ascension. This yoga has been taught by all the Messengers of the Great White Brotherhood. Even the prophets of Israel were practitioners of fire yoga.

In the 1920s, Nicholas and Helena Roerich began releasing the teachings of El Morya and other Masters of the Great White Brotherhood through books published by the Agni Yoga Society. Agni yoga is the yoga of the sacred fire of the Mother, the sacred fire of the Word Incarnate as the spoken Word (the dynamic decree), the sacred fire of the Father and the Holy Spirit. El Morya speaks of agni yoga as the yoga of the coming age:

"All preceding Yogas, given from the highest Sources, took as their basis a definite quality of life. And now, at the advent of the age of Maitreya, there is needed a Yoga comprising the essence of the entire life, all-embracing, evading nought, precisely like the unignitible youths in the biblical legend who valiantly sacrificed themselves to the fiery furnace and thereby acquired power.[26]

"You may suggest to Me a name for the Yoga of life. But the most precise name will be Agni Yoga. It is precisely the element of fire which gives to this Yoga of self-sacrifice its name. ... Fire will not lead away from life; it will act as a trustworthy guide to the far-off worlds....

"Let us see in what lie the similarities and differences between Agni Yoga and the preceding Yogas. Karma Yoga has many similarities with it when it acts with the elements of Earth. But when Agni Yoga possesses the ways to the realization of the far-off worlds, then the distinction becomes apparent. Raja Yoga, Jnana Yoga, Bhakti Yoga are all isolated from the surrounding reality; and because of this they cannot enter into the evolution of the future. Of course, an Agni Yogi should also be a Jnani and a Bhakta, and the development of the forces of his spirit makes him a Raja Yogi. How beautiful is the possibility of responding to the tasks of the future evolution without rejecting the past conquests of spirit!"[27]

There is no progress without fire. This is what the path of the saints is all about.

Those who do not internalize the sacred fire—for they have not bent the knee before our God who is a consuming fire[28]—experience the fire as stress. They seek to escape both the fire and the stress by "getting away from it all."

Those who experience fire as fire learn to internalize it through interludes of meditation, communion with the Earth Mother, yoga, breathing exercises, devotions, decrees or physical activities that balance and quicken the organs. Other methods that stimulate the assimilation of fire in the four lower bodies are listening to classical or religious music, engaging in rhythmic and creative activities, raising the Kundalini[29]—even deep sleep during which you take leave of the body temple for service with the heavenly hosts on the etheric plane. Work itself is a means of assimilation of fire.

In the book *Heart* we read, "Even the highest beings must become aflame in spirit in order to act."[30] When you reach a certain level on the path of spirituality, unless you become a flame in that moment and ever thereafter, you may suffer setback and disaster in your life. It is impossible to retain and manifest a certain level of spirituality without acquaintance with the fire.

Place your hand at the center of the chest cavity and visualize the Atman as the manifestation of Brahman, the clearest visualization you can give to yourself of the presence of Brahman in form. So the Atman, at the very center of this place, nearest the heart chakra, that Atman is the replica of Brahman in your being. That presence of that God-manifestation and that flame is the open door to your soul's reunion with God.

The soul is mutable and only becomes immutable through reunion with Atman and reunion with God. This is why there is a path of light and darkness, why there is good and evil, because the soul must make her choices and choose to thresh out the evil and to enter in to the Atman. Then you can walk about in the ecstasy of the Atman.

When you know that God lives within you, you feel as though you are carrying God on a bier and bearing him hither and thither and along the way. And you feel that you have this precious presence, this precious cargo that you carry about. It is this miniature of the LORD in your heart. And so the temple is filled with light because God dwells in you and you give devotion to this presence.

All Paths Lead to the Heart of God

The plethora of Hindu views about God has caused much confusion about Hinduism in the West. But the great nineteenth-century saint Ramakrishna said that there should be no conflict about the nature of God: "Really, [the divergent opinions about the nature of God] are not contradictory. As a man realizes him, so does he express himself. If somehow one attains him, then one finds no contradiction.... Kabir [a fifteenth-century Hindu mystic] used to say: 'The formless Absolute is my Father, and God with form is my Mother.'"[31]

The great understanding that Lord Krishna imparts is that there is only one God. And that one God—call him by any name—may direct his light rays to us through Archangels, through Ascended Masters, through Cosmic Beings or through the person seated next to us. But the Source is always God. It always comes from the one God.

So God has many disguises. Each of us is a mask for God, and behind the mask there is the living presence of the Lord. Krishna disguises himself in many ways so that we can show our devotion to those who are seemingly imperfect—and yet we know that the Lord of Love lives within them.

As Krishna says in the Bhagavad Gita: "Whatever path men travel is my path: no matter where they walk it leads to me."[32]

So we can see that all paths lead to the heart of God. As long as we are not idolators of self or another we can perceive God in all beings and know that God alone is the giver of whatever we receive from those beings.

Archangel Michael is a mask for God—as is Archangel Gabriel, as is El Morya—but their masks tell us a vast story of their path, their momentums, their cause for sainthood. How did they achieve such a unique internalization of a virtue of

God? By their love and by their path. So if we desire that virtue of God we go to one of them as we go to a professor or a teacher or a scientist, because we want to excel in what he knows and what he is. But it all comes back to one and only one living God.

Many people in the world have fixated themselves on the mask instead of on the God behind the mask, the one universal God. And so they argue, "If you do not believe in Jesus Christ you will go to hell." Likewise, if you do not believe in Lord Krishna, if you do not believe in Moses, if you do not believe in Gautama Buddha, you will go to hell. People have lost the magnificent conception of God's appearing to us in so many manifestations. It's not pantheism. It's not idolatry. It's not many gods. It's that God is infinite and we have a finite habitation, and therefore just a portion of God appears through each one.

So we take the bow and we shoot the arrow into the heart of our highest conception of God. Then we pray to that highest conception of God. The light returns to us and we are raised up to that level. What you can conceptualize, what you can know, what you can touch, what you can see—that point of contact with God is the all and everything for you. And perhaps when you reach it and attain union with it, then you will be at another level of the mountain and you will see the next mountain beyond—which you did not see before. And so step by step we attain union with God.

The Sacred Fire Breath

The Elohim Cyclopea sums up the Masters' intentions on how to integrate yoga into our daily practice. He says: "We have approved and advocated various systems of yoga for the maintenance of the rhythm of the flow of life. When these are combined with the four-point breathing exercise [taught by Djwal Kul—see below] and the visualization of the threefold flame for the light to flow in the chakras, the rhythm of yoga, the rhythm of the dynamic decree, right diet, exercise, and a facing of the sun once a day for ten minutes as you give the call to Helios and Vesta* (taking care not to expose the eyes to the direct glare of the sun)—this will give you the contact to a mighty reservoir of light in the heart of Helios and Vesta that is the balancing action for this solar system."[33] This is the call to Helios and Vesta:

> Helios and Vesta!
> Helios and Vesta!
> Helios and Vesta!
> Let the light flow into my being!
> Let the light expand in the center of my heart!
> Let the light expand in the center of the earth
> And let the earth be transformed into the new day!

Djwal Kul explains the importance of the breath as a means of attaining enlightenment. He gives us this exercise in the highest yoga, a meditation on the sacred fire breath to balance and expand consciousness:

"As the inbreathing and the outbreathing of God is for the integration of cosmic cycles, for the sending forth of worlds within worlds and for the return of those worlds back to the heart of God whence they came, so man, as a cocreator with God, is endowed with the gift of the sacred fire breath. And if he will use that breath for the consecration of the energy of the Holy Spirit within the chakras and within the aura, he will find

---

*Every solar system has a focalization of the Father-Mother God personified in twin flames who include in their own self-awareness the entire solar system and all of its evolutions. Helios and Vesta are the masculine and feminine polarity of God who hold the flame in the Sun behind the sun in the center of our solar system.

himself becoming the very fullness of the Presence of God....

"The very air that you breathe can be qualified with the sacred fire breath of the Holy Spirit. Indeed, the air is, as it were, the latent potential of the breath of the Holy Spirit. It is energy that is passive which can be activated by the Christ Flame as the energy of the heart chakra is drawn up through the throat chakra and released as the sacred Word. . . .

"Let us now consider the two most important functions of the chakras: first, to be the vortex of the outbreath that is the giving-forth of God's energy as the action—the sevenfold activation—of the seven rays of the Holy Spirit; and second, to be the vortex of the inbreath, the drawing-in of the sacred fire breath as the universal essence, the passive energy of the Holy Spirit. These functions are most obvious in the throat chakra; and therefore the purpose of this study is to give the devotees of the Holy Spirit a truly practical exercise and a fundamental understanding of the use of the throat chakra for the integration of the four lower bodies through the inbreathing and outbreathing of the sacred fire breath.

"Just as you breathe in and breathe out through the throat chakra, so all of the chakras are taking in and giving forth the energies of God according to the frequency assigned to each specific chakra. As the energies that are drawn in through the chakras are of the Holy Spirit and the Mother and relate to the functions of the soul in Matter and the nourishment of the four lower bodies, so the energies that are sent forth from the chakras are of the Father and the Son and relate to the functions of the soul in Spirit and the release of its spiritually creative potential....

"This is an illustration of the mathematical equation that is always present in the cosmic exchange of energy from God to man and man to God.... The outbreath—the outward thrust of Spirit—is the plus factor. The following exercise will enable you to increase the inbreath—the inward thrust of Mater, the minus factor. And so you will come to know the balance of both as the regenerative action of the currents of Alpha and Omega within your form and consciousness and world.

"First, place yourself in a meditative posture, sitting in a comfortable chair before your altar, the physical focus of your worship. If possible, you should set aside a chair that is used only during your meditations and invocations....

"Place your feet flat on the floor, your hands cupped in your lap, your head erect, eyes level, chin drawn in for the disciplined flow of the energies of the heart chakra through the throat chakra.

"The Call to the Fire Breath [see next page], the invocation of the Goddess of Purity given to the devotees of the Holy Spirit, should now be recited three times. Give it slowly, rhythmically, with feeling. Absorb each word and each concept with the conviction held in heart and mind that you are here and now a joint heir with Christ.[34] And as the beloved son, the beloved daughter, you are claiming your inheritance ... of the sacred fire....

"It is essential that you hang above your altar the Chart of the Presence [see chart facing page 44]....Establish in mind, then, the concept of a perpetual flow from the heart of the individualized God Self to the heart of the Christ Self to your own threefold flame pulsating in the rhythm of God's heartbeat. The sealing of your aura within the very heart of the expanding fire breath of God is accomplished by your I AM Presence through the Christ Self in answer to your call. Remember, it is God in you who is the decreer, the decree and the fulfillment of the decree.

"Visualize your aura as an ovoid of white light extending beneath your feet and above your head....See the aura increasing in the intensity of the light as that energy is expanded from the heart chakra and thence from all of the chakras as the sacred mist that is called the fire breath of God. Let its purity, wholeness and love fill the ovoid of your aura, and feel your mind and heart disciplining that energy and holding it in the creative tension of your cosmic awareness. Conclude the giving of the call (three times) with the acceptance, the six concluding lines:

> I AM, I AM, I AM the fire breath of God
> From the heart of beloved Alpha and Omega.
> This day I AM the immaculate concept
> In expression everywhere I move.
> Now I AM full of joy,
> For now I AM the full expression
> Of Divine Love.
> My beloved I AM Presence,
> Seal me now
> Within the very heart of
> The expanding fire breath of God:
> Let its purity, wholeness and love
> Manifest everywhere I AM today and forever! (3x)

> I accept this done right now with full power.
> I AM this done right now with full power.
> I AM, I AM, I AM God-life
> Expressing perfection all ways at all times.
> This which I call forth for myself, I call forth
> For every man, woman and child on this planet!

"Now you are ready for the exercise of the integration of the eighth ray. To the count of eight beats, draw in through your nostrils the sacred breath. When you first begin this exercise, you may wish to count the eight beats by the gentle tapping of your foot.

"The breath is drawn in through the nostrils. As you breathe in, push your abdominal muscles out, letting the air completely fill your lungs. Let your lungs be inflated like a balloon. See the air that you draw in as the pure white light.

"Now to the count of eight beats, hold in the air and visualize it penetrating your physical form as the essence of the Holy Spirit, which nourishes, stabilizes and balances the interchange of energy in the physical atoms, molecules and cells. Visualize this sacred energy flowing though your veins, moving through your nervous system, anchoring the essence of the balancing energies of the Holy Spirit in your four lower bodies and absorbing from them all impurities, which you now see being flushed out of your system as you exhale to the count of eight beats.

"Let the exhalation be deliberate and disciplined as you slowly release the air as though it were a substance being pressed out of a tube. You may round your lips to increase the tension of the exhalation. Imagine that breath being pushed out from the very pit of the stomach as the abdominal muscles contract. You may lean forward if this helps to press out the last bit of air remaining in the lungs. Now let your head resume an erect posture, and hold without inbreathing or outbreathing to the final count of eight beats.

"Repeat this exercise daily, as you are physically able, until you have established a rhythm—mentally counting, if you wish, 'One and two and three and four and five and six and seven and eight and one and two and three and'—and so forth. Be careful that in your zeal you do not overdo. Each one must in Christ discern his capacity, which may be anywhere from one to twelve repetitions of the exercise per daily session.

"This fourfold exercise is for the balancing of the four lower bodies. The inbreath comes through the etheric body; the first hold is an action of energizing through the mental body;

the outbreath is the release through the emotional body; and the final hold is for the anchoring in the physical form of the balanced action of Father, Son, Mother and Holy Spirit.

"When you have mastered the inbreathing, holding, out-breathing and holding in this fashion and the accompanying visualization of the sacred fire releasing light, energizing the consciousness, extracting impurities and finally anchoring the energies of the Christ, then—and only then—you may add to your exercise the affirmation 'I AM Alpha and Omega' to the count of eight beats. This you mentally affirm once for each of the four steps of the exercise. This affirmation is for the estab-lishment within you of the cloven tongues of fire, the twin flames of the Holy Spirit that are the energies of the Father-Mother God.

"By thus invoking these energies and using the breath as the means to convey that energy to the four lower bodies and to anchor it in the physical form, you will be building the bal-anced action of the caduceus—the intertwining of the Alpha and Omega spirals along the spine that are for the ultimate vic-tory of the masculine and feminine polarity that raises the ener-gies of the chakras, merges in the heart as the Christ, and flowers in the crown as the Buddhic enlightenment of the thou-sand-petaled lotus....

"Without the balance of the spirals of Alpha and Omega within you, O chelas of the sacred fire, you can go no further in the expansion of the aura....

"This, then, is the beginning of your exercise of expansion. It is also the ending of your exercise; for ultimately in the com-pleted manifestation of the Father-Mother God, you will find that your being and consciousness has become the aura, the forcefield, of the Holy Spirit. You will find that you have thereby magnetized that Presence of the I AM and that you are magnetized by it in a literal conflagration which is, blessed ones, the ritual of your ascension in the light. Thus from beginning to ending, the Alpha and Omega spirals within you are the fulfillment of the very living Presence of God."[35]

Mantra Yoga

Like hatha yoga, mantra yoga is an adjunct to the principal forms of yoga. A mantra is a brief prayer that is given over and over again to develop the momentum of a particular virtue within the soul. The word *mantra* is taken from the Sanskrit, meaning "sacred counsel" or "formula."

The repetition of the names of God—and of sacred mantras containing the names of God—is used by Hindus and Buddhists throughout India as a means of reunion with God. For the name of God *is* God, because the name is a chalice, a formula that carries his vibration. So God and his name are one. He gives you his name, you recite the name, then he gives you all of himself.

Today in the West, many people have a difficult time meditating because their minds are so yin. They eat too much sugar and drink too many liquids like coffee and soft drinks, most of which have caffeine in them. These yin foods—and especially alcohol and recreational drugs—make it difficult to concentrate. This weakness has become ingrained in our bodies.

To compensate for this weakness, we give mantras during our meditation. The mantras help us focus on words and on word pictures and visualizations. As we meditate and give these mantras, we are becoming one with the object of our concentration. The mantra keeps the mind in line. This was the grand solution of Saint Germain for all of his disciples in the West.

Many of Jesus' statements, in addition to being sacred counsel, are also prayer formulas to increase the disciple's awareness of God. For example, the following statements of the Law may be used as prayerful affirmations of Truth; and when so used, they become precious mantras of the devotee of the sacred fire: "I AM the way, the truth and the life;" "I AM the resurrection and the life;" "I AM the light which lighteth every man that cometh into the world."

When we utter a mantra properly, we attain fusion with the object of that mantra, which is always an attribute of God. And an attribute of God is simply a ray of light that goes back to God. If we recite mantras to Shiva, we become one with Shiva.

We repeat mantras because union with God is a gradual process. It occurs step by step. Each time we repeat a mantra, we are gradually drawing ourselves into union with God. As we repeat the mantra, it is effecting change in our heart and mind.

Westerners often do not understand the value of repetition. Some think it is mindless. Some even say it brainwashes the giver of the mantra and causes him to lose his willpower. But the real value of the repetition of mantras is that it helps us attain the state of remembrance of the Divine. It also assists us in balancing the karma we have made with the throat chakra by the misuse of the science of the spoken Word. That is why it is good to have a mantra on the lips.

As the great prophets and patriarchs journeyed, wherever they camped they would set up an altar to the LORD. Archangel Gabriel and Archangel Michael would be with them, and wherever they were, they offered their prayers to God.

Saint John Chrysostom teaches: "Everywhere, wherever you may find yourself, you can set up an altar to God in your mind by means of prayer. And so it is fitting to pray at your trade, on a journey, standing at the counter or sitting at your handicraft." Saint John says that the person who develops this habit will eventually "train himself to the uninterrupted prayerful invocation of the Name of Jesus Christ." This spoken prayer becomes "prayer of the mind" and ultimately "prayer of the heart, which opens up the Kingdom of God [the consciousness of God] within us."[36]

After giving a mantra for a period of time, the devotee's ignorance is purged. He may have a mystical experience when, in a flash, he has a direct perception of the truth of the mantra. The next step is *moksha,* reunion with God.

As we focus upon the sun of our Mighty I AM Presence, we can fill the chalice with the words of the mantra. All of the mantras in our decree book[37] are dictated by the Ascended Masters. So the mantra or decree is a little pouch of their Causal Bodies, a little formula all tied up. And when we repeat the words, we have made attunement with and created the counterpart of the Master's vibration in ourselves.

We speak of the Master as the yang (Spirit) force and ourselves as the yin (Matter) manifestation, a polarity of plus and minus, masculine and feminine—which is why the soul is always referred to as "she." So we become the anchoring point for the Master in the planet when we say his mantras and combine mantras with meditation.

As you pick your Guru, pick your mantras. Do them on a regular basis and see how they begin to sing in your heart. As you say a mantra again and again, it says itself back to you. This is not auto-hypnosis. It's not self-programming. The mantra is alive. It is the extension of the Guru who gave the mantra, which is now being brought back to you through the very voice of your Guru who is inside you.

Pick the Master who is most like you and whom you are most like. Then pick a second Master whose very manifestation of mastery you need so much that you know you are obliged to also give mantras to that Master. Choose the Master who embodies so greatly that quality you are lacking that you can through the heart of that Master gain balance in the qualities of God within you.

Perhaps you think you need to love more or to be more kind or more merciful. Kuan Yin is a great one to whom to give mantras, because there is no such thing as ever having enough mercy or enough compassion toward life.[38]

The Transfer of the Life Record

The transfer of the life record from one embodiment to the next must be studied in view of the fact that it is necessary to purify this record to attain the highest yoga.

All of the good that men do is conveyed by the power of light into each one's Causal Body—the Body of Causative Good. There it is stored as a reservoir of great strength and spiritual abundance in a shimmering sphere of splendid reality. The negative patterns that men generate by wrong action become a part of the lower self and are recorded (so to speak) within the "bones" or densified structure of the electronic belt.

As Lord Lanto teaches, "This belt extends from the waist to beneath the feet. It is shaped like a large kettledrum. It contains the aggregate records of your negative thoughts, feelings, words and deeds, hence your negative karma."[39]

Of course, the longer we've been around (millions of years of incarnations, creating after the human ego) the larger that kettledrum has become. Its many layers are compressed like dinner plates—almost like a Greek pastry, layer upon layer upon layer. And locked in that electronic belt is all your human creation and karma.

If the entire contents of your electronic belt were dumped on you today, it would kill you. So God assigns to each of us for one lifetime only a certain portion of this kettledrum, the portion that according to our attainment we are able to deal with. And other people whom we must serve or work with are scheduled to be in embodiment at the same time.

Through a special process that takes place at the close of each embodiment, the life record is transferred to an electronic envelope that holds the aggregate substance of the individual's world. This he is required to pick up and deal with in his next life. When he reembodies, the records that correspond to the emotions, the thoughts and the memory are placed within their respective vehicles. The soul continues to evolve from the place where she left off in her previous life.

The record and the substance of the personality are transferred to the physical structure of man through the genes, the chromosomes, the hormones, the blood, the fluids, the nerves, the bones and the brain. Man's unredeemed substance is deposited not only in the atoms of the physical body but also in the atoms of the emotional, mental and etheric bodies and in the energy mass that is called the soul.

It is through the patterns that man has stamped on the four lower bodies and on the soul that he retains his personality from one embodiment to the next. Until he has found his spiritual identity through the highest yoga, he retains the patterns of his personal momentums. Often physiological similarities are noted from one embodiment to the next. For these traits are merely a reflection of the soul personality, which remains unchanged.

According to the law of attraction (like attracts like), parents often draw to themselves souls of similar personality traits. Thus the incoming lifestream may pick up through the genes and chromosomes of his parents those traits that are also native to his own evolution. In those cases where parents and their offspring seem to have nothing in common, one may conclude that karmic ties drew them together for the sole purpose of balancing wrongs that were mutually imposed.

Here we see the operation of the law of opposites, intuitively felt by Job when he said, "The thing which I greatly feared is come upon me."[40] If we are honest enough to look beneath the surface of our own worlds, we often find that those characteristics we despise in others (especially in members of our own family) are the very weaknesses we were sent into embodiment to overcome in ourselves.

Until we get rid of our antipathies and our anathemas, we cannot overcome them. For the energy that is qualified with repulsion becomes the magnet that draws the object of our disdain to us. How true it is that what we see in others, we are likely to become.

The Transmutation of the Life Record

It should be clear to everyone who aspires to be free from the karmic wheel, from the round of reembodiment, that he must first transmute his life record together with the cause, effect, record and even the memory of every wrong act.

Man does not escape his personal karma through the transition called death, although he loses his form and he may temporarily lose his identity. For where man goes, there goes his life record. The life record must be purified before he can attain the highest yoga—and conversely, the practice of the highest yoga will teach him how to purify his life record.

Enter Saint Germain and Portia with their dispensation of the violet flame for the Aquarian age. The violet flame cuts across the electronic belt and may begin to penetrate, dissolve, transmute and balance that energy and send it back to your Causal Body transmuted even if you never meet the people you owe karma to, even if you're born at the wrong time and the wrong century as many people think they are. They go back and relive previous centuries in fantasy, in plays and so forth.

The violet flame is the universal solvent in the sense that it solves a universal problem—and the universal problem is having all of these leftover loose ends of ancient and recent karma to tie up, and having the opportunity at the end of this age of Pisces to make our ascension.

In earlier ages, we were required to balance 100 percent of our karma before we could return to the heart of God. Every jot and tittle of the law had to be fulfilled; every erg of energy misqualified throughout all our incarnations had to be purified before we could ascend. Perfection was the requirement of the Law.

Thanks to the mercy of God and the Lords of Karma, the old law has been set aside. Now, those who have balanced only 51 percent of their debts to life can be given the gift of the ascension. They can then balance the remaining 49 percent from the ascended realm through service to earth and her evolutions.

Lord Lanto tells us: "Beneath the surface calm of your being are caverns of consciousness that may be in a state of turmoil. This is often indicative of a polarization of negative karma within the psyche. This karma, spawned in near and distant epochs of personal history, is the underlying cause of schism within the self.

"To cast out the enemy within by invoking the sacred fire is a necessary process. When you do this, transmutation takes place and the energies that you have imprisoned in matrices of imperfect thought and feeling are released.

"Immediately after having been dislodged from the electronic belt and purified by the flames of God, these energies ascend to your Causal Body. This is the body of First Cause, and it is the repository of all God-good that you have ever externalized.

"Just as the electronic belt bears the record and the

misqualified substance of negative human karma, so the Causal Body bears the burden of light that records all positive karma. The Causal Body, then, is of the spiritual order and universe, and the four lower bodies and the electronic belt are of the natural order and universe.

"The glory of the celestial body is the means whereby we overcome and transcend the terrestrial body. In the words of Saint Paul:

> [The terrestrial body] is sown in corruption; it is raised in incorruption.
>
> It is sown in dishonor; it is raised in glory. It is sown in weakness; it is raised in power.
>
> It is sown a natural body; it is raised a spiritual body. There is a natural body, and there is a spiritual body.
>
> And so it is written, The first man Adam was made a living soul; the last Adam was made a quickening spirit."[41]

The Lost Doctrines of Karma and Reembodiment: Keys to the Highest Yoga

A great deal of truth has been preserved in the perpetuation of orthodox Christian dogma, even while much has been distorted. The truth about karma and reembodiment is virtually unrecognized in Western theology, yet this truth is essential to understanding and practicing the highest yoga.

El Morya points out: "One of the most pernicious errors of orthodoxy this day . . . is the lie that Jesus is the only Son of God, and furthermore that Jesus came into embodiment in the full mastery of Christhood and did not himself have to follow the Path and realize his own inner God-potential before beginning his mission.

"These things are plain in scripture, but the scriptures have been read and reread so many times that the true intent is no longer heard by the soul. The layers of misinterpretation and then the removal of the very keys themselves have given to Christianity today a watered-down religion that does not have the fervor or the fire to meet the challengers of civilization— whether it be in World Communism or in pornography or all manner of perversion or immorality that does steal the light of the soul.

"I tell you, nothing can move forward in life unless the individual has a true understanding of God and his relationship to that eternal Spirit. Therefore, realize that Jesus did not come from God a new soul, born for the first time in his incarnation in Nazareth. Nay, I tell you! He was embodied as Joshua, the military hero of the Hebrew people. He was embodied as Joseph and wore his coat of many colors as the favorite son and did go through all manner of trial and persecution by his own brothers who were jealous of him; and yet he found favor in the sight of Pharaoh.

"You know the soul of Jesus in Elisha, the disciple of the prophet Elijah. And you know that Elijah came again in the person of John the Baptist as was prophesied and as it is written. Jesus gave to his own disciples the confirmation that this John the Baptist was Elias come again,[42] thereby ratifying the teaching of reincarnation. . . .

"You cannot believe in reincarnation unless you will also stand, face and conquer the deeds of the past. Thus, the non-accountability, due to the upbringing of children in the West today, does not prepare warriors of the Spirit to meet the inroads that are being made by all forces of lust and greed after this nation's light and after this citadel of freedom.

"Understand, then, that your understanding of the one God and the one Christ enables you to see that that one God and one Christ has vouchsafed to you the I AM Presence and Christ Self as the manifestation of pure divinity—not many gods, but one God. And the pure Son of God is the universal Christ whose body and bread are broken for you. And therefore, as partakers of the light, as one with the Holy Christ Self, you also may pass through the initiations of discipleship as Jesus did. And you ought to look forward to and expect the fullness of that Christ dwelling in you bodily.

"Wherefore evolution of a spiritual nature? Why have the prophets come? Why have the avatars appeared? Because they are favorite sons and all the rest are sinners? I tell you, no! And it is the most pernicious lie, as I have said, for it stops *all* short of the mark of that high calling in Christ Jesus of which the apostle spoke.[43] And none dare become heroes or leaders or examples. And those who do are set on a pedestal of idolatry rather than seen as the example!

"What one can do, all can do. And this is the philosophy of the Darjeeling Council that we would impart. We would quicken and enliven you, as God has empowered the saints to do, to unlock that potential of your heart, that divine spark, and to show you that lifetime after lifetime you have been moving toward that point of the courage to be who you really are and not to accept the philosophy that you are evolved from animals and that you cannot exceed the matrix of the animal creation."[44]

Those who pin their faith on the present form of the recorded word and fail to take into account the Word of God as the original divine intent will often be misled. Yet there is no power of argument that can dissuade them from their wrong course, which seemeth right unto them.

In the Book of Proverbs we find the statement "There is a way which seemeth right unto a man, but the end thereof are the ways of death."[45] The death that is referred to here is the death of Self-awareness—of the awareness of the Higher Self or the I AM Presence. When men are raised from death unto life, their awareness of higher Truth is restored. This Truth is actually a part of the life that lives in every man. And this life, which is God, can commune with them daily through the mediation of the Christ. He can teach them to unravel the tangled threads within the garment of their consciousness, for he is the only one who can make that garment seamless.

The Truth that God imparts to man when he is called upon is linked with the great mysteries of life that have been handed down from teacher to disciple during epochs of darkness as well as in periods of relative enlightenment. Many who are concerned about the preservation of right knowledge will be relieved to know that through the long historical stream spanning ancient and unknown civilizations to the present time, the thread of contact between God and man has never been broken.

As Saint Germain says: "Because of my dedication to holy freedom, I have consistently maintained, by cosmic decree and by the approval of heaven, a contact with one or more lifestreams embodied upon earth during every decade since my ascension, with few exceptions. Jesus and other great luminaries who have descended in the fullness of the divine plan have likewise appeared and do occasionally manifest to men and women of today with no more effort than that which is employed to turn a dial to receive a television picture."[46]

Knowledge Held in the Retreats of the Great White Brotherhood

It is a fact that the greatest truths have been periodically withheld from the masses because of their abuse of these truths during the decline and fall of many great civilizations, when the people turned from their God. Yet the torch of knowledge has been held within the sanctity of the retreats of the Great White Brotherhood. There since the dawn of time, the rites practiced by those who have overcome the world have been taught. And there they are still being taught. All through the ages up to the present time, the hierarchs of these retreats have made available to evolving souls the true teachings of the Ancient of Days.

These retreats of the Great White Brotherhood are anchored in what is called the etheric plane—a dimension that is above our physical, mental and emotional world. It is a high dimension, close to the octaves that we call heaven or the Ascended Master octave.

In these levels of consciousness, the Ascended Masters of the Great White Brotherhood anchor certain energies on behalf of mankind. And to these retreats come the souls of those in embodiment who desire to be trained at night while their bodies sleep. Their souls journey to these places where the Masters hold sway as the teachers of mankind. Before they incarnated, our great religious forebears—the saints, Mother Mary and Jesus—also studied in these retreats to prepare themselves.

We do not always remember that we have been to these retreats in the heaven-world, but sometimes we awaken in the morning with a memory of a certain experience. We think it was a dream, but many times it was not a dream at all. It was an actual experience of meeting people of light, teachers, avatars, angels, Christed beings, counselors.

People who have had near-death experiences have actually seen certain advisors whom they thought were like a supreme court. They remember being reviewed before these judges. These are the Lords of Karma, and they do advise and counsel us. They prepare us each time we take embodiment and receive us afterward. Before each embodiment, they tell us our assignment and our mission for that life, and it is recorded in the very depths of our souls. When we are little, we want to be a policeman, a fireman, a nurse or a doctor. Gradually we form in our hearts the concept of what is our mission in life, and we seek education in order to be able to reach that goal.

There is a saying "When the pupil is ready, the teacher appears." And so, when he has proven himself worthy to be entrusted with the higher truths that cannot be imparted safely to the masses, the disciple is escorted to one of the retreats on the etheric plane. There he may sit at the feet of the great Masters of Wisdom. There he is given the opportunity to learn the same techniques given to Jesus, which he used to attain self-mastery. But like all who have gone before him, the disciple must prove himself each step of the way.

Thus the highest yoga is practiced not only by unascended men (would-be overcomers battling in the fields of life), but also by those who have already overcome—the Ascended Masters, who return to the scene of their own victory to find union with the God who dwells in the evolving consciousness of unascended man. Truly, this is the highest yoga.

The Seamless Garment: Wedding the Soul to God

In the Bible we find many examples of souls who are on the path of the highest yoga. In the story of Joseph, one of the twelve sons of Jacob, reference is made to his "coat of many colors."[47] The wearing of this coat signifies that the initiate is passing through certain tests of the Brotherhood prior to his manifestation of the seamless garment of the Christ.

This splendid coat, the envy of all of Joseph's brothers, was composed of bands of colors of the rainbow—the colors found in the Causal Body of man: white, pink, gold, yellow, green, blue, purple and violet. Thus we see that Joseph—the idle dreamer sold into slavery by his brothers, who became an interpreter of dreams in the court of Pharaoh and then governor over all of Egypt—had the protection, the power and the providence of a son of God whose mission was sponsored by the Great White Brotherhood.

Students of history will recall similar cases of the rise of a soul to the zenith of power and achievement on behalf of humanity. Such figures fulfill the destiny of the Christ in their respective fields of endeavor. In so doing, they move on in the order of the hierarchy.

Returning to the symbology of the coat of many colors: It will be noted that the division of the white light into seven rays (seven aspects of identity) is achieved through the breaking down of the high frequency of the light itself. In this case, the whole (the white fire) is equal to the sum of its parts (the six lesser rays). Together with the pure white light, these make up the sevenfold nature of the Deity as he expresses himself through the evolutions of this planetary home.

The Rainbow Rays of the Days

Each day of the week there is released to this solar system from the heart of Alpha and Omega the concentrated action of one of the seven rainbow rays of God. This is the rainbow of light which flows into the world of form through the prism of the Christ consciousness. Each of the sun's rays carries a particular quality or attribute of the Godhead.

The order of precipitation begins on Sunday, the day of the Son's illumination concerning the intent of the Father (the yellow ray). As the saying goes, "All things begin with an idea." Thus an idea intact and complete in the Mind of God—the very desire of his heart—is released out of Spirit's own omniscience.

On Monday it gathers the flame of love (the pink ray) and

with it the creative potential of the Godhead. On Tuesday, having equalized within itself the inherent patterns of wisdom and love, this desire-idea is awarded the activating power (the blue ray) necessary to a balanced manifestation.

On Wednesday it is infused with the life-giving properties of the chlorophyll green. On Thursday it is nourished by the ministrations of the angelic hosts, the gold and purple of the Spirit and Body of God of the masculine and feminine rays. On Friday its manifestation is complete in the sevenfold purity of the Christ consciousness (the white ray), and it is sustained in the world of form by the ritual and freedom of the violet flame that is released on Saturday. Thus are the seven days of creation fulfilled with cyclic regularity.

Those who desire to dedicate their lives to unbroken communion may wish to amplify the light in their worlds and their service to humanity by wearing the "color of the day." Wearing the color of the day will help you to visualize yourself as a flame and to focus the qualities of the flame in your consciousness.

The Masters suggest that their disciples wear the seven rays as solid colors so that the heavenly hosts may focus through them their personal momentums of spiritual victory attained through service on one or more of the seven rays.

In their service to life, men do express an affinity for a specific color or ray, of which they become a very real part. In chapter 4, "Hierarchy," we will discuss the seven rays and the members of hierarchy who serve on these rays. We will also explain how the talents and services of mankind are distributed according to the same principle of the division of the white light into its components.

The core of each ray of manifestation (the center of the flame) is always composed of the white fire of purity. As all of the colors merge into white when a color wheel is spun rapidly, the white fire core of each ray embodies the other six colors. Therefore, no matter what ray an individual may be serving on (and this may change from one embodiment to the next), he is required to hold the balance of the other six rays in his service to life. A balance of mastery on all of the rays is one of the requirements of the ascension (the manifestation of the pure white light). But candidates for the ascension often have developed a "major" concentration on one ray and a "minor" on another ray, as they might have a major and minor field of study at a college or university.

The seamless garment of the Christ represents the fundamental unity of God and man. It is the wedding garment that signifies man's alchemical union with his Higher Self. The seamless garment also focuses God's desire to unite people of various backgrounds and experience into an activity of light. For God intends that men come together without fear to blend the many facets of the God-life within themselves in the service of all. Through this joint service they create a seamless garment of protection whereby the members of the Lord's Body (of the church universal and triumphant) become one in action even as they are one in spirit.

Forces Working against the Highest Yoga: Contamination through Mass Thoughts and Feelings

But there are many forces working against the union of God and man, and against the union of man and man. For instance, the tremendous weight of human miscreation, which is charged into the atmosphere of the world daily by all who are evolving upon earth, makes everyone a potential victim of mental malpractice. This mass effluvia is either funneled into his world by people whose attention may be upon him (as they contact him) or it is magnetized by similar vibrations hidden

The Chart of Your Divine Self

within the folds of his own subconscious mind. The targets of this type of malpractice, as well as those who may be instruments for it, are often totally unaware that this is taking place.

We insert here the comments of the Great Divine Director on the subject of contamination through thought and feeling. He makes clear the need for perpetual protection from the world's negative thoughts and feelings:

"There has been a great deal of study and experimentation by members of the medical profession and other investigators in the material sciences concerning the effect of the mind upon the body. In that connection I would like to point out that the planet is one, but this idea is too big for most people to understand. Each nation is one, and this idea is also too big for many to understand. The community is one, and this idea some can assimilate.

"For those who are able to understand it, I must state that the body of the world (civilization as a whole) is subject to each individual's thoughts and feelings taken singularly and to the thoughts and feelings of mankind taken as a whole.

"The thoughts and feelings of the masses have created famine, hunger and disease, war and natural disaster. The thoughts of the masses have conspired to shake the foundations of heaven itself and to bring forth avatars with divine missions to correct the conditions mankind have brought upon themselves through this untoward use of divine energy.

"The thoughts of the masses are a vital factor in the manifestation of individual and planetary happiness or unhappiness. Today, men are witnessing more than ever the spread of violent ideas through the mass media. I would remind that the spread of peace, of beauty, of harmony, of culture and of reality can also be activated by the correct use of media, of science and of the mind of man.

"It is a great pity that many of the orthodox leaders of the world, with the exception of a few such as Dr. Norman Vincent Peale, have not been active in teaching the people the power of positive thinking, of mind over matter, and the control of emotions. So lacking is the education of the people in these matters that many successful professional men actually project feelings of hostility against individuals and segments of society that are not to their liking, and they are totally ignorant of the great harm and the great karma that they thereby incur. Because of the dearth of right knowledge in high places concerning the laws governing thought transference, the thought-power of energy misused goes out into the world and stimulates frictions.

"If the clergy and the laity of the orthodox movements of Christianity and other religious orders would wake up and recognize the power of right thought and right feeling to magnetize more of their kind and to galvanize right action, they could provide a sound basis for the power of right example in the world community.

"For as subtle and invisible as the stealthy vibrations of mortal wickedness and hatred that now radiate in the world are, the power of good would swallow up the power of darkness, and light would be shed upon many of the problems now disturbing mankind—if those to whom the masses look for leadership would take an uncompromising stand for righteousness (the 'right use' of thought and feeling)."[48]

Floating Grids and Forcefields

The Great Divine Director teaches further on the subject of mass thought and feeling: "Mindful now of the cherished words of the Psalmist of old 'Yea, though I walk through the valley of the shadow of death, I will fear no evil: for thou art with me; thy rod and thy staff they comfort me,'[49] I would speak of the insidious mechanical grids and forcefields that exist invisibly but subtly in the planetary atmosphere.

"The lovely sweet earth upon which God has bestowed so much abundance has become a treacherous abode in many unexpected places, for the very atmosphere itself has been charged with large floating grids or forcefields embodying crosscurrents of human thought and feeling. And the conflicting harmonic rate of vibration of these fields is such as to bring about great discomfort to elemental life as well as to mankind. . . .

"As you know, whenever an individual uses energy (and this always occurs whenever thought or feeling is exercised), the energy itself is not destroyed even after passing through the nexus of consciousness where qualification with bane or blessing occurs. Hence, energy is continually being released by all of mankind into the atmosphere.

"Now, because of the law of harmonics dealing with affinities, like seeks out like; and therefore, a strengthening occurs in the strata of misqualified energy as well as in that of properly qualified energy as line upon line of similarly qualified vibrations are added thereto. Many have noted that in spiritual places, temples and churches they can receive a greater inrush of peace than in the busy streets and businesses of the outer world. Contrariwise, when entering into places qualified with feuds or destructive and trivial passions, mankind are often ensnared in feelings that do not sustain the vibratory action of God-happiness and peace. . . .

"There do exist, then, in the atmosphere throughout the entire planet, floating forcefields or grids containing the scapegoat energies of mankind's wrong thought and feeling. These abide in larger quantities in the so-called ghettos of the large cities and such places as are rampant with the ravages of crime and poverty. Yet I can recall but few spaces upon the landed area of the earth where these large forcefields do not occasionally drift to bring about potential destruction where taken in.

They are like floating minefields in the sea. Insidiously existing beneath the level of visibility, they drift to affect the unwary of mankind and to bring about results little dreamed of by most contemporary men. . . .

"I cannot deny that some of them, by reason of size and density patterns, are particularly lethal and hence deadly to those who are unsuspecting and therefore unprotected against them. Just as a cloud will cover the face of the sun preceding a storm, so in many cases a sudden feeling or drop in the normal level of happiness or well-being will indicate the presence of such an invisible forcefield.

"There are two simple defenses available to mankind against these unseen pitfalls. One is to recognize that mobility can soon bring an individual into an area out of the center of the thrust; hence, many times a distance of one or two miles will give absolute safety. At other times, for various reasons when individuals cannot conveniently flee the invaded area, they can make mighty application to the Godhead, to the Cosmic Beings and the Ascended Masters including Jesus and Archangel Michael, for spiritual assistance in moving these forcefields away or transmuting them into light.

"Now I do not for one moment wish any to accept that no matter how deadly these forcefields may be, they cannot be made to yield to the invincible power of God. Yet just as Don Quixote was unable to defeat the windmills with the point of his lance, so it is senseless to, in the words of Saint Paul, fight as one who beateth the air.[50]

"You see, there are few in physical embodiment today who are able on the instant to cope with the more malevolent of these conditions from the level of mankind's externalized personal grace. But I am certain no call goes unheeded by heaven, and therefore mighty inroads can be made into these forcefields. Sometimes they can be reduced or cut in half by a thrust of the sword of blue flame invoked by a chela.

"It is not my wish to have the student body overly conscious of these conditions, yet it is not wise to be wholly unconsciously subject to them either. Therefore, in a state of perfect mental and spiritual balance, mankind ought to understand that these conditions do exist and that they function almost mechanically—not always as fixed monsters either, but frequently as predatory roaming beasts of the air subject to unconscious driftings and magnetization by minutely affinitized centers in individuals or in groups.

"This means then that those who permit themselves to be subject to vibratory actions of fear, anger, human viciousness or hatred, or even a sense of wrong or injustice may draw to themselves from various parts of the planet either small or large focuses of the exact type of the quality of negation they permit to play through their mind and feeling consciousness. Is this not a sound argument, then, for the constant maintenance of thoughts of beauty, holiness, protection and grace?...

"I must admit that there are certain activities of the black magicians and insidious actions that we may well term vicious witchcraft, which deliberately foster and encourage the building up of such reservoirs of negated energy....

"Do you see, then, that reservoirs of negative force can also be accumulated in these drifting banks of negation to be used by the brothers of the shadow to draw upon when needed to fight against Good? This misqualified energy becomes available to the powers of darkness, then, to use in confusing the mind of man and in upsetting his world whenever possible so as to create more and more mass confusion.

"This is why undesirable television programs, vile movies and destructive books are so effective in disturbing the very young as well as people of all ages. These tie emotionally into these clouds of negated energy and feed through the consciousness, holding an absorbing fascination for mankind once they become emotionally involved in the drama. The plot sequences of most of these unwholesome stories are often mere duplications of themselves in a new format. We do not deny that many of the authors thereof enjoy great popularity with mankind, but they must bear well in mind that they will one day give account of their stewardship of life....

"Let it be made clear that we do not frown upon drama; for your own Lord Maha Chohan, in his epic releases while embodied as Homer, did bring about cultural understanding that flows forth to the present age. Your beloved Saint Germain, in his magnificent Shakespearean releases and his many other writings, did bring about the renaissance of virtue and culture to the world....

"It is absolutely true that there is no power but God. It is also true that good will ultimately triumph. But in effectively seeing to it that good does triumph over the veil of misqualified energy called evil, we must now invoke the forces of mercy that shall swiftly respond to the imploration of the saints, 'How long, O LORD?'"[51]

The Use of Thoughtforms in the Expansion of Consciousness

In the same way that mankind's thought and feeling energy is used to create forcefields of negativity in the world, the practitioner of the highest yoga may consciously use thought and feeling energy to create forcefields of great benefit to himself and to the world. The first step in this science is the study of thoughtforms.

The subject of thoughtforms is concerned with mentally creating designs of perfection to draw forth from spiritual octaves creative power and creative manifestations. To hold a concept in mind attracts the physical manifestation of that concept. It almost happens effortlessly. Consciousness is constrained, restrained and expanded by creating thoughtforms that relate to the geometrizing of God. It is a sort of cosmic trigonometry. It is a magnificent thing, a cosmic calculus. It is a form of the Divine Mind used for expansive purposes.

Lord Himalaya, a great Master from India, does not speak to his disciples; he receives them in silence. They are taught to meditate before him and perceive his thoughtforms through an intense attunement with his mind. We have received dictations from him and instruction through his Christ consciousness.

He suggests that we close our eyes and visualize every saint and Cosmic Being holding the thoughtform of the blue gentian or the blue lotus—a fiery, deep sapphire-blue flower of the heart. Through that visualization we can see the oneness of all cosmos and of the entire Spirit of the Great White Brotherhood.

The Ascended Masters often use thoughtforms in their instruction. Saint Germain uses the thoughtform of the Maltese cross in his teachings on alchemy.[52] We meditate upon the thoughtform, it is filled in, and it finally becomes a manifestation in form.

One thoughtform such as the Maltese cross can produce a variety of manifestations. As a result of this thoughtform being held in the minds of many students of Saint Germain, its image was transmitted to jewelry designers, who then began to design Maltese crosses. They captured a thoughtform that was waiting in the air (so to speak), and for a time jewelry in the form of Maltese crosses was in vogue throughout the land.

This principle can also hold true for inventions. When you hold a matrix in your mind, it is as though you were suspending it in the ethers. Others may also tune into it and precipitate it or even patent it.

So the great mystery is the alchemist's understanding of

consciousness as the supreme ingredient. With God, all things are possible. If you possess his consciousness, then all things are immediately possible to you in manifestation.

If you have a perfect thoughtform in your mind, the thoughtform itself is a magnet and it attracts to you in manifestation the outpicturing of that image. For instance, in the multiplication of the loaves and the fishes, Jesus held in his mind the thoughtform of bread and of the fishes. He was an adept in this science, and so it manifested.

There is a great responsibility in holding any concept in your mind, because as the concept is, so will the manifestation be. We can sow good seed and bad. We have to be responsible for stray thoughts, because our desires magnetize their manifestation.

Thoughtforms that elevate consciousness may include such objects as wings. To evoke wings, choose some appropriate classical music, such as Beethoven's Ninth Symphony, the Grail music from *Parsifal* by Richard Wagner, the "Ride of the Valkyries" or other classical renderings that are inspiring and elevating to your consciousness. The music from *Lohengrin* is also excellent.

As you play this music you may envision a pair of wings, perhaps on an hourglass. See the wings raising the hourglass. The idea is to elevate time into its proper use—and how better can you use time than to understand that God, who is eternity represented in the rising, is also magnetized or drawn into your image and then transferred to you because you have given authority to your God Presence to act for you.

Gautama Buddha has used the thoughtform of the anchor in his instruction. He explains that this thoughtform is for you to look upon in the same manner in which the children of Israel looked upon the caduceus—the brazen serpent that Moses put upon a pole and held up in the wilderness. When the children of Israel looked upon it, they were healed of the bites from the fiery serpents that the LORD had sent for their judgment.

As you see this thoughtform of the anchor and visualize it, you can pour into it, as a matrix, all of your hopes, your plans, your destiny and the distillation from your being of all that is the transmuted essence of your karma and your psychology. And if you fix your hope upon the anchor, even as the anchor represents hope, you will find that you will retain what is real about yourself and discard the unreal as all things permanent coalesce in the thoughtform of the anchor.

Lord Maitreya uses the thoughtform of a clipper ship, of which we are the anchor: "O hearts of light, indeed you are anchor points—under the sea of the astral plane and in the heart of the earth—of the great, great light of the mother ship of our Brotherhood. So it is that the clipper ship is my symbol and the symbol of your soul's journey in time and in space."[53]

The healing thoughtform was created by the Archangels and released by Raphael, Archangel of the fifth ray. It is another gift of God's love, scientifically formulated to remagnetize and restore the elements of your four lower bodies to Nature's design. The healing thoughtform is composed of concentric spheres of God's healing light—a sphere of white surrounded by a sphere of blue suspended within a globe of green.

Whenever you pray for healing, know that the call compels the answer. Then call upon the LORD and know that he will answer: "In the name of Jesus Christ and his presence with me in the person of my own Christ Self, I call to the heart of my own beloved I AM Presence and the angels of healing for the beautiful healing thoughtform to seal me in the perfect light of God's own consciousness of my wholeness—now made manifest!"

Then visualize spheres of sacred fire descending as the

pulsating presence of the Holy Spirit. Visualize the white-fire core centered in the scintillating, sapphire-blue flame wrapped in the leaping, emerald-green fires.

By your unspeakable love for the Holy Spirit, magnetize this healing thoughtform from the Mind of God first to your heart and then to any distressed, disturbed or diseased area of the body.

Other thoughtforms the Masters use include the Sacred Heart of Jesus; the purple, fiery heart of Saint Germain; Astrea's circle and sword of blue flame; Archangel Michael's blue-flame sword; Portia's scales of justice; El Morya's diamond heart; Mother Mary's white rose; Lanello's bluebird of happiness; and Saint Germain's fleur-de-lis (the threefold flame).

Gautama instructs us: "In contemplation of the beauty of God, do not rest your weary eyes with the mere fixing of them upon the form of the mountain or of the rain or of the river or of the sun or of the flower or of the tree or of the beautiful face of a child, of a loved one, of a soul purified and made white. Penetrate beyond the form lest you become worshipers of form. Discover the key, the inner pattern. And when you have the pattern, you will have the key to creation itself, for the pattern that you contain is the pattern that you can multiply."[54]

As you begin to meditate on spiritual thoughtforms, you will learn to condition your mind and spirit to their creative abilities, and these creative abilities will come out in all of your work. You will begin to understand how to use your physical senses in an improved manner, because you will understand that you are working with the fingers of the mind in the use of these thoughtforms. Later you will transfer your sensory awareness to your fingertips.

By doing it under God's direction through your Presence, you will find that you have greater control of your creativity than ever before. You can do this, and you can do it better and better each day if you get a momentum on prayer, on talking to God, on speaking to the angels and giving them assignments, and on keeping your chakras open to God instead of to the pollution of the world.

Invoking the Protection of the Seamless Garment

Because men send out torrents of discordant thoughts and feelings each day through the misqualification of God's energy, the individual must find a means of protecting himself. Unless this be achieved through a conscious rejection of these ill-fitting thoughts, he will find that, either consciously or subconsciously, this effluvia will penetrate the domain of self. The banal effects of such penetration invariably come to the surface later. But from the moment they gain entrance into the individual's subconscious world, they can produce a vibratory response to negativity that burdens the soul and produces feelings of unhappiness, depression and sickness, thus thwarting her total creative output.

There is a way in which every person on earth can call to his Divine Presence and ask that Presence to enfold him in the seamless garment of the living Christ. This garment is a high-frequency manifestation of vibrating light that can actually be drawn down daily and hourly to enfold the self with tremendous protection. Through regular devotion and invocation on the part of the supplicant, the power of this garment of light can become more and more real.

It has been reported that some of the great adepts of India have developed such a momentum in drawing down this garment of light into tangible manifestation that it has actually deflected a bullet from an elephant gun, the lead being flattened upon contact with the light and falling to the ground a few feet from the body.

Of course, sensible students will neither claim nor test such development of the armor of God ("Thou shalt not tempt the LORD thy God"[55]). But they will maintain implicit faith and trust that when the need arises the light of God will defend them against all attacks on their person.

The seamless garment is a powerful thoughtform for the protection and sealing of the aura against negative thoughts and feelings emanating from the mass consciousness. You may put on this seamless garment as a surrounding tube of light by pouring out your love to your God Presence, saying:

> O my constant, loving I AM Presence, thou light of God above me whose radiance forms a circle of fire before me to light my way:
>
> I AM faithfully calling to thee to place a great pillar of light from my own mighty I AM God Presence all around me right now today! Keep it intact through every passing moment, manifesting as a shimmering shower of God's beautiful light through which nothing human can ever pass. Into this beautiful electric circle of divinely charged energy direct a swift upsurge of the violet fire of freedom's forgiving, transmuting flame!
>
> Cause the ever expanding energy of this flame projected downward into the forcefield of my human energies to completely change every negative condition into the positive polarity of my own great God Self! Let the magic of its mercy so purify my world with light that all whom I contact shall always be blessed with the fragrance of violets from God's own heart in memory of the blessed dawning day when all discord—cause, effect, record and memory—is forever changed into the victory of light and the peace of

the ascended Jesus Christ.

I AM now constantly accepting the full power and manifestation of this fiat of light and calling it into instantaneous action by my own God-given free will and the power to accelerate without limit this sacred release of assistance from God's own heart until all men are ascended and God-free in the light that never, never, never fails!

Or you can use this shorter prayer, which is also highly effective:

Beloved I AM Presence bright,
Round me seal your tube of light
From Ascended Master flame
Called forth now in God's own name.
Let it keep my temple free
From all discord sent to me.

I AM calling forth violet fire
To blaze and transmute all desire,
Keeping on in freedom's name
Till I AM one with the violet flame.

As you offer these prayers, look at the Chart of Your Divine Self, which depicts the tube of light (facing page 44). Visualize the tube of light as a concentrated stream of vital, intelligent energy that weaves an armor of invincible protection, a cylinder of spiritual light substance around your whole being. You may think of yourself as standing in a giant milk bottle. Your tube of light is approximately nine feet in diameter and extends three feet beneath the soles of your feet into the earth.

As you balance and expand your threefold flame, the tube of light increases in stature. The tube of light of an Ascended

Being such as Jesus the Christ or the Lord Buddha is as large as the planet.

Visualization is an important part of the ritual of perfectionment in which you participate each time you use the violet fire and tube of light decree above. Therefore, meditation on the Chart of Your Divine Self will assist you in daily drawing forth the full potency of the light of God that never fails.

Focusing this powerful tube of spiritual light around your physical form insulates your mind and consciousness. As long as you sustain the action of the tube of light, you have an impervious armor that shields you against the play and ploy of the psychic effluvia of the planet.

But if you then become involved in any kind of discordant activity whatsoever (be it gossip, argument, anger or despair), you must quickly call upon the law of forgiveness and the violet transmuting flame and then invoke the tube of light once more. Any rent in the spiritual garment caused by the introduction of inharmony into your forcefield should be mended as soon as you have recovered your balance through the mercy of the Christ.

A tremendous power of protection is afforded the soul who surrounds herself with the unfailing light of God. Archangel Michael, the Defender of the Faith, speaks of God's desire for every man:

"Grace, perfection and victory are the full intention of God for everyone! God does not intend that mankind shall dwell in an unprotected or vulnerable state. God does not intend that mankind shall be subject to domination by the feelings and thoughts of one another. God does not intend that mankind shall make improper suggestions to one another, nor does he intend that as a result of these suggestions individuals shall be led away to fall into error, pain and unhappiness.

"God intends that the protection of that great transcendent Niagara of light that flows down from their own God Presence shall be a tangible substance of Ascended Master light (which you call your tube of light) and that it shall so fortify them against all the hordes of darkness and shadow that nothing—I say, nothing—shall ever pass through!

"Individuals have accepted into their consciousness the idea that the tube of light can be easily rent. And because they have thought that the tube of light could be easily penetrated, it has become so qualified. Therefore, through this tube of light slings and arrows of outrageous fortune have passed—and as a result, unhappiness and struggle have entered into their consciousness.

"When they realize that this great power of light flows down from their own God Presence (which abides above them in space) and radiates around them as a Niagara—a literal torrent of Ascended Master light from the heart of God (from their individualized God Presence), which cannot be pierced— and when they shall so qualify that wall of light, I tell you, man shall have a freedom that he has not known before!"[56]

Could it be that the prophet Jeremiah saw the tube of light and the violet fire inside it when God foretold the judgment of the Moabites that would surely come? The record in Jeremiah 48:45, when understood in its esoteric interpretation, suggests that he did:

"They that fled stood under the shadow of Heshbon because of the force [the negatively qualified energies of mankind, mass thoughts and feelings called the sinister force]: but a fire shall come forth [the same Presence that was in the pillar of fire or tube of light that provided protection and direction for the Israelites when they crossed the wilderness now exacts judgment upon the consciousness of idolatry] out of Heshbon [the Hebrew word for 'accounting' suggests a place of karmic reckoning], and a flame [the violet transmuting flame] from the midst of Sihon [a cult center], and shall devour [transmute] the corner of Moab [the portion of substance misqualified by the Moabites], and the crown of the head [the cause and core] of the tumultuous ones [of their emotional substance]."

Words That Key the Energies of God

The power of affirmations that use the name of God to draw down his light should be understood in connection with the violet flame and the tube of light decree. In fact, the science of being is based upon God's own affirmation of his flaming identity, given to Moses: "I AM THAT I AM!"[57] But it is not necessary for us to probe this science or the far reaches of God's consciousness in order to understand one important and immediate verity: The words "I AM" key the energies and the very living Presence of God himself whenever and wherever they are spoken.

Man cannot utter this scientific statement of being without experiencing a portion of the divine consciousness. Therefore, whenever the words "I AM" are spoken, they should be followed by constructive statements that will fix in mind the regenerative nature of the Christ Self (the true man of God) as well as the divine intent of wisdom and power for the freeing of the whole man.

We offer a simple decree that you can memorize and use often to affirm the nature of God in man as a flame—a violet flame. Each time you say the words "I AM" you are affirming that "God in me is . . . " Now you see that whatever follows in your invocation is being activated by the Presence of God right where you are, in the very heart center of your being and consciousness.

I AM the violet flame
     In action in me now
I AM the violet flame
     To light alone I bow
I AM the violet flame
     In mighty cosmic power
I AM the light of God
     Shining every hour
I AM the violet flame
     Blazing like a sun
I AM God's sacred power
     Freeing every one

The Washing of the Water by the Word: The Violet Flame

When you conclude the ritual of invoking the tube of light as an expression of the highest yoga, it is essential that you draw forth in greater measure the violet fire of freedom's love in, through and around yourself within the tube of light.

The violet flame is not always felt, and it is usually not visible to one who is just beginning to practice this ritual. However, it can become visible and tangible in a very short time. Therefore, when calling forth the flame, always hold in consciousness the vivid memory of a roaring, crackling fire—a violet fire. Envision the action of the flame intensely, to the point where you can feel and hear its pulsations in the pores of your physical body, in your brain, your bones, your nerves, and in every cell and atom of your entire being.

There are certain activities in the flame involving elemental life—the dancing electrons, the fiery salamanders and the very energy components of the flame itself. These are magnetized in the service of man through intense visualization. This visualization must include not only a mental image but also the feeling of the heart—a great love for the light and an empathy with the flame that enables you to experience a unity with God bordering on spiritual ecstasy. The stronger the visualization, the stronger will be the action of the flame. And the action of the flame must be experienced with all of your spiritual faculties. In like manner, these faculties will come alive as you use the violet flame.

A simple method of visualizing the flames is to fix in mind the memory of a blazing campfire. Retaining the concept of the action of the physical flames, see them take on the color of the God Flame you desire to invoke—in this case, violet.

Now enlarge your image of the flames to fill your entire consciousness. Then visualize yourself stepping into the center of God's flaming Presence. Feel his love enfold you as a thousand-petaled lotus—each flame a petal of God's all-embracing consciousness.

Through the conscientious use of the "violet singing flame" (as it has been referred to by Archangel Zadkiel[58]), the cause, effect, record and memory of all errors and harmful momentums of the past are loosened from your entire consciousness, being and world. By the power of the light of God that never fails, these are changed in the twinkling of an eye into spiritual energy, which may then be used to implement your forward movement and regeneration into the domain of freedom.

As a vital adjunct to your devotions, the violet fire should be made an integral part of your visualization of the tube of light. Originating in the heart of the Presence, the light ray descends into your forcefield. When it reaches the "ground" (the point of invocation), it springs up as a violet flame. See it leaping and pulsating through the folds of your consciousness as the purple lining of the seamless robe.

In olden days, the cloak of violet transmuting flame was

worn by rulers sponsored by the Brotherhood. This mantle of protection (the divinely vested 'rite' of kings as a focus of the flame of freedom—the royal purple) assisted them in transmuting unwanted conditions in their own worlds, as well as in repelling the vicious thoughts and feelings of others.

The power of the violet flame and of all of the flames of God is known as "the power of the three-times-three," because it contains within it the action of the threefold flame. It is through this power to make you whole that the violet flame readies you for initiations to come.

As you know, the zero that is added to one to make ten introduces the next place in a column of figures. Spiritually speaking, the step from grade 9 (which is the power of the 3 x 3) to grade 10 is the step of initiation. It is your graduation into the next order of magnitude of the God Flame within. Here the cycle of transformation moves into the ascending spiral of the transfiguration. Here you are expected to have readied yourself through the ritual of transmutation for the divine testing.

Saint Paul referred to this test as a daily challenge when he said, "I die daily." He also said, "The fire shall try every man's work of what sort it is."[59] For when the violet transmuting flame is called forth on the altar of being, it does ready your consciousness for the cycles of initiation that follow.

The violet flame, as the pen of the Architect of your noblest aspirations, focuses the power of the Holy Spirit, which assists you to transmute your negatives and to make way for the great positive onrush of divine perfection into your world.

If you will call upon the violet flame at least once but preferably two or three times a day, you will find that the causes and core of unhappiness, fear, distress and a host of knotty human problems will gradually be eliminated from your world. This takes place as the lower self is stripped of its records and momentums of past mistakes. As the violet flame transmutes the energies that you have invested in imperfection, they rise into your Causal Body and are stored there until you need them.

As a generous application of the violet flame dissolves the penetrations of the psychic effluvia of the world and the wrong thoughts and feelings of others, there occurs what we may call a "washing of the water by the Word."[60] This is a spiritual cleansing. It is the baptism by fire that John the Baptist was referring to when he said, "One mightier than I cometh, the latchet of whose shoes I am not worthy to unloose: he shall baptize you with the Holy Ghost and with fire."[61]

The "Getting" of the Holy Spirit

Now, it is true that through persistent prayer made to God and Christ, the followers of some religious movements do invoke a descent of the Paraclete (the Holy Spirit), whose presence causes great changes to be wrought in them if they are receptive to the leadings of the Holy Spirit.

However, the gift of the Holy Comforter is not always retained. Sometimes the recipients return to the world and once again take up its ways, thereby spilling the precious oil from the cup of their consciousness. And even those who are wholly sincere may lose the blessing conferred because they do not know how to hold the essence of the divine light and how to protect it from the vampire activities of the psychic forces who, whenever possible, feed upon the pure energies of the devout.

It should be noted in this connection that the infilling of the consciousness with the power and radiance of the Holy Spirit can also come about through the consistent use of the violet flame. This is the process of gradual conferment, whereby an individual can invoke in his world the baptism by fire of the Holy Spirit as he passes successfully through the orderly steps of initiation. If he desires with all of his heart to "get" the

Holy Spirit, he may use this gradual method to ensure that he retains in his world the love and light of the Paraclete.

But the consecration of his life to the Holy Spirit places great demands on the disciple. He must be willing to be self-disciplined if he would be God-taught. He must maintain a great inner reserve and an outer calmness that he might retain in the chalice of his consciousness the essence of the sacred fire that he invokes. The process of putting on the LORD's Spirit is cumulative; therefore, he cannot afford to dissipate the sacred energies of life through self-indulgence or the condemnation of any part of the Body of God.

On the other hand, if the disciple adheres to the precepts of the flames, the results of his efforts to be an instrument of the Holy Comforter can bring about a complete change in the nature of his consciousness and outlook.

The spiritualization of consciousness is an altogether natural process that involves not only the violet flame but also all of the flames that issue forth from the heart of God. The consciousness of the Holy Spirit is the prism through which these flames pass as they travel from God to man. One approaches the Holy Spirit most rapidly through the violet fire because this is the flame that consumes the human creation that stands between man and his God and prevents his union with the Highest. But just as all roads lead to Rome, so all rays lead to the Holy Spirit. We would, therefore, acquaint you with the many paths that lead Home.

Blazing the Homeward Path with the Flames of God

Following is a list of the flames of God that may be invoked by those who desire to practice the highest yoga. Regardless of their color, all of the flames have a white fire core of purity that embodies all of the attributes of God.

*Flame of faith, power, perfection, protection and the
    will of God:* blue—an activity of the first ray;
Flame of wisdom, intelligence and illumination
    (focusing the Mind of God): yellow—
    an activity of the second ray;
Flame of adoration, love and beauty: pink—
    an activity of the third ray;
Flame of purity (focusing the inherent design of all
    creation), also known as *the ascension flame:*
    white—an activity of the fourth ray;
Flame of healing: emerald green—
    an activity of the fifth ray;
Flame of precipitation, abundance and supply:
    Chinese green tinged with gold—
    an activity of the fifth ray;
Flame of ministration and service: purple and gold—
    an activity of the sixth ray;
Flame of freedom and transmutation, also known
    as *the violet singing flame:* violet—
    an activity of the seventh ray;
Mercy flame: shades ranging from pink-violet to
    orchid and deep purple (visualizing a pink center
    around the white fire core of the mercy flame
    will intensify the action of Divine Love within
    the quality of forgiveness)—an activity of the
    seventh ray;
Mighty Cosmos' secret rays: five flames whose colors
    have not been revealed, which may be invoked
    with great personal and planetary benefit;
Threefold flame, also known as the flame of the
    Christ because it focuses the balanced action of
    love, wisdom and power, a prerequisite to
    Christhood: pink, gold and blue, three plumes

anchored in the heart of the God Presence, the
Christ Self and the physical body of man—
an activity of the first, second and third rays;

Resurrection flame: mother-of-pearl—
an activity of the sixth ray;

Flame of comfort (also known as *the flame of the
Holy Spirit*): white tinged with a delicate pink—
an activity of the third and fourth rays;

Cosmic honor flame: white tinged with gold—
an activity of the fourth and sixth rays;

Flame of peace: golden yellow, often used in
conjunction with the purple flame—
an activity of the sixth ray;

Fearlessness flame: white tinged with green—
an activity of the fourth and fifth rays.

The use of the violet transmuting flame and of all of the
flames can lead man far along the path of the highest yoga. For
they enable him not only to decree a thing and to establish it in
his world[62] ("accentuate the positive") but also to negate negativity ("eliminate the negative"[63])—to remove the cause and
core of, and therefore the propensity toward, wrong action.

Putting Off the Old and Putting On the New

Lord Lanto teaches: "Each man's cultivation of his consciousness is dominated by the patterns of mind and soul that
are layered deep within his subconscious. It is because of these
unseen influences that people say they don't understand themselves. They don't know why they do what they do. It is not
possible for them to pry open the doorway of consciousness, to
roam the corridors of memory and see each habit as it develops, and then to weed out undesirable thought patterns.

"There is a better way. And that way is the saturation of one's consciousness with the flame of cosmic worth. . . .

"We dare not eliminate the tares from the field of human consciousness without taking into account that if we do so prematurely we may also uproot the good wheat.[64] It is known that when the shoots are young the tares and the wheat look alike. And so they are left to grow side by side until the harvest. When they are mature and ready to harvest, they are easily separated. The tares are gathered and bound in bundles to be burned, and the wheat is gathered into the barn.

"The safest way to eliminate the tares of the human consciousness before they choke the wheat of the divine consciousness is to use the flames of God. But men seldom realize just what the flames are, and when we speak of them they are often puzzled.

"Let us repeat, then, that there is a natural order and universe, and there is a spiritual order and universe. . . . The flames of God are of the spiritual order; and these, by the grace of God, penetrate the natural order with the transforming power of the Holy Spirit."[65]

Of course, Nature abhors a vacuum. Thus you cannot continue to use the violet transmuting flame and the other flames of God and not become wholly constructive in your thoughts and feelings. Simultaneously with the destruction of imperfect models, the construction of right thoughts and feelings must take place.

Jesus compared a man from whom an unclean spirit had been cast out to a house swept clean, freed from human miscreation and demons of human thought and feeling. Jesus said that unless such a man were careful, the unclean spirit would go and find seven others worse than himself and return to inhabit the house. "And the last state of that man is worse than the first."[66]

To guard against such an occurrence, the tube of light should always be used in connection with the invocation of the various flames of God—and certainly the building of a Christ-like character should become a temple ritual. The use of the violet flame prepares man's temple to be the dwelling place of the Holy Spirit. Thus, purifying his temple "even as he is pure,"[67] man is able to retain the new wine of the Spirit.

Old things must pass away and all things must become new. Saint Francis of Assisi understood well this process of putting off the old and putting on the new, and he expressed it in his prayer:

> Lord, make me an instrument of thy peace.
> Where there is hatred, let me sow love;
> Where there is injury, pardon;
> Where there is doubt, faith;
> Where there is despair, hope;
> Where there is darkness, light; and
> Where there is sadness, joy.
>
> O Divine Master, grant that I may not so much
> Seek to be consoled as to console;
> To be understood as to understand;
> To be loved as to love.
> For it is in giving that we receive,
> It is in pardoning that we are pardoned, and
> It is in dying that we are born to eternal life.

Harmony: The Key to the Key

A key requirement for those who would pursue the highest yoga is maintaining harmony. God Harmony is a Cosmic Being who so espoused the flame of harmony that he became known by that name.

He tells us: "Harmony is a science, even as music is a science; and the notes of mathematics strike the chords of cosmic principles. . . .

"The flame of God's harmony creates a magnet of the Central Sun. That supreme magnet of love harmonious is all-attractive of all good and all-repelling of all evil. Therefore those who would survive when the earth is in chaos and disintegration and death must understand clearly that the antidote for all of this is the purity of harmony. . . .

"Harmony, then, is the balance of light, of sun centers, electronic forcefields. When there is balance, then there is harmony. When there is balance and harmony, then and only then can there be acceleration.

"You may have wondrous gifts of virtue, but often in a lifetime or many lifetimes an individual lifestream does not exceed a certain level of attainment professionally or a certain level of virtue because the individual reaches the line where there is no longer balance, where he cannot carry into an accelerated momentum that virtue which may function at a lesser vibration.

"Take, for example, a top that spins. In order to spin, it must have a certain acceleration and a certain balance. Thus when the law of harmony functioning within you goes below the level of a certain acceleration, it can no longer be maintained. And this is when discord enters in with disintegration and ultimately self-destruction. Thus in order to have the key of harmony, you must have the key of the acceleration of love. . . .

"Wherever energy is tied in knots of self-deception, of dissonance, of selfishness, of hatred—all of these manifestations, including anxiety itself, cause the deceleration of that which is God-harmony within the very fiery core of the threefold flame itself. Thus when the momentum of dissonance becomes too great, the top of the threefold flame cannot spin. When its three plumes are of differing height (out of balance), it cannot spin, and therefore the resurrection fires do not glow.

"Thus when considering, then, those who have certain virtues that they cannot exceed, we contemplate individuals who, for example, under normal conditions may express patience or mercy or kindness, but as soon as stress and distress is introduced into the life pattern, then the individual is no longer kind, patient and merciful. This is because these qualities have received only a certain impetus to acceleration. They have not accelerated further because of the impediments within the four lower bodies.

"These impediments are as islands of darkness in a sea of light—that is, it is hoped that that is the condition of consciousness. For where consciousness is a sea of light with islands of darkness, these islands can be inundated with the flame of love and freedom and transmutation and therefore they can be readily dissolved. But when individuals are not attentive to maintaining the cosmic sea of consciousness and they allow the precious gift of the receptacle of life to now become more and more dominated by larger and larger islands of blackness and despair and darkness, sins that go unconfessed, these islands become continents. And soon they occupy more space and time within the energy field than the sea of light—and they swallow up that sea. And therefore the individual has not the ability to press forward and to accelerate any gift of life, any flame of creativity, or to see through the completion of a simple project. Therefore we turn the attention of our chelas to the science of God's own flame of harmony. . . .

"May God-harmony, as the white fire core of all being and light and radiation, come to mean more to you than all else in life. May God-harmony provide you with the key to light— which itself is the alchemical key. Thus harmony is the key to the key.

"Think upon these words and ask yourself this question:

'How many doors will I pass through, how many keys must I find to finally enter into the Holy of holies of my very own God Being?'"[68]

The Mystery of the Threefold Flame

Pursuing our study of the highest yoga, we approach the mystery of the threefold flame of Christ-illumination that God has placed within each heart. Although less than one-sixteenth of an inch in height in the average person, this flame can be expanded until it penetrates the entire physical envelope and passes into the atmosphere of earth as a greater expression of the Christly nature of man.

The three plumes of the flame should be seen in the following order: the pink (love) to one's right, extended through the right hand in service; the yellow (wisdom) in the center, illumining the mind and heart; and the blue (power) to one's left, drawing in the strength of God.

While there are seven rays in manifestation and each person has a special affinity with one or more of the seven, all hold in common the manifestation of the Holy Christ Flame within the heart. This threefold flame of life is projected as a ray of light from the heart of the Presence through the crystal cord. This ray descends first to the Christ Self (the Higher Mental Body), where it springs up as a flame. The ray continues its descent into the heart of man, where it produces another flaming focus of the threefold nature of the Christ.

The Ascended Master Saint Germain has used the fleur-de-lis (the golden lily with three petals) as his personal insignia and as the emblem of the cause of freedom that he has so nobly espoused. The fleur-de-lis is a replica of the flame of life resident in every man. This tripartite flame is in reality the one flame of life that beats all hearts.

Love, wisdom and power constitute the trinity of the divine nature manifest in man. A man or woman who possesses these qualities in perfect balance is known as a Christed one. When one of the plumes is out of proportion, there is a corresponding imbalance in the outer personality. The rebalancing of the threefold flame is the only means whereby such personal imbalances can be corrected. This process is absolutely essential before the divine union can take place. For the threefold flame in man must become congruent with the threefold flame in God, ere God and man can be truly one.

Of what value is power, for example, when the rest of a man's nature exhibits very little wisdom and very little love? And when an individual has a larger concentration of the yellow plume, he is intellectually brittle; he lacks the qualities of loving understanding and the willpower to employ his mental skills effectively in the domain of world action or for his personal success. Then again, an individual may be, so to speak, "all heart." His manifestation is all love—but he lacks the ability to convey this love actively to others and often expresses little intelligence as to how to convey it in a proper manner.

All in all it can be observed by anyone that an unbalanced activity of the threefold flame of life will not produce harmony in the world of the individual. Therefore, the decree "Balance the Threefold Flame in Me," given at the end of this chapter, is a plea to the Godhead and to the Christ Self to strengthen the plumes of the threefold flame according to individual need. For it must be recognized that every disciple has a need to amplify in his own nature the qualities of the Christ in which he may be lacking. To do this he must be objective about his personal weaknesses and deficiencies of character, realizing that the light of the Christ is always present—even at the very door of his heart—to raise him from the valleys of discouragement and defeat to the summits of attainment.

Those who come to Luxor to sit at the feet of the Master Serapis and to learn the precepts of self-mastery hear the following instruction on the balancing of the threefold flame in one of the first lectures they attend:

"When men fail to progress, it is always because there is imbalance in the threefold flame of life. The life that beats your hearts is a triad of motion, consisting of tripartite energies. The Holy Trinity of Father, Son and Holy Spirit—of body, mind and soul; of thesis, antithesis and synthesis; of Brahma, Vishnu and Shiva;[69] of love, wisdom and power—is also the pink, blue and gold of divine consciousness.

"The will of God is a predominant third of the whole; but lacking the wisdom of God, the golden illumination of his supreme knowledge, even power is stifled of action; and without love, power and wisdom become but the brittleness of self-preservation. The balance of the threefold flame creates a pattern of the ascension for all.

"Dominant emotions are controlled by love and by the power of love in action. Because the wisdom of men is foolishness with God,[70] they perceive that not in the psychology of the world but in the balance of the energies of the heart do men bank the fires of the ascension against the day of their victory. The furnace of being, heated white-hot, must needs manifest the colors of the sacred fire. And the coil from the serpent's nest must needs rise upright, being lifted by wings of faith, hope and accomplishment (faith, hope and charity) until the Christ-man is enthroned in all. This is a scientific victory of the Spirit.

"Not without precedent was this universe created. No idle experiment was behind the program but the ageless wisdom of the infinite Creator, whose purposes are dimly perceived by men of lesser vision. Emotions controlled by love in balance with wisdom create a sharp etch of power that life cannot resist. Progress stems, then, from attunement with all of the triune aspects of God in perfect balance.

"If your tendency is to excessive study and the feeling of egoistic wisdom gleaned from the world's storehouse of knowledge, remember that with all thy getting, unless thou hast wisdom thy knowledge is but a tinkling bell or a clanging cymbal. And if the love that thou art manifesting is a love in expectation of return as a dowry from the beloved, thou art not cognizant of the will of the Great Giver, whose every desire is to give the allness of himself unto the beloved. If thy power is as a flood or a raging fire that covers the mountains and the plains or consumes that which it seeks to benefit, thou must then master holy wisdom and holy love that thy power may be within the reins of the trinity of balance."[71]

The one flame of life is the same for all. And yet, because of the various qualifications that men have stamped upon the energies that flow hourly from the heart of the Presence, it does not manifest the same in all. To balance one's nature, then—in the realization that the divine nature of man is the essence of God's love, God's wisdom and God's power—is an important phase of temple work that may be engaged in immediately by all and will convey immediate benefits.

In this chapter we have conferred the rudiments of the highest yoga upon all who would receive them as a little child. The practice of these simple precepts requires but a little time each day with the expenditure of naught else save your energy and attention.

Will you not try to utilize this highest yoga, not only for your own freedom but also for the freedom of all mankind? If you will practice the highest yoga consistently and follow the other instructions given in this book, you can well become a God-free being. Following in the footsteps of the Nazarene Master, you will find your cosmic destiny unfolding before you as the infinite path of life.

Decree to Balance the Threefold Flame

In the name of the beloved Mighty Victorious Presence of God I AM in me and my very own beloved Holy Christ Self, I call to beloved Alpha and Omega, beloved Helios and Vesta and the threefold flame of love, wisdom and power in the heart of the Great Central Sun, to beloved Morya El, beloved Lord Lanto, beloved Paul the Venetian, beloved Mighty Victory, beloved Goddess of Liberty and the Seven Mighty Elohim, beloved Lanello, the entire Spirit of the Great White Brotherhood and the World Mother, elemental life—fire, air, water and earth!

To balance, blaze, expand and intensify the threefold flame within my heart until I AM manifesting all of thee and naught of the human remains.

Take complete dominion and control over my four lower bodies and raise me and all life by the power of the three-times-three into the glorious resurrection and ascension in the light!

In the name of the Father, the Mother, the Son and the Holy Spirit, I decree:

> Balance the threefold flame in me! (3x)
>   Beloved I AM!
> Balance the threefold flame in me! (3x)
>   Take thy command!
> Balance the threefold flame in me! (3x)
>   Magnify it each hour!
> Balance the threefold flame in me! (3x)
>   Love, wisdom and power!

[Give the decree four times using "blaze," "expand" and "intensify" in place of "balance" the second, third and fourth times. End with the following paragraph.]

And in full faith I consciously accept this manifest, manifest, manifest! (3x) right here and now with full power, eternally sustained, all-powerfully active, ever expanding, and world enfolding until all are wholly ascended in the light and free! Beloved I AM! Beloved I AM! Beloved I AM!

Chapter 2

The Ascension

And Enoch walked with God:
and he was not; for God took him.

GENESIS

The Ascension

IF YOU COULD SIT AT THE FEET OF THE greatest Master and ask him, "What is the purpose of life?" he would reply, "It is to prepare yourself for the ascension."

Serapis Bey, hierarch of the Ascension Temple in Luxor, Egypt, tells us: "Men must return to the pristine, to the reality of the inner walk with God, to the high temple magic embodied and captured by living Truth."[1]

The purpose of man's incarnation, as the Great Divine Director defines it, "is to ascend back to the heart of God after the manifestation of victorious overcoming. Unless this purpose be served, mankind continue to reap the effects of their own sowings, which are usually cumulative in the sense that more discord is created than balanced in any given period of time. Therefore, there is always a balance of payments required, necessitating their return to the planet earth through the ritual of reembodiment. This continual extension of the mercy of God to man is a necessity as well as an opportunity for those who try and try again, finally to succeed.

"Those who succeed in the kingdom of God to balance the accepted portion of their debts to life find the natural expansion of the flame of life pouring through their flesh forms, through their consciousness, through their thoughts and feelings—until the spirit of the resurrection, penetrating the universe with the power of the Sun behind the sun, draws the mighty light rays of the Presence of God into the physical form, and the consciousness ascends in ever-expanding awareness. These find, as did Elijah when he was caught up into heaven in the chariot of fire, that the very atoms and electrons composing their beings begin to draw forth from the Godhead increasing radiance, and their forms and four lower bodies are literally transfigured."[2]

What Is the Ascension?

What, then, is the ascension? The ascension is the victorious return to God of his beloved Son, whose descent into form is solely for the purpose of expressing below the qualities of heaven that are Above. We refer not to place, but to condition. Once the individual son has overcome outer conditions, he can say with Christ, "I have meat to eat that ye know not of."[3] For his every surge of joy is the joy of God, of the angels, of fulfillment.

Saint Germain says: "When the gift of the ascension is given to anyone by his own I AM Presence and the Karmic Board, the appearance of age drops from him as swiftly as a smile can raise the lips, and the magnetism and energy of that one becomes the unlimited power of God surging through his being. The dross of the physical body, the weariness of the emotional body tired of the creations of hatred, the ceaseless rote of the mental body—all drop away and are replaced in perfect ease by their divine counterparts. The feelings become charged by the love of God and the angels. The mind is imbued with the diamond-shining Mind of God—omnipresent, omniscient, omnipotent. The total being is inspired and aspiring."[4]

Through the ascension the Son becomes one with the Father. He can no longer remain wedded to the earth, for he is filled with the light of the Sun and he has no further need for the physical body. In a moment, in the twinkling of an eye, he is changed: his flesh becomes transparent, his veins are filled with golden-pink light, and the very atoms of his being become lighter and lighter. In this weightless condition man's buoyant, God-free form can no longer be bound to earth. Therefore he must rise "into the air," where a cloud of white light receives him out of mortal sight—and the Son, reuniting with the Father, merges into his omnipresence.

The ascension, then, is a raising action that affects the entire being of man. The rising of the form into the air is actually a side effect that results from the acceleration of the electrons revolving around the nucleus of every atom in the four lower bodies. Through this process of acceleration the individual consciousness blends with the Christ consciousness of the Eternal Preceptor.

In the ritual of the ascension, the soul attains permanent reunion first with the Christ Self and then with the I AM Presence. From this level of God-centered Be-ness, distinguished from earthly planes only by an increase in the velocity of the electrons or in their vibratory rate (as some have called it), ascended man can "so come in like manner" as he went into heaven.[5]

This does not mean that Ascended Beings reembody in physical form, but rather that they possess the power after the ascension to appear at will to unascended men, thereby extending the blessings and healings of the octaves of light to those who have not yet attained. Thus did Jesus appear on Patmos to beloved John.[6] Since that time he has appeared to many of his disciples.

"The ascension is an inevitable part of the divine system," says Serapis in his introductory lessons to neophytes. "It consists of these initiations: the transfiguration into the divine configuration, the ritual of the crucifixion upon the cross of Matter, the resurrection from dead substance, and at last that of the ascension flame itself, which raises man out of the domain of his recalcitrant energies and all treacherous activities, mortal imperfection and error. The ascension is the beginning of the kingdom for each one. And when every soul is taken and none left, the world itself will ascend back to the heart of God, a planet victorious."[7]

The Initiations of the Transfiguration and the Crucifixion

The Maha Chohan explains: "The transfiguration is when the light of the Cosmic Christ descends to fill you, and the power of the Holy Spirit and the Father-Mother God, until every atom and cell of your being is a vessel of light. And those near you should see then the glistening white of your garments.... You pass through the initiation of the crucifixion because you have experienced the transfiguration."[8]

John the Beloved, the disciple who witnessed Jesus' transfiguration, crucifixion and resurrection, gives invaluable instruction on the initiation of the crucifixion: "Do you understand that you can pass through this initiation without surrendering the four lower bodies? Do you understand that the atonement that you can make is an atonement of energy factor?

"Through the surrender of all energy that God has ever given to you into the flame of the sacred fire you can hold the balance for the planet by the weight of light. ('My burden is light!'⁹) The burden of light that you carry comes from the transmuted efforts of the sacrifice of all that is less than perfection.

"The day will come when God will claim the four lower bodies also. But you can be a living witness to the purging of the cells and of many cells in the Body of God upon earth that these lively stones in the temple might be the electrodes that keep the whole consciousness of humanity intact, preserved for the coming of the great glory of the law of love.

"There are some in every age who elect to become stars in the firmament of being. And as one age is concluded and another begins there must be those who make the arc, carrying energy spirals from one dispensation to the next, from one level of consciousness to the next. These form the bridge over which all of humanity pass into a golden age of enlightenment and peace. . . .

"You are living in the time when the drama, the reenactment of the sacred ritual of Good Friday of the descent of Jesus into the planes where those departed spirits dwelled is to be reenacted by the many and by the few on behalf of the many. The initiation of the crucifixion involves the descent of the soul to the darkest levels of the planet where there are those rebellious ones who have refused to acknowledge the Christ as the light 'which lighteth every man that cometh into the world.'¹⁰

"Therefore, you see, while the body of Jesus lay in the tomb, his soul, his higher mind was active in the depths of the astral, in the place that has been called purgatory, where the souls of the departed ones from the days of Noah (the days of the sinking of Atlantis) were held because they refused to submit to the law of God. Therefore they had been denied rebirth and entrance to the screen of life.

"It was the assignment of Jesus (and it is the assignment of every man and woman who would follow through in the ritual of the crucifixion) to go to the darkest places of the earth and to preach the light, to compel the spirits to come into alignment with the Presence of God. At the moment, then, just before the quickening of the body cells with the resurrection fire, it is necessary to bear witness of the Truth to the mass consciousness. Thus you will see how you will find yourselves teaching the Word of Truth in places you had not expected to be. And you will understand that this is part of a sacred ritual and that you cannot partake to the fullness of the resurrection spiral until you have accomplished this mission.

"It is necessary that in the hour of trial these rebellious ones see the glory, see the sacrifice and the victory upon your brow. It is necessary that they come in contact with those who are willing to make the final sacrifice on their behalf. When the contact is made and the Word as the sacred bread of life has been broken, you can return for the celebration of the resurrection spiral. And then the quickening of the body temple, the soul, the heart and the mind will also be for those to whom you have preached."

Remember well these words of John the Beloved, "Without the cross, there can be no crown. Without the crucifixion, there can be no resurrection."[11]

The Resurrection Flame and the Ascension Flame

"The future is what you make it, even as the present is what you made it," Serapis Bey says. "If you do not like it, God has provided a way for you to change it—and the way is through the acceptance of the currents of the ascension flame."[12]

Man identifies so closely with his physical body, his emotions, his thoughts and his memory patterns that he seldom realizes who or what he really is. In actuality, man is a flaming spirit who descended into mortal form and consciousness to prove his mastery over self and substance in order that he might ascend back to the Spirit from whence he came.

As a result of his identification with form consciousness (which always involves duality), man has created a personal record of good mingled with evil. Whereas the good has risen to his Causal Body, the evil has accumulated in a negative spiral that surrounds his form as an electronic belt. This accumulation of negative qualities has been called human effluvia. It is an actual accumulation of substance—an energy veil qualified with mortal thought and feeling—which has density and weight. In addition to clogging the four lower bodies and thereby hindering the flow of purity through man's being, this negative spiral (sanctioned by the ego, the intellect and the will of the human) directly opposes the ascension spiral and confines the soul to the gravitational pull of the earth.

Throughout the history of the planet, certain lifestreams have proved that this negative spiral of human limitation can be overcome through the scientific qualification of God's energies—that is, through invoking the sacred fire. In studying the magnificent example of the Master Jesus and the initiations that he publicly demonstrated for and on behalf of mankind, we find that during his ministry he employed specific aspects of the sacred fire to prove certain aspects of the Law. Each demonstration of the superiority of Divine Law over human law fulfilled in his life a phase of one or more of the thirty-three initiations that every ascending soul must pass.

In this chapter we are concerned with Jesus' overcoming of the last enemy—death. Using the powers of the sacred fire, first as it manifests in the frequency of the resurrection flame and then as it pulsates in the ascension currents, Jesus proved life to be the natural and death the unnatural state of being.

The first biblical records of Jesus' use of the flame of

resurrection to restore life to the physical body were the raising
of the widow's son and Jairus' daughter. Subsequently, with the
raising of Lazarus[13] and ultimately with his own resurrection,
Jesus proved for all time the superiority of divine science over
the laws of death and decay.

The resurrection flame is an acceleration of the threefold
flame whereby the pink, blue and yellow plumes blend as one
flame having the rainbow iridescence of mother-of-pearl. The
presence of the color spectrum within the flame signifies that its
intensity or velocity is just beneath that of the pure white fire of
the ascension current.

The resurrection flame is used to resuscitate and to heal the
four lower bodies by releasing the power locked within the
white fire core of every atom of man's being. The ascension
flame is used to accelerate his bodies to the point of total
reunion not only with the white fire core of his atoms but also
with his own I AM Presence. Thus in the invocation of the resurrection flame, the light from within the atoms is drawn without to heal man's "flesh." In the invocation of the ascension
flame, the flesh itself is accelerated to the frequency of the light
within the atom.

When man is able to sustain the frequency of the ascension
flame within his flesh, nothing can prevent his reunion with the
white fire core, which is the ascension in the light. Jesus was
one in whom the glory of God, in the fullness of the divine
descent, pulsated through the flesh form as the white light. This
light, surging and resurging from the heart of God, entered into
the blazing sun of every atom of substance in his world and
changed the corruptible into the incorruptible.

Gautama Buddha describes the power of the resurrection
flame: "The effect of this flame upon the environment where it
descends may be comparable to the energy released in the splitting of the atom. By resurrection's flame not only was the stone

rolled away, but boulders were cleaved asunder, the mountains moved, the thunder and the lightning descended, and that which was mortal was set aside as Jesus walked the earth to complete his life span and service, fully the embodiment of the spirit of the resurrection.

"The blessed one, as the Son of man, did demonstrate what must be demonstrated by the evolutions of the planet in this hour."[14]

During the three-day initiatic period following his crucifixion, Jesus drew the resurrection flame into his four lower bodies, where it quickened the action of the threefold flame of life that forms the nucleus of every cell. The resuscitation of his physical body was made possible by the overpowering radiance of his eternally conscious, immortal spirit, which was transferred to his form through the impelling currents of the resurrection flame. The flame of life, magnified by the Holy Spirit and the ministering angelic hosts, was thus breathed into his form once again. The ritual of the resurrection, reenacted in the nature kingdom each spring, was fulfilled in the Son of God on behalf of the Son of man on that first Easter.

However, you can receive the initiation of the resurrection without having to go through the process called death. There are initiates who walk this earth in the resurrected state, having passed through the initiation of the resurrection. This is a pre-ascension initiation in which you walk the earth in a physical body yet bear the flame of the resurrection, the spiral of mother-of-pearl radiance whereby you emit the rainbow rays of God.

For a prescribed period of forty days following his resurrection, Jesus instructed his disciples in Cosmic Law. At the same time, sustaining the momentum of the resurrection flame within his being, he was able to anchor the hope of the resurrection in the four lower bodies of the planet and in the evolving consciousness of humanity.

When the cycle of his victory came full circle, it was the cosmic moment for the resurrection flame, spiraling through his world, to be accelerated to the frequency of the ascension flame. As this action was taking place, the beloved Master walked up Bethany's hill and there, in the presence of many witnesses, he ascended into the cloud of his I AM Presence. The sacred fire within his being merged with the sacred fire swirling without. Thus the flaming spirit of man became one with the Flaming Spirit of God, and he disappeared from mortal sight because his being no longer vibrated at the level of the mortal consciousness.

Thus as the onlookers gazed at Jesus' form, they perceived that it rose from Bethany's hill in a glory of such transcendence and inspiration as to stir their souls for all eternity. The wind blew upon his garments and the majesty of his expression was beyond description. The pulsations of his love for each of them quickened the flame of response in their own hearts. The more illumined among them knew within themselves that there by God's grace they would one day be, following him in the regeneration.

Higher and higher into the air he rose, and by and by a great covering of white fire, resembling a cloud, concealed him from their sight. While they yet looked steadfastly toward heaven, two angels stood by them in white apparel. These spake and said, "Ye men of Galilee, why stand ye gazing up into heaven? This same Jesus, which is taken up from you into heaven, shall so come in like manner as ye have seen him go into heaven."[15]

And so he did, for Jesus did return from the cloud of his I AM Presence. The event on Bethany's hill was not the conclusion of Jesus' life on earth, although he there demonstrated his ability to become one with his I AM Presence and one with

Lord Maitreya (whom he called "Father"). Jesus yet walked the earth in the full glory of the resurrection flame. He left Palestine to travel to the East, where he taught until his ascension at the age of eighty-one.

Gautama Buddha outlines the path that Jesus took: "What a joy it is to know that the blessed one, Jesus, did walk the earth in the resurrection flame from the hour when he did quit the area of Palestine, did take his leave for other assignments and ultimately did finish out that beautiful life on earth at the age of eighty-one in the power of the nine and the nine-times-nine and the three-times-three. Such a beautiful fulfillment!

"All of these years the earth received the anchoring of his resurrection flame through the mountain chains and the waters, through the fastnesses of the Himalayas. Thus the Lord and Saviour did fulfill all things, even the fullness of the law of the resurrection, that you might follow in his footsteps. Thus did the blessed one abide in Kashmir. Thus did the blessed one ascend in his final Parinirvana from the very heart of Shamballa."[16]

Since that day, many have witnessed the coming of the Lord Christ out of the light into manifestation, proving to them that he is not dead, but alive forevermore—a *living* Master! Jesus bids us follow in his footsteps and gain the attainment to walk the earth in the fullness of the resurrection flame.

Having reached that level of God Self-awareness born of the Spirit, the consciousness and being of the Ascended One is as the wind that bloweth where it listeth.[17] It may go and be wherever it desires to focus the flame of identity. As the Ascended Master Serapis Bey says:

"Consciousness can move. It can penetrate. It can fly. It can break tethers. It can loose itself from the moorings of life and go out into the sea, the briny deep where the salt tears of my joy are a spume of hope, renewed again and again. I am gladdened as never before, and there is no remembrance of the former conditions. These are put aside as finite, as trite, as a passing fancy of the mortal mind.

> Now I engage my consciousness
> With the beings of fire,
> With the seraphic hosts—
> Now I see God's desire
> To be the most intense,
> Glowing white radiance—
> A furnace white-hot
> Whose coolness is my delight.
>
> I see the shadows and the veils
> Of human thought and human foolishness
> Melt and evaporate,
> Vanish in the air;
> And all that I AM is everywhere,
> And everywhere I AM."[18]

John the Beloved asks: "How can we convey to those of you who have not experienced the influx of the great current of the ascension spiral what this energy is? Shall we say that it is like the splitting of a thousand or ten thousand atoms, and man himself being in the center? Shall we say that it is like the explosion of worlds or sun centers? Or shall we say that it is like the unfolding of a lily or a rose?

"Perhaps the poetry of the ascension ought to be written by you as you experience that great ritual—perhaps at the close of this life. For as you have been taught, the doors are open to all who will make the call and give the service and apply for each test. For line upon line, precept upon precept the victory is won. You are ascending daily. You are ascending the spirals of your own being and your own consciousness. You are not as you were yesterday or last week, and if you are giving daily devotions to the Most High you are light-years beyond your former self."[19]

Requirements for the Ascension: Purity, Discipline and Love

Purity, discipline and love are requirements for the ascension, for in these virtues the Law is satisfied: purity of consecration, of heart and mind and soul; discipline of motive and desire; transparent thoughts, feelings and acts, shining in the crystal-clear stream of consciousness flowing back to its Source.

Purity is the discipline of directing all of one's energies in loving action. Purity is going all the way with Christ. It is ministering to the poor in spirit. It is healing the sick and raising the dead. It is submitting to the tests of the Great Initiator. It is surrendering totally and praying without ceasing.

To be pure in the discipline of the Law is to "love the LORD thy God" with one's total being, to "love thy neighbor" as one in whom the Christ Self lives, and to love the Christ in every Ascended Being with enough devotion so that one can put behind him the things of the world and say, "What is that to me? I will follow thee!"[20]

The ritual of the ascension is the goal for everyone who understands his reason for being. This initiation can and will come to anyone—even to a little child, when he is ready: when he has balanced his threefold flame; when his four lower bodies are aligned and functioning as pure chalices for the flame of the Holy Spirit in the world of form; when a balance of mastery has been achieved on all of the rays; when he has attained mastery over sin, sickness and death and over every outer condition; when he has fulfilled his divine plan through service rendered to God and man; when he has balanced at least 51 percent of his karma (that is, when 51 percent of the energy given to him in all of his embodiments has either been constructively qualified or transmuted); and when his heart is just toward both God and man and he aspires to rise into the never-failing light of God's eternally ascending Presence.

The ascension process also involves the passing of those initiations given at Luxor: the transmutation of the electronic belt, the correct use of the chakras and the caduceus, the raising of the seed atom (the Kundalini), and the building of the cone of fire for the transmutation of the last vestiges of one's human creation.

Originally, the complete balancing of personal karma was required before a man could return to the heart of God. Every jot and tittle of the Law had to be fulfilled; every erg of energy he had misqualified throughout all of his incarnations had to be purified before he could ascend. Perfection was the requirement of the Law.

Now, however (thanks to the mercy of God dispensed by the Lords of Karma), the old occult law has been set aside. Those who have balanced only 51 percent of their debts to life can, by divine decree, be given the great blessing of the ascension. This does not mean that man can escape the consequences of his acts, nor does it imply that through the ascension he can evade any unfulfilled responsibilities. This dispensation does, however, enable man to obtain the freedom and perfection of the ascended state more quickly in order that he may from that plane of consciousness balance all remaining debts to life.

Then, when the Great Law has been fulfilled and 100 percent of the energies allotted to him since he came forth from the heart of God have been qualified with perfection, he can proceed on the high road of cosmic adventure and service in the eternally perfect reunion of man with God.

Every man is worthy of God's purity, his love and his discipline, for the Christ is the Real Man who has never sinned and never died. The Christ who lives in all receives the energies of God on behalf of the soul. Therefore, all may invoke purity in his name without fear or shame for past failures, for "he is the propitiation for our sins." By invoking purity, every child of God can dissolve the veil of errors past that has separated him from his true identity. When the veil of his misqualified energy is finally consumed, the Spirit of God will descend upon his unified consciousness and say, "This is my beloved Son, in whom I AM well pleased."[21]

To this end you may use the following meditation technique* to prepare your consciousness for the inflow of purity, which must be invoked daily if it is to be sustained.

White Fire Ball Meditation

Begin by placing your attention upon the Chart of Your Divine Self (facing page 44). When you are at peace and in harmony with all life, center your consciousness in the white fire core of being, which you may visualize as a small white ball at the base of the threefold flame within your heart. Withdraw your senses from their perceptions of the world—your ties to other persons, your thoughts of outer things—for only by so doing can you draw your total being into the white fire ball.

Become first the ball and then the flame within the center of the ball. Picture yourself within the ball, rising up the shaft

---

*Students should beware of meditation techniques performed through the descent of the consciousness by a "countdown" method, in which they are taught to feel themselves descending into a sublevel of awareness rather than ascending from the point of contact within the heart. Such attempts to contact the Spirit of God are not only fraught with danger but also with ultimate failure, for through meditation upon the chakras below the heart man can contact only unreality.

of the crystal cord to the center of your Christ Self-awareness. Tarry here and absorb the radiance of the pure love, pure wisdom and pure power focused in the threefold flame of your Christ Self. Retaining the vision of yourself within the white fire ball, continue up the shaft of the crystal cord to the center of the Divine Monad, the threefold flame in the heart of your own I AM Presence.

Feel yourself becoming one with God until you are no longer consciously defined apart from his Being but are aware only of your Self in God, as God. Bask in the bliss of reunion and realize that here in the Holy of holies you are experiencing a fragment of that which will one day come to you through the ritual of the ascension.

After some moments, feel yourself returning slowly down the shaft of the crystal cord. Concentrating both your God Self-awareness and your Christ Self-awareness within the white fire ball, descend to the point of contact in form, the threefold flame within your heart. Realize that here in the chalice of the four lower bodies you are anchoring the potential of the Father, the Son and the Holy Spirit.

As long as you remain in the consciousness of the flame of life, you have the authority to command—and life will obey. God will speak through you, the Word (the Christ) will go forth and the Spirit will fulfill your decree. Therefore, conscious of the dominion of the Trinity, in humble reverence for the Presence of the Three-in-One, give this prayer for purity:

> In the name of my own beloved Mighty I AM Presence and Holy Christ Self, beloved Jesus the Christ and the Holy Spirit, I humbly invoke the flame of God's purity:
>
> Open the door to purity!
> Open the door to purity!

Let the breezes blow and trumpet purity
Over the sea and over the land:
Let men understand
The voice of Cosmic Christ command!

I come to open wide the way
That men without fear may ever say:
I AM the purity of God
I AM the purity of love
I AM the purity of joy
I AM the purity of grace
I AM the purity of hope
I AM the purity of faith
And all that God can make of joy and grace combined!

Lord, I AM worthy of thy purity! I would have thy purity surge through me in a great cosmic burst to remove from the screen of my mind, my thoughts and my feelings every appearance of human vibratory action and all that is impure in substance, thought or feeling.

Replace all that right now with the fullness of the Mind of Christ and the Mind of God, the manifest power of the resurrection spirit and the ascension flame, that I may enter into the Holy of holies of my being and find the power of transmutation taking place to free me forever from all discord that has ever manifested in my world.

I AM purity in action here, I AM God's purity established forever, and the stream of light from the very heart of God that embodies all of his purity is flowing through me and establishing round about me the power of invincible cosmic purity which can never be requalified by the human.

Here I AM; take me, O God of Purity. Assimilate

me and use me in the matrices of release for the mankind
of earth. Let me not only invoke purity for myself, but
also let me invoke purity for every part of life. Let me
not only invoke purity for my family, but also for all
the family of God neath the canopy of heaven.

I thank thee and I accept this manifest right here
and now with full power as the purity and authority
of thy words spoken through me to produce the
instantaneous manifestation of thy cosmic purity in
my four lower bodies, intensifying hourly and accelerating those bodies until they attain the frequency of
the ascension flame!

The Mechanical Ascension

Before we proceed to unveil some of the greater mysteries
of the ascension, we are obliged to warn the reader of the dangers inherent in certain wrong motives and methods used in
seeking the ascension.

First of all, the pursuit of the ascension must not be based on
a philosophy of escapism, the desire to rid oneself of the world
before one has actually met the challenges of being the Christ in
action in the very midst of turmoil. The ascension is for overcomers and for the lonely ones who dare to love whether or not
they are loved in return, simply because they never tire of seeking the Christ behind the mask of the human consciousness.

Second, the pursuit of the ascension must not be based on
ambition, pride in spiritual powers, or the desire to be exclusive
or above one's fellowmen. Those who use their spiritual powers to produce phenomena by means of controlling elemental
forces, discarnate entities and demons are likewise wrongly
motivated.

A person's ability to produce phenomena such as apporting objects (or other types of materializations), suspending the functions of the physical body or engaging in astral projection is no guarantee that he has met the requirements for the ascension. In fact, with the setting aside of the occult dispensation (in which certain requirements of the Great Law regarding the ascension and the guru-chela relationship were relaxed), the Masters ceased to use phenomena as a means of proving the existence of higher worlds, beings and laws to their unascended chelas.

The reader will recall that the LORD produced many phenomena through Moses in order to move the Egyptians toward compassion for the Hebrews and obedience to his laws. Nevertheless, Pharaoh's heart was hardened. From the prophets of the Old Testament to Jesus, Paul, John and the saints, we find records of miracles witnessed by many that prove beyond the shadow of a doubt the extraordinary contact these chosen ones had with hierarchy. But in the majority of cases, those who should have benefited from such demonstrations remained unmoved by them.

Although such holy experiences, often involving unusual phenomena, have by no means ceased in our day, the Brotherhood has for the most part abandoned this method of teaching a wayward generation. For the record clearly shows that in all cases those who did not wish to believe refused to accept the phenomena even of miraculous healings and visitations as proof of their own higher destiny. Nevertheless, the hierarchy reserves the right to reveal its most sacred miracles to receptive souls who have passed certain initiations and to the humble of heart who wait upon the LORD.

Furthermore, the dark forces often produce phenomena in order to deceive the elect and cause the children of God to follow those dark stars that appeal to and teach the development of the personality consciousness instead of the Christ consciousness. Therefore, in these latter days the Brotherhood is emphasizing the raising of the individual as well as the planetary consciousness through the widespread dissemination of their teachings. Instead of employing the materialization of objects, voices and forms as proof of hierarchy, the accent is now on the dematerialization (that is, the spiritualization) of the human consciousness.

Closely related to the various power complexes that have become the basis for some men's desire for attainment—even for the ascension itself—is the desire to control the universe (including man) through material science, without acknowledging the supremacy of Spirit as First Cause. Within the framework of this mechanical world view, this intellectual approach to immortality, we find the forced opening of the chakras and the premature raising of the Kundalini to be one of the greatest dangers to aspiring souls who lack the attainment to deal with the energies—both good and bad—that they thereby invoke.

In his dissertation on the mechanical ascension, the Great Divine Director discusses a number of vital concepts that no one who has set his sights upon the ascension should be without:

"The mechanical sense of attainment is usually behind the violence of mankind who seek to force their way of spiritual grace and their unfolding divinity through the erroneous supposition that the secrets of the universe can be mechanically mastered, including the ascension itself.

"Filled with abundant curiosity concerning the mysteries of life and seeking ever to probe the unknown, man has discovered many laws governing the partial control and use of energy. Likewise he has mastered in part simple manipulations of the power of mind over matter. In both cases, men have used knowledge without principle and caused a betrayal of the covenant between the Father and the Son in order to wrest from the universe, by violence if necessary, the mysteries of the kingdom of heaven.

"A clear example of the perversions that arise when partial knowledge is substituted for impartial wisdom is seen in the concept of the mechanical creation of man and in the mechanical creation of matter. This idea is based upon the erroneous notion that man is no more than a well-put-together machine whose components may be duplicated through scientific processes known or discoverable.

"When all of Truth is known and the akashic records are laid bare, mankind will understand how the principle of mechanization—if it can be said to have principle—was used long ago in the Lemurian and Atlantean ages, prior to the flood of Noah, to produce monstrous human forms that posed recurring problems to the earth and its evolutions. But the mechanistic concept has also taken the form of doctrine. Religious cults and political philosophies have arisen that propound a mechanical victory for man. These affirm that by the performance of a certain ritual or by the creation of a superstate, mankind will be assured of entering into the kingdom of God.

"We must admit that the desire of the hierarchy *is* for everyone to obtain Christ-victory—but not at any price or method. . . . The end can never justify the means, for the means of spiritual attainment are just as important as the goal. This is why no mere mechanistic attitude toward the obtaining of victory in life could ever be a substitute for divine grace or for the spirit of the Christ light, which is intended to be the Mediator for every man between the outer evolving soul personality and the immaculate creation of God—the perfect Father image or I AM Presence of God individualized for and in each man.

"As we explore the mechanistic theory as it pertains to the resurrection, let us state that there are individuals who proclaim that a mechanical method is in existence whereby mankind can literally raise the dead or be raised themselves by artificial means without the understanding and use of the spirit of the resurrection and its divine processes.

"Now let no one misconstrue our words to imply that we do not favor the use of the scientific healing arts as a form of resuscitation and continuation of life for mankind. But let all understand the use of true healing, which should always have as its primary objective the reinstallation of divine harmony in the being of man rather than the mere temporary alleviation of physical distress by those material methods that have come to replace the spiritually scientific understanding of the spirit of the resurrection.

"... Let us point out the doctrine of the mechanical ascension whereby, following methods that we may term 'rote and performance,' individuals are guaranteed their ascension through the observance of certain ritual and the performance of certain mechanical acts....

"I do not deny that some have attained to the powers of the kingdom of heaven through an attempted action of rote and partial elements of cosmic science. Yet in all such cases, because the grace of God is greatly absent and the power and pressure of individual attainment is utilized rather than the reverent attitude of 'Thine is the power,' such a one must sometime, somewhere, painstakingly retrace each stitch of partial accomplishment until all is properly placed by that divine grace in the seamless garment of the eternal Christ, the high priest of man's true being.

"Let me affirm, then, concerning the ascension, that while it is true—as in the case of the form of man himself and in the composition of matter—that electrons and atoms, cells and organs do play a part in the outer substance made manifest, it is the polarization of spiritual energies that assures the successful functioning of the outer form.

"Therefore, while it is true that the micro- or macro-universe could be considered a great machine or motor, it is also true that the currents of energy intelligently flowing through the outer form of that motor are derived from spiritual levels of universal love and power whose holy design can be found in the very Word itself—and, in this case, in the verb *to geometrize*. The *g* in the word is symbolical of God, the first and only Cause; *e*, the energy that emanates from that one Source; *o*, the output of that energy; *met*, the meter or unit of that energy; and *ize*, the automatic action of that energy, derived solely from the divine impetus of the love-wisdom of the Godhead.

"Let me point out to you the power of divine grace and how mankind, through infinite and holy prayer ('infinite prayer' being the great inward groanings of the soul and 'holy prayer' being the conscious implorations to Deity made with the purity of right concepts) may draw forth from the Godhead the grace that is sufficient for every hour, which will expand the light and consciousness to such Christlike proportions as will literally draw God-awareness into the individual focus of consciousness. This enables each one to rise, not only through the balancing of karma (through overcoming error) but also spiritually through the attainment of the fullness of God's gift of divine Sonship, the 'right-you-all' (or ritual) of the ascension whereby the Sun-ray of individual being is drawn up the ladder of light to the Great Sun Source. . . .

"Let all recognize, then, that mere mechanics are not the prime requisite in the knowledge of God, but the pure power of love is the perception of the infinite. The Creator's expanding love will enter into every area of life (when invited) until the temple is flooded with such ineffable light as will automatically raise every facet of your life into its victory and freedom."[22]

All Can Ascend through Christ

Serapis points out: "Because the ascension in the light is the goal of all life upon earth (whether or not the individual parts are aware of it), it is essential that life should cognize that the fruit of striving is God-realization. There is no need to have a sense of struggle about this, but only a sense of acceptance as stated by Saint Paul, 'Believe on the Lord Jesus Christ, and thou shalt be saved'[23]—which is to say, 'Believe in the power of this infinite-finite example as attainable by thyself; cast aside the sense of sin, sickness and death; and enter into the beauty of wholeness (holiness) and Christ idealism.'

"If God so loved the only begotten Son, the Christ, and if the Christ is the Divine Image, then this is the image of God in which all men are created.... A return to this image need not be a complicated maneuver or a dogmatic charisma, but it can become, through absorbing the simple consciousness of the Messiah, the means whereby all may enter the kingdom of heaven that is within. So will thy consciousness become refined and ascendant toward the Deity into which all life must merge."[24]

In truth, the mysteries of God's creation are many. In making his ascent into the cloud of his I AM Presence a public demonstration, Jesus unveiled one of life's greatest mysteries. The ascension is God's desire for every man. Hence, all heaven stands ready to assist the man, woman or child who, having faith, will seek in holy innocence to express his true Christ-identity as a Son of God. All life should welcome the opportunity of following in the Master's footsteps. Jesus was a way-shower, one of many. For Enoch, the seventh from Adam, also ascended into the heart of God,[25] as have many others of whom the Bible mentions but a few: Elijah, Melchizedek, Mary the mother of Jesus, and John the Beloved.

When the goal of the ascension is kept before the eyes of the soul, it ennobles the life of the individual and all whom he contacts with the divine intent; and this dedication reaches out into the world to fulfill the purposes of God.

There are many avenues of service and creative endeavor open to those who make the ascension their central goal in life. Each one of the seven rays of God provides the opportunity for splendid achievement on behalf of God and man. Those who fail to ascend in one embodiment but who have earnestly worked toward that end are prepared at inner levels after the transition called death, so that the succeeding embodiment will be the victorious one.

On the other hand, some who earn their ascension forgo the prize. They do not take their ascension but volunteer instead to reembody in order to assist those who are still struggling to overcome. (See "The Bodhisattva Ideal," pages 145–47.) In any case, service that men render is never lost but contributes ultimately to their victory in the light.

We begin to see, therefore, how the divine plan is timeless, how it transcends the ages. The declaration of the Christ "Before Abraham was, I AM"[26] is a statement of being; it is a statement that issues from the consciousness which comes forth from the Mind of God. The fact that all men can say, "Before Abraham was, I AM" shows the power of the Divine Logos (the Word) to penetrate cosmos and to manifest as individual being and consciousness within time and space while transcending both. This is the power of every man who is born of the Spirit. This is the power of the First Cause by which all things are made.

Each individual who accepts his divine destiny passes from death unto life, becoming that which in reality he already is. Conceived of God and born in liberty that they might ascend into cosmic purpose, all of God's children can obtain the fullness of Christhood and thereby manifest the very nature and being of God. There is no blasphemy in such concepts, but only the sweet sense of fulfillment that is the divine plan for every son and daughter of God.

The ascension is the fulfillment of the will of God for every man. As the Christ descended to the earth he cried, "Lo, I AM come to do thy will, O God!" The descending consciousness of man, as it identifies with the Divine Ego, affirms the intent of God for his creation. This intent was revealed to Moses when God appeared in the burning bush. Affirming the supremacy of his universal Being, which was individualized within the flame, the LORD spoke the simple words that proclaim the beginning and the ending of man's fiery destiny: "I AM THAT I AM."[27] Here the LORD was referring to the true nature of his Being, and he made plain the image of the being that is not conditioned by circumstance but that conditions circumstance—being that is not mastered but masters.

Thus having descended to do the will of God, man completes the cycle of life through the ritual of the ascension, which unfolds the true eschatology of each lifestream. The ascension is the predestination—the preordained destiny—of all who will study to prepare themselves for the return to the heart of God over the pathway of light that is the ascension flame.

How to Reenact the Ritual of Reunion

The ritual of reunion with the Presence is reenacted each time the individual elects (1) to identify with the Christ Self of his own being, (2) to purify himself by making invocations to the sacred fire, and (3) to balance his karma through ministration and service to life.

As Serapis Bey admonishes: "Cause, effect, record and memory of all that is incomplete, of all that is darkness and of all that is intransigent must be willfully abandoned by the soul who aspires to the freedom of the ascended state. If you are content merely to wallow in episodes of your personal history, to seek for an intrapsychic declaration of your past records, you can have it by pursuing it diligently enough—but it will be only a conglomeration of banal circumstances from which, like a bad dream, you will one day seek to escape. Or it will become an astral lure, as pretty trinkets and sparkling baubles, to distract you from the track that leads to your immortal freedom.

"In order to ascend, you must abandon your past to God, knowing that he possesses the power by his flame and identity to change all that you have wrought of malintent and confusion into the beauty of the original design that, by the power of his love, did produce the fruit of eternal goodness. Cast aside illusion, then, veil after veil, of the 'personal person,' and possess the willingness, in the name of Almighty God, to change your world!"[28]

Through the use of the violet transmuting flame, through the implementation of right thought and action, and through the power of right qualification, the body of man's energies, the substance of his soul, once again becomes God-identified. This is not the practice of self-righteousness, but it is the illumined righteousness of the Higher Self, as God acts through his creation to provide a new and living way for the Son to manifest in his flesh that life which God truly is. Thus is man restored to the divine image and likeness.

That which has departed from perfection cannot by a mere thought return to perfection. Can the leopard change his spots? "Which of you by taking thought can add one cubit unto his stature?"[29] The redemptive process involves the total consecration of the mind, heart and soul of man. Only through the daily baptism of the Holy Spirit, lovingly invoked by the disciple, can the fires of creation reestablish the individual in the secret place of the Most High God.

Saint Germain explains: "The constant embroilment of the human ego in karma-making conditions, wherein hatreds are exchanged between lifestreams and the only satisfactions of life are derived from the assertion of the human personality, is a pitfall that does hinder the evolution of the soul. Obviously, if all came forth from the One, then all must return to him. Therefore, in preparing for the merging of souls that occurs in the Great Return, one must consider the natural outpouring of true brotherhood in all that he does. Old ancestral hatreds and desires for vengeance, stemming in many cases from karmic conditions of long standing, must be transmuted. For as long as the flame of forgiveness is not active in mankind, it is impossible for them to win their ascension."[30]

The forgiveness of sins is not brought about, as so many think, by a simple declaration of faith in the Son of God. This declaration is but the foundation stone of the divine pyramid upon which the supplicant must rebuild his temple line upon line, stone upon stone, according to the divine blueprint, until he has fulfilled all things—and the capstone of his edifice is the victory of his ascension in the light.

"The process of the ascension is one of utter forgivingness," Saint Germain continues. "It is one of transmutation and transformation. It is the drawing in of holy energies and the purification of all abused energies of the past. It is a regenerative process that begins not only in the physical form but also in the very heart and soul of man. It is the Christ command to the great Cosmic Law itself to draw within the form the magnetic properties that will attract more and more of God to the individual monad. As the great inner radioactivity of the cosmic light flows in and gathers intensity to become the inner lodestone of man's being, that being reflects more and more of the regenerative properties of the Creator."[31]

Consciousness and life must be used as tools to implement individual reality. The individuality of a man may be defined as that portion of the consciousness of God with which he identifies, whereas the personality is only the mask of illusion that comes forth from the mortal mind and is wedded to the consciousness of mortality.

The Christ Mind is victorious over all outer circumstances. It focuses the power to heal, the power to raise the dead and the power to do greater things because the Christ is one with the Father.[32] These powers are given to those who faithfully pursue the upward path. Entering into the ineffable light behind the veil of flesh, these find the cup of divine union into which all must one day drink—and having drunk, never thirst again.

The Deathless Solar Body and the Caduceus

The manifestation of the deathless solar body and the mastery of the caduceus are signs of victory on the Path. Serapis Bey gives the following commentary on these signs of Christ's appearing:

"When man functions under divine direction and activity, either in or out of the body, he takes the energy dispensed to him (which in ignorance might have been misused) and creates instead a great body of light, called the immaculate seamless garment of the living Christ, which will one day become the great spherical deathless solar body.

"Born of the energies of the sun and of the energies of the Sun behind the sun, the deathless solar body becomes a magnet. The magnetism of the Divine is a lodestone that will transmute shadow in the human octave and transform the consciousness of the ascendant one so that, little by little, there will gradually occur in his world a lessening of the tenacious ties that mankind over the centuries have woven to persons, places, conditions and things. Simultaneously there will occur a renewal of the ancient covenants of the soul with the Father, whereby the Son recognizes that the return home to the heart of God is most imperative.

"Thus the divine lodestone and the deathless solar body are activated. And because there is a response mechanism created in the consciousness below, it becomes an occasion whereby the Father, through the choice of man's own free will, now has the authority to choose the hour when the Son shall return back to himself. Unless, however, the pathway of the flame is created in the caduceus fashion, the soul will not be able to make its winged flight back to God.

"The caduceus takes advantage of both centripetal and centrifugal forces. It utilizes the energy known to the Hindus as Brahma and Shiva, the Creator and Destroyer. Thus are mankind made aware of the forces of disintegration, which flow in a counterclockwise spiral and bring basic structure back to Spirit, and of the forces of creation, which flow in a clockwise spiral from Spirit into the realm of manifestation. The caduceus action gives man victory over both hell and death—and with the ascension, the last enemy, death, is destroyed.[33]

"The wings at the top of the caduceus symbolize the fact that the holy and vital energies of both sympathetic and central nervous systems around the spinal column have been raised toward the spiritual eye of perception. Here the wings of spiritual perception raise the individual and trigger the cosmic mechanism of the ascension.

"Thus the flame above (in the heart of the Presence) magnetizes the flame below (the threefold flame within the heart) and the wedding garment descends around the crystal cord to envelop the lifestream of the individual in those tangible and vital currents of the ascension.

"Tremendous changes then take place in the form below, and the four lower bodies of man are cleansed of all impurities. Lighter and lighter grows the physical form, and with the weightlessness of helium the body begins to rise into the atmosphere—the gravitational pull being loosened and the form enveloped by the light of the externalized glory that man knew with the Father in the beginning before the world was."[34]

Signs of the Ascending Consciousness

"In the past," recounts Serapis, "many of the saints who levitated into the atmosphere did so by reason of the intensity of their magnetization of the energy of the God Flame above. The floating into the air of these saints was an attest to their devout and intimate relationship with the God Presence. Thus the winged God Self will raise man back to God's own heart, and that which descended will also ascend. The alchemical marriage (the union of the lower self with the Higher Self) will take place when the lower self has shown good faith and the willingness to fulfill all obligations set forth in the covenant of divine reunion.

"Some may say that during the ascension the flesh form will rise, leaving a pile of white ash upon the ground beneath the feet of the aspirant. This is true in some cases where the alchemy of the ascension is performed a bit prematurely and for cosmic reasons. In this instance the white ash is the untransmuted residue of the lifestream. In other cases this residue is absent from the spot where the individual ascended, having been transmuted by an intense caduceus action.

"It is true, although the form of an individual may show signs of age prior to his ascension, that all of this will change and that the physical appearance of the individual will be transformed into the glorified body. The individual ascends, then, not in an earthly body but in a glorified spiritual body into which the physical form is changed on the instant by total immersion in the great God Flame. Thus man's consciousness of the physical body ceases and he achieves a state of weight-lessness. This resurrection takes place as the great God Flame envelops the remaining shell of human creation and trans-mutes, in a pattern of cosmic grids, all of the cell patterns of the individual—the skeletal structure, the veinal and arterial sys-tems, the central and sympathetic nervous systems—and all bodily processes go through a great metamorphosis.

"The blood in the veins changes to liquid golden light. The throat chakra glows with an intense blue-white light. The spiritual eye in the center of the forehead becomes an elongated God Flame rising upward. The garments of the individual are completely consumed and he takes on the appearance of being clothed in a white robe—the seamless garment of the Christ. Sometimes the long hair of the Higher Mental Body (the Christ Self) appears as pure gold on the ascending one, while eyes of any color may become a beautiful electric blue or a pale violet.

"These changes are permanent, and the ascended one is able to take his light body with him wherever he wishes. Or he may travel without the glorified spiritual body. Ascended Beings can and occasionally do appear upon earth as ordinary mortals, putting on physical garments resembling those of the people of earth and moving among them for cosmic purposes. This Saint Germain did after his ascension, when he was known as the Wonderman of Europe. Such an activity is a matter of dispensation received from the Karmic Board. Jesus' appearance to John on Patmos is another case in point.[35]

"Merely to be carried by the Spirit from one city to another, as was Philip,[36] or to be raised temporarily into the atmosphere in levitation is not the same as the ascension and should not be so construed. Elijah the prophet, in his ascension, was taken up into heaven in a chariot of fire.[37] This so-called chariot symbolizes the rumbling of the atomic densities of mankind turning as chariot wheels in the fiery substance of the ascension flame until every atom, cell and electron is purified of all dross. Thus man is propelled into the ascension flame as these 'wheels within wheels'[38] are stepped up in vibratory rate, until they spin with the intensity of light itself and the divine tone sounds forth from within them the note of individual victory.

"Whether it be Zarathustra, who ascended back to God in the great flame, or Elijah, who went into heaven in the chariot of fire, the flame of the ascension is the key that unlocks the door to immortality for every man. The flame is the vehicle that conveys the ascending one back to the heart of his Divine Presence. He retains full consciousness of this entire ritual, and once ascended, he becomes on the instant an emissary of the Great White Brotherhood in carrying out its various aims, which always come under the direction of the Fatherhood of God."[39]

The Ascension Temple and Its Hierarch

Serapis Bey, Chohan of the Fourth Ray of purity, is known as the Great Disciplinarian. It is his service to prepare the disciples of the Holy Spirit for the ritual of the ascension at his retreat, the Ascension Temple in Luxor, Egypt. Students are admitted to this retreat only after they have successfully passed certain initiations given by other members of the ascended hierarchy, who act as the sponsors and Gurus of unascended initiates.

Speaking of the entrance requirements to the Ascension Temple and its service to humanity, the Master advises:

"Immortality is of a high price, and it demands the allness of men from the smallness of men. Yet men can only give that of which they are capable. The capacity of their externalized selfhood must be given in toto, and there is no need for men to seek our treasure without giving all. The holding back of the smallest particle of individuality as possession is forbidden in our retreat. Total surrender is the order of the day.

"We are not hungry for chelas, but for quality in those who come. And while many are turned away (even as many leave of their own free will), those who are left understand that the planetary needs must be served from the unique standpoint of the spiritual design in order that on this planet the yearly quota of ascensions may be met. Some may ask, 'Why is this so?' I shall reveal the answer in part.

"When the Lords of Karma make their yearly examination of the world aura with a view to ascertaining whether or not the continued allotment of light should be granted to the planetary body, thereby providing harmony in nature and the perpetuation of the four seasons, there is always the need to answer the question, How many students have graduated from the planetary curriculum, from the school of earthly experience?

"One of the demands of the Lords of Karma is that a stated number of individuals must graduate each year in order to renew the grant of light that is necessary to maintain the stability of the planet.* Therefore, our training school is of utmost importance to the destinies of the people of earth, and whether or not they are aware of the greatness of this school does not matter. We are aware of it, and those who come here for training are aware of it. And the striving of their spirits to hold congruence with the triads of light is very beautiful to behold."[40]

"Men must seek to raise themselves before they can come

---

*Earth's quota at the present time is one ascension per year.

to the point of the transfiguration," says Lord Maitreya, the Great Initiator. "To raise the self is to bring it to a point where the power of the light can penetrate the substance of the individual's own world, not only by his request but also by his invocation.

"Examine the word *raise*. The first two letters focus the power of the Son of God, the power of light itself, the power of <u>Ra</u> (taken from the Egyptian *Ra*, whence comes the word *ray*). The third letter is the <u>I</u> ('eye') or *lumen*, the organ of vision, or the ego of being. This is followed by <u>se</u> ('see'). The full meaning of the word, then, in all of its glory, becomes 'the light of God I see.' *Raise*, which is synonymous with *rays*, denotes the extension of the power of the Sun from its center out into the field of darkness. John described this extension of the forcefield of the Almighty when he said, 'The light shineth in darkness; and the darkness comprehended it not.'[41]

"The purpose of our work in this day and age is to see to it that men do comprehend the light and that they walk upon the path of faith. The meaning of raising the self, then, is to bring the self to a place where it is capable of discerning the light. When the light is discerned, it cannot help but reveal the shadows that exist in the lower self.

"Whereas some men have said to themselves before the light shone in the darkness of being, 'We are very good', after they have perceived by the power of the light the conditions they were in, they were ready to cry to the mountains, 'Fall on us, and hide us from the face of him that sitteth on the throne.' Yet punishment or estrangement is never the divine intent, for 'there is nothing hid that shall not be known' and 'his mercy endureth forever.'[42]

"By the power of Truth the exposure of the darkness of the self takes place, and then mankind is able to bring the darkness to the light in order that the light can transmute and redeem that darkness. This is the process of the resurrection. It is a resurging of the uprightness that is now and always has been within the spirit of man."[43]

Divine Humility

Pointing out the need for divine humility on the Path, Serapis cites the Master Jesus as the perfect example: "I recall full well that when the Master Jesus came to Luxor as a very young man, he knelt in holy innocence before the hierophant, refusing all honors that were offered him and asking to be initiated into the first grade of spiritual law and spiritual mystery. No sense of pride marred his visage—no sense of preeminence or false expectation. Albeit he could have well expected the highest honors, he chose to take the low road of humility, knowing that it was reserved unto the joy of God to raise him up.

"To raise an individual is a glorious thing when that individual lies prone in hope, in faith and in charity, awaiting an act of God to reconsecrate the self to the simple quality of humility. For there is an act of false pride that manifests as false humility and causes individuals to appear humble, whereas in reality they reek with pride. This false humility is often manifest in subtle ways, and it is always a mockery of the real.

"Shun, then, all that is not real and virtuous in the thoughts of thine own heart, and mend the thoughts of thy heart if they seem to be trifling with eternal purpose. You came forth for one cause and one cause alone, and that to manifest God's light. No greater purpose has come to anyone, and no lesser purpose. While our mastery stands as a rainbow of promise to unascended men, this promise can never remain their guiding light unless they shed human pride.

"Quite frankly, many individuals on the spiritual path use their contact with us as a means of attaching importance to their own egos. They but harm our cause, for the awful majesty of the divine light is able to probe men even to the depths of their very bones, and the flame of divine penetration that tests men before their ascension reveals the very naked recesses that are often unknown to the individuals themselves.

"I urge upon all, then, that they seek the banner of divine humility. If the Masters and the Divine Presence of men, through the mediatorship of the Christ, have ever recognized any of the errors that have hindered men from becoming that which they long to become, they have recognized the error of their pride. Pride takes many forms, and true humility but one. True humility must be worn eternally. It is not a garment that you don for a moment, for a day or for a year, or during periods of testing. It is an undergarment with which God himself is clothed and unless it surround thee, thy hopes of attainment are slim indeed."[44]

A More than Ordinary Discipline

"It is most unfortunate but true," the hierarch tells his students, "that in the disciplining of men, we find that their hearts often become so familiar with the lines and cadences of Truth that scar tissue forms upon the folds of their consciousness to the extent that they can no longer derive satisfaction from the holy tenets of our faith.

"Our faith is in purpose, and men must learn to still the mind as one would grasp a blade of steel and thrust it not forward one quarter of an inch until the command to do battle is given. A soldier exercises control and heeds the call of the captain.

"The disciplines of life must be inflexible. Otherwise, there can be no discipline.

"The seemingly cold calculations of the aspirants to our

temple are, in reality, the refinements of the fires of the hearts of those who have heard our voice and prepared themselves by reason of need, of weariness to the bone, and by the density of mortal desires. These have perceived that they must forsake the way of the flesh, shunning it as a plague and determining to pursue the best gifts and graces of the Spirit.

"There are many young men in the world today who consider themselves to be fearsome and tough, who consider that they are well equipped to meet the challenges of the world—but the challenges of the Spirit, they think, are for sissies.

"I think they have much to learn. Their premises are wrong. The foundations of their thinking are wrong. They lack compassion; they lack understanding. They lack Wisdom and in her place they entertain baneful thought. They know it not.

"To be ignorant is understandable, but to know not that one is ignorant is a tragedy of considerable dimension. Our lamentation is made, then, in order that men may awaken to a realization of their stature in the eyes of God.

"Now, men do not need to come to Luxor in order to find liberation. Only the strong may come here—those who aspire to overcome a sea of troubles during an episode called a lifetime. There are those who are content (and I do not think that beloved Kuthumi will mind my saying it) to sit at the feet of the Master Kuthumi or at the feet of Jesus. I would remind them that when Jesus was ready to fulfill his great mission, he came to us in Egypt and offered himself in the service of the light.

"Just as Egypt has been a land of shadow and pain, a land of bondage, a land of sand and brick and mortar, of confusion and sensuality, so has Egypt been the repository of great stature and great light under God. We here at Luxor have held firmly to the rigors of the disciplines of the infinite. We have determined to uphold the Cosmic Law and the cosmic effort and to make it, where possible, translatable into understanding on an individual basis so that any part of life might be able to embrace the tenets of our temple and to comprehend that out of darkness light can come."

Serapis, with his usual candor, continues: "We are interested in maintaining a stable community here at Luxor, and we have no need for emotional sycophants who come here and then cry for their earthly mothers. Men and women who come here are selected because, in essence, they are the lonely ones whose every thought and desire is the fulfillment of cosmic purpose as a finalizing act of their embodiment in the world of form."

Serapis stresses the need for the disciplines of the Spirit to those who would overcome the limitations of the flesh: "To you, I say, a more than ordinary discipline must be given. You must understand that to embrace in principle a certain goal, without having the willingness to do all in your power to achieve that goal, is a sign of great weakness that ought to bring some element of shame into manifestation in consciousness. But this shame is without virtue unless it serve to goad an individual to seek the disciplines of Spirit.

"These disciplines will enable him to perform the somewhat complicated maneuvers that will provide him with the necessary spiritual energy to oppose the opposing forces, to close in upon and to join in the battle against the destructive elements in his own nature that are residual from all of his many embodiments, For these have a tendency to come up at the very moment when the individual determines that he is going to make the greatest progress.

"Because darkness is always evoked by light (the presence of light brings out its opposite), men must understand that theirs must be the forte of vigilance.

"I shall give you an example. When individuals begin to seek their ascension and they begin the process of externalizing divine grace in sufficient quantity to assist them to that end, there is always a very definite action of shadow and darkness that converges upon the forcefield of their identities and seeks to thwart the plan that they have begun to conceive. We call this process the testing of the mettle. Just as the dross is skimmed off and discarded as the fire of refinement is applied to the gold ore, so the impurities of consciousness must be brought to the surface and removed ere the aspirant can absorb in greater measure the purity of the ascension flame.

"You will always find those who, like Don Quixote and his windmills, will fight against the paper tigers of the air and thrash their energies in a vibratory action of resistance to life. This is not needful. All resistance should be turned not against life but against death, for death is an unnatural state."

A Matter of Perspective

Concerning the temptation to seek a place for oneself in the world rather than pursue the spiritual path, Serapis points out: "In reality, the men and women who choose the world will lose their souls. Thus some who have come to our retreat have said, 'Beloved Serapis, as long as I will lose my soul anyway if I choose the world, why should I not lose it in divine seeking?' And I have answered, 'To plunge into the ocean of infinite love, even though the soul would be absorbed and not recognize that love, would be better than to dwell in the tents of the world's greatest sheiks.'

"And it is true; for when the last breath goeth out, when Yama* has fulfilled his activity and the flesh attains to the dubious quality of corruption, the sustainment of the soul and its own standard is all that endures of the man. Family, friends, treasures and riches are no more—even the flow of ideas ceases

---

*Yama: the Hindu god of death.

in the mortal consciousness and brain. But all externalized Truth and obedience to Cosmic Law is etched by the angels of fire and record upon akashic substance for each lifestream.

"Thus it was recorded of old in the archives, 'Whatsoever a man soweth, that shall he also reap'.[45] There are none who can defeat this law. Neither sobriety nor levity will produce in the consciousness of man any change in this unalterable substance, the substance of Cosmic Law.

"I wish to say at this time that it is in little ideas, such as those I am conveying to you, that men are able to summon the best virtues for the moments when they are tested and reality is born in the soul. The soul is the substance upon which is reflected the reality of God. The actualizing of that reality is similar to the process used in the manufacture of rubber known as vulcanization.

"Individuals should reckon with the factors of mind and memory and understand that the folds of memory are filled with unclean substance. This substance cannot create a pattern of adherence. The best materials must be used in order for individuals to weld those energies of mind and heart that will cause their consciousness to become wholly unified. There is never any need, then, for individuals to expect that those qualities of thought and feeling which are less than the Christ-perfection of life will be joined unto the God Flame of reality that is within.

"Men cannot build immortal bodies out of mortal substance. They cannot build out of mortal thoughts immortal ideas. They cannot build out of mortal feelings divine feelings that enfold the world and create the great pyramid of life."[46]

Lest some feel unworthy or unable to meet the requirements of the Ascension Temple, we quote from Serapis one final word on the subject:

"Some have sat before me at Luxor when I have given this

very same lecture and they have said, 'Send me back, for my consciousness is but a sewer of human reason and I am without hope.' To these I have turned with a look of withering scorn and spoken these words: 'You have disgraced divine purpose for centuries and now you stand at the doorway of freedom, this by divine grace. Would you return, then, to the turgid sea of human emotions and frustrations without receiving the benefit of our instruction, when you stand nigh unto the portals of a complete escape?' Out of an entire class I have seen no more than one turn back—and frequently, as that one has lingered near the portal, he has silently slipped back into his seat and gone on.

"Do you see, precious ones, it is all a matter of perspective? Those who minister in the world to men's spiritual needs do so from the standpoint of pleasing men. We act solely from the standpoint of pleasing God. Our desire is to get the job done, to show men how to find their freedom.

"Men require spunk and a straight spine. There is no question that they have pampered themselves, and that with illusion. Straight talk and straight thought will do much to clear the way, and it will not place any individual outside the citadel of hope but wholly within it.

"Men stay on the merry-go-round of human thought and feeling because they fear lest they fall off. But it will keep on going. So jump off the round of delusion and the mad whirl of human confusion. Come to Luxor, to the place where I AM."[47]

And so it is through the wisdom of the hierarch of Luxor that we come to know him who waits even now for your knock at the portal of the Ascension Temple. Let all who apply for admission know that the only way to leave honorably is through the open door of the ascension flame.

Cremation: Freedom through Fire

The problem of disposing of the physical body arises at the time of transition, or death. Not all are able to ascend physically as did Elijah, for the actual raising of the physical body into the atmosphere occurs only when the individual has achieved a certain degree of self-mastery before the transition is made.

It is, however, altogether possible to translate the physical body in this day and age. None should dismiss this supreme demonstration of the Divine Alchemy as either unnecessary or impractical, for as Jesus proved the law of life two thousand years ago, so it can be proven today—either in public or in private. The ascension of the physical body is an attainable goal and, we might add, one that is well worth striving for. In the case of those who do not translate their physical bodies, the ascension may take place immediately after death or during the following three days.

Those who do not raise their physical bodies at the time of their passing may ascend from inner levels, elevating the etheric, mental and emotional bodies together with their soul consciousness. This may occur immediately or within twenty-four to seventy-two hours thereafter, or even from several months to several decades as the Law may require.

Whether the soul ascends leaving behind the physical body or prepares at inner levels for reembodiment, the physical body must pass through the natural process of dissolution. Therefore, in order to facilitate the soul's transition to higher octaves, either to complete the requirements for the ascension or to enter into temple training for the next life, Serapis Bey has recommended that the physical body be placed on ice for a period of three days after death and that it then be cremated.

Sanat Kumara gives these detailed directions for cremation: "Place the body on ice, dry or otherwise, two days and two nights. And on the third day, the commemoration of the resurrection is the invocation of the resurrection flame. Whether on a funeral pyre or in a modern crematorium, let the physical fire pass through the body that is untouched; for both flesh and blood must be intact, and embalming is forbidden by the Brotherhood of Luxor.

"This method is safe and sane and healthy for all. It allows the soul the freedom from all earthly ties as the four lower vehicles are demagnetized simultaneously by the physical fire and the spiritual fire. The soul, as the winged symbol of the *ka,* takes flight with the flying eagle to pursue the initiations of the Mother in the retreats of the Great White Brotherhood."[48]

Through this ancient ritual, the light in the heart of the physical atoms is released by the fire element, and the energy that was used to sustain the form is immediately returned to the heart of the God Presence. In most cases the three-day period of rest is required for the soul and its vehicles to withdraw from the form. Cremation eliminates the possibility of the form exercising dominion over the soul through what is called residual magnetism; for the records of the individual's thoughts and feelings do leave a residue of substance that creates a magnetic forcefield in the body even after interment, which tends to keep the soul earthbound.

The passage of the soul to higher octaves is facilitated by the blessed fiery salamanders,* who consume not only the physical body but also that portion of untransmuted substance lodged within it. If the soul has gravitated toward the things of the Spirit during its sojourn on earth, it will be taken to etheric retreats and temples of the Masters or to one of the fourteen etheric cities, where the lifestream may either prepare for his

---

*The fiery salamanders are nature spirits of the fire element—impressive, fiery beings who appear in rainbow flames. They can be extremely tall, extending themselves from nine to fifty feet in height.

ascension or take instruction for service in his next embodiment.

When the physical form is not cremated, the pull of the records and of the residual magnetism within the forcefield of the body is so great that the soul usually remains in the lower astral levels between embodiments. And since little or no progress can be made in the astral realm, the lifestream will return to embodiment in the same frame of mind in which he left.

The soul's obligation to release the energies imprisoned within the physical form is not fulfilled until the body is committed to the eternal Flame and the light-energy in each atom is returned to the Great Central Sun for repolarization (that is, purification of the impressions stamped upon the energy through the reestablishment of the divine polarity of Alpha and Omega). Due to custom—based on the mistaken concept that the physical body will be raised at the time of the Second Coming of Christ—most people have had their bodies interred at the close of many lifetimes, so that their responsibility to transmute their human creation necessarily includes the transmutation of the images of their former selves that lie buried in the earth. Without the assistance of either the fire element or the violet transmuting flame, the release of the energies imprisoned within these discarded forms must occur through the slow process of decay, in some cases delaying the process for thousands of years. Needless to say, embalming is a means of even further prolonging the soul's bondage to the form.

If the body is embalmed before cremation, the blood is removed, discarded as waste, and allowed to mingle with the elements; therefore, it is not consigned to the flame with the remains. Since the blood carries the light and the identity pattern of the soul, which cannot be removed except by fire, it is wise to see that the body is not tampered with prior to being placed on ice. Where state laws prevent this practice they can be challenged on the grounds that they interfere with religious freedom. Nevertheless, it should be remembered that the power of the Holy Spirit, when invoked through the violet flame, is able to transmute body, mind and soul, including the cause, effect, record and memory of all that is left of the human, wherever it may appear in the earth's crust. Truly the universal grace of God is sufficient for man's salvation.

Where the Spirit of the LORD Is

The release of the soul into the octaves of light at the close of each embodiment is vital not only to its own progress but also to that of the entire planetary body in the eternal cycles of being. Therefore it behooves all who would serve the world need to call to the hosts of light to cut free from astral entanglements those who are in the process of making the transition from this plane to the next.

Archangel Michael, that great defender of the faith, has dedicated himself to the freeing of all mankind from the effluvia of the astral plane. He wields a sword of blue flame, a pillar of blue fire that he has magnetized in the shape of a sword to literally cut mankind free from their own human creation.

This Prince of the Archangels has made a promise so wonderful that we include it here in order that all might avail themselves of his transcendent blessing:

"Some of you are of advancing years, and it will not be long before you will vacate your body temples. Some of you will do so through the ascension, and some will enter the realms of our world through the change called death. I shall, therefore, make you one promise: If you will call to me secretly now within your heart and ask me to come to you at that hour, I, Michael, will materialize to you at the hour of your passing and you will see me as I AM!

"And I promise you that I will help to cut you free from the remaining unredeemed portions of your karma. I will help you to enter into the realms of light with less of the attendant pain that results from human fear in passing through the gate. This is a mighty privilege and a gift I give you from my heart. I flood it forth...to those throughout the world who have the faith to accept it, to request it, and to realize that God walks and talks with men today in the same manner as he did of old."[49]

At the end of this chapter we have included a decree that you may use to cut yourself free from astral entanglements that would otherwise interfere with the fulfillment of your life plan both now and after your transition. The same decree may be given with the suggested insert to facilitate the passing of loved ones into the octaves of light. On countless occasions we have witnessed the release of souls from the lower astral plane (which some have called purgatory), thanks to the intercession of the angelic hosts who have come forth in answer to the prayers of the faithful. Truly "where the Spirit of the LORD is, there is liberty."[50] Let us therefore invoke the assistance of those Ascended Beings who have become one with the LORD's Spirit so that all mankind may rise in the ascending spirals of cosmic liberty.

Opportunity after the Ascension

The thought of the cessation of worldly activities should in no way cause the aspirant to shrink from the glorious opportunities that the ascended realm affords. To render assistance to mankind from inner levels and to become involved in the progressive unfoldment of the evolutions of other systems of worlds is certainly a most rewarding experience and one that is not without challenge, even to an Ascended Being. The only difference between life on earth and life in heaven is that in the latter state the individual has unlimited time and unlimited energy to lavish on creative endeavor, on the pursuit of cosmic wisdom and on service to his brethren, both ascended and unascended. This is the means whereby the individual expands the universe as he himself expands.

Through the ritual of the ascension, each soul attains her freedom. She enters into the communion of the saints and into service with every Ascended Master who has ever lived upon this or any other planet. The return of the lifewaves of this system has been referred to as the bringing in of the sheaves into the Father's granary. There is purpose in this plan—there is victory, there is life, there is fulfillment. In the ascension eternal values come full circle, and in the majestic upsweep of the ascension flame all can find their immortal freedom in Christ. "Then shall be brought to pass the saying that is written, Death is swallowed up in victory. O death, where is thy sting? O grave, where is thy victory?"[51]

Being fitted for the goal of the ascension is the most rewarding experience that can come to any man. The glowing response of man's purified consciousness to the Father's love enables the soul to rise into the rarefied air of reality; and the vibratory connection that is established with all Ascended Beings everywhere is the return to heaven that Jesus foretold. For indeed, "in my Father's house are many mansions: if it were not so, I would have told you. I go to prepare a place for you... that where I AM, there ye may be also."[52]

The Cone of Fire and the Pyramid

The following notes are given by Serapis Bey for the benefit of those who are willing to submit to the disciplines of the Ascension Temple. Let all who read them bear in mind that none are excluded from the teaching except those who exclude themselves:

"The cone of fire pulsates from dullness to the brilliance of the white light, and the residual ash is itself consumed. The egg of the serpent must not be left, for it might well bring forth not only a serpent or a sea serpent but also a dragon. And thus the cone of fire must be preserved until the blinding light of transposition, of transmutation, does consume the dross and produce the fruit of the Cosmic Egg. The ovoid of the infinite is within the capacity of mortal men—but when it is invoked, they are no longer mortal. . . .

"The cone of fire is necessary in order for individuals to understand the circle of fire and the dot in the center of the circle, signifying the First Monad and the expansion of the monad from the base of the circle to the apex of the cone.

"The cone of fire is involved with the constructive spiral of manifestation. For out of this energy is given the pattern by which man may rise in divine symmetry, without flaw, in the ideational patterns of his existence. Unless this occur, the smoothening of the way will not be possible—it will not be possible for individuals to shape their tube of light as they ought in preparation for the ascension.

"Now, I do not expect that those who are not actually readying themselves for their ascension by an extensive preparation will understand the meaning of the cone of fire. But when it is understood and the terms *light* and *fire* become synonymous in their consciousness, individuals will understand how space can be hallowed by divine thought and feeling. They will understand how a given amount of space—so many cubits of space—can actually reflect either light densities or vacuums of consciousness. If vacuums of consciousness are filling that space, this indicates that there is indeed a lack of light within the cone of fire, and intensification must occur.

"I know of cases on record, and one in particular where long ago in France an individual near Paul the Venetian's retreat actually started the creation of the cone of fire at seven o'clock in the evening. By midnight he had created a matrix of such strength that he ascended the following day at one minute after midnight. In other cases I have seen individuals strive alchemically to create the cone of fire, beginning in an embodiment during medieval times and culminating in their ascension at the beginning of this century.

"Do you understand what I am speaking about? I am speaking about the span not of ordinary, earthly centuries, but the span that leaps across the centuries. It is like a spiral of wire: the energy does not necessarily travel around the wire circle by circle, but through magnetism and induction it suddenly animates the whole by the principle of the divine soul.

"This principle is universal cosmos; it is cosmic essence. And this principle can, as a spark leaps a gap, flash forth through the coils of manifestation. The residual ash will then fan out from between the coils and fall to the floor or to the ground. . . .

"I would like to point out that there is a certain waste in the white ash. Actually, the white ash ought not to manifest at all, but often it does because of a lack of preparation on the part of the aspirant.

"Let men understand that by constructive spirals of thought, by discipline of mind and heart, and without engaging in any strange states of consciousness, individuals can fashion the ascension spirals. Some are prone to use the power of mortal imagination, and they fail to recognize that we are dealing with the true geometric figure.

"We are dealing with true geometry. We are not dealing with imagination. We are dealing with fact, with the spirals that are closely knit, with the spirals that follow the cone pattern, with the spirals that stem from the base of the circle of identity, and with the desire for cosmic purity, which is akin in miniature to the Cosmic Central Sun behind the Central Sun.

"By the power of the three-times-three, the triad of manifestation can produce the fruit of the ascension within the forcefield of the individual. But men must understand that as these spirals become closely knit, there is a definite responsibility to the cubit stone. The cubit stone of identity must conform to the necessary patterns whereby there will come about the manifestation of individuality in accordance with cosmic principle.

"Today men are functioning haphazardly, attempting to produce individuality through personality aspects instead of recognizing the nature of true being. When we are involved with Cosmic Law, we are involved with an identification with unity. When you identify with cosmic unity, you will have a similitude made in the likeness of God. Therefore, there will be a very definite pattern of similitude in all.

"While Ascended Masters do differ from one another after their ascension because of individual patterns that are retained as the result of their individual contributions to life, I wish to point out that there are certain inescapable acts that must be accomplished by each individual. These must conform to a definite spiritual similitude, and they cannot vary one iota. Unless these formulae be followed, the mercury, the salt and the earth will not be properly proportioned, and our experience, your experience and the experiences of mankind will not conform to the same cosmic pattern.

"Unless there is a conformation to the laws involved in the hallowing of space and the creation of the cone of fire by those who seek this light, they will produce only another spiral of error, which must later be undone. It is like dropping a stitch in a knitting: one must unravel one's work all the way back to the place where the stitch was dropped and commence all over again. Some individuals are not willing to do this, preferring to abandon the project—and thus the weaving of the wedding garment is discontinued in that embodiment because they allowed discouraging tendencies in their nature to influence the course of events.

"The science behind the ascension is very great indeed. And if the necessary conditions were met by mankind, there would be built in the world order a pillar of great beauty, a pyramid of lives in harmony, a pyramid of architectural grandeur.

"When that day comes, the greenswards will stretch toward the four corners of the earth. Then the pyramid will glow. Then the fire of the Spirit will transmute first the base stones, and the capstone will be the last to glow. All energy in the capstone is from on high, and that which is in the base is from below; but the qualifications of the base must conform, by reason of thought and devotion, to the pattern from on high. Thus, the fire will draw down first to the base stones. Then the capstone, supported by the base stones, will glow as the sweep of the great electronic stream from the heart of God moves down symmetrically and in perfect divine order through the entire structure and then rises from the base as a mighty cone of fire, causing the entire pyramid to glow on the greensward.

"And it shall come to pass that, with the accomplishment of the capstone crowning man's achievement, the civilization of the permanent golden age will begin. Then the destiny of America and of the world will be outpictured, because the pyramid of lives will have adjusted itself in conformity to divine principle. The Grand Mason of the Universe, the eternal God, will himself express satisfaction by causing to descend out of heaven the hand that carries the torch. When this occurs, that which is below will manifest that which is Above. . . . "53

Serapis says: "To this end we must work and serve. The pyramid of cosmic Truth, builded on lively stones, must rise from the great plain of Mamre[54] ('Mam-Ray,' symbolizing the Motherhood of God...). The Eternal Mother must shield the Eternal Son. The shell of cosmic purity must trumpet forth the victory of man in accordance with the divine plan. The course of life may wend its way over a variegated terrain and under a multitude of circumstances, but when the stream becomes crystal clear and purified, it merges with the sea of glass[55]—the cosmic cube of perfection, the white stone which signifies that purpose, ideal and action have been purified in man.

"The divine geometry, through the symbol of the pyramid, draws the aspiring consciousness of man into the idea of an ascendant life. To ascend is to blend in cosmic unity with the heart of the Eternal. It is the destiny of every man. Those who understand this will rejoice in the consolation of their own ultimate freedom from every earthly travail, as cosmic purpose is enthroned in consciousness both now and forever."[56]

"O God, here am I, here I AM!
One with thee and one to command—
Open the doorway of my consciousness
And let me demand as never before
My birthright to restore.
Thy prodigal son has come to thee
And longs once again to walk with thee
Every step of the way home."[57]

Freedom from Astral Entanglements

Beloved mighty victorious Presence of God, I AM in me, O thou beloved immortal victorious threefold flame of eternal Truth within my heart, Holy Christ Selves of all mankind, beloved Saint Germain, beloved El Morya, beloved Jesus, beloved Mother Mary, beloved great God Obedience, beloved Archangel Michael, beloved mighty Astrea, all Ascended Beings, powers, activities and legions of light, angels and activities of the sacred fire, beloved Lanello, the entire Spirit of the Great White Brotherhood and the World Mother, elemental life—fire, air, water and earth!

In the name of the Presence of God which I AM and through the magnetic power of the sacred fire vested in me, I decree for my freedom from all astral entanglements and for my permanent victory in the light!

> Cut me loose and set me free!
> Cut me loose and set me free!
> Cut me loose and set me free!
> From all that's not Christ-victory!*
>
> [Repeat verse between the following endings.]

1. Beloved I AM, by Christ-command (3x)
2. In the Ascended Masters' love and names
   and by the power of their cosmic flames (3x)
3. By the spiral blue flame (3x)
4. In Archangel Michael's love and name
   and by the power of his sword of blue flame (3x)
5. In the Great White Brotherhood's love and name and
   by the power of their threefold flame (3x)
6. By God's blue ray, it's done today (3x)
7. By cosmic I AM fire, manifest God's desire (3x)

---

*Suggested alternate insert: I decree on behalf of all souls confined in mental hospitals, convalescent homes, general hospitals, state institutions and places of incarceration for their freedom from all astral entanglements and for their permanent victory in the light!

> Cut them loose and set them free!
> Cut them loose and set them free!
> Cut them loose and set them free!
> From all that's not Christ-victory!

8. In joy I know that this is done, for Freedom's flame
    frees everyone (3x)
9. I command it done today, I command it done to stay,
    I command it done God's way
  I expect it done today, I expect it done to stay,
    I expect it done God's way
  I accept it done today, I accept it done to stay,
    I accept it done God's way
  It is done today, it is done to stay, it is done God's way

And in full faith I consciously accept this manifest, manifest, manifest! (3x) right here and now with
full power, eternally sustained, all-powerfully active,
ever expanding and world enfolding until all are
wholly ascended in the light and free! Beloved I AM!
Beloved I AM! Beloved I AM!

The Covenant of the Magi
by El Morya

Father, into thy hands I commend my being. Take
me and use me—my efforts, my thoughts, my re-
sources, all that I AM—in thy service to the world of
men and to thy noble cosmic purposes, yet unknown
to my mind.

Teach me to be kind in the way of the Law that
awakens men and guides them to the shores of reality,
to the confluence of the river of life, to the Edenic
source, that I may understand that the leaves of the
Tree of Life, given to me each day, are for the healing
of the nations; that as I garner them into the treasury
of being and offer the fruit of my loving adoration to
thee and to thy purposes supreme, I shall indeed hold

covenant with thee as my guide, my guardian, my friend.

For thou art the directing connector who shall establish my lifestream with those heavenly contacts, limited only by the flow of the hours, who will assist me to perform in the world of men the most meaningful aspect of my individual life plan as conceived by thee and executed in thy name by the Karmic Board of spiritual overseers who, under thy holy direction, do administer thy laws.

So be it, O eternal Father, and may the covenant of thy beloved Son, the living Christ, the Only Begotten of the Light, teach me to be aware that he liveth today within the tri-unity of my being as the great Mediator between my individualized Divine Presence and my human self; that he raiseth me into Christ consciousness and thy divine realization in order that as the eternal Son becomes one with the Father, so I may ultimately become one with thee in that dynamic moment when out of union is born my perfect freedom to move, to think, to create, to design, to fulfill, to inhabit, to inherit, to dwell and to be wholly within the fullness of thy light.

Father, into thy hands I commend my being.

Chapter 3

Ascended and Unascended Masters

The glory of the celestial is one,
and the glory of the terrestrial is another.
THE APOSTLE PAUL

Ascended and Unascended Masters

Many students of the occult, of mysticism and of spiritual law become involved in a search for the masters. To sit at the feet of a master is a goal to which many aspire. They feel that if they can contact a living master, their own victory will be assured—while not a few aspire to be the master of other men.

These seek to gather around themselves those to whom they can give advice, while often they themselves are unable to manifest their own victory over the very conditions from which their students seek deliverance. Of these Peter says, "While they promise them liberty, they themselves are the servants of corruption."[1] Thus many have found that the pathway to the masters is not all that they thought it would be. And they have returned to their own hearth, the spiritual quest unfulfilled.

Nevertheless, there are indeed what we may call true unascended masters, just as there are Ascended Masters. Unascended masters are those who have attained a degree of mastery but who, for various reasons, have not taken their ascension.

Ascended Masters are those who have mastered life on earth, fulfilled their divine plan, balanced a minimum of 51 percent of their karma and taken their ascension.

The Ascended Master Djwal Kul points out: "There are some people who ponder why it is necessary to have Masters. The answer is simple and can be accepted as such with impunity. The Masters are as necessary as the Godhead, for they are an extension of the Deity in his contact with mankind. Without hierarchy and without the assistance of the Brothers of Light, man would be forced to pursue his search for God alone— without chart or compass or the benefit of the experience of others who have gone before. He would be forced to rise to heights beyond the margin of safety and thus suffer the effects of his blindness even while in search of cosmic illumination.

"The Masters are Mediators. They have safely risen to the highest contacts with great Cosmic Beings and back to the very heart of God. They have maintained a state of willingness to enter into human consciousness—with all of its degradations and all of the accompanying uncomfortability that the Masters face in descending into human consciousness—all in order that they might do the work of God and restore man to his rightful place so that he can safely rise into the arms of the waiting Deity, who longs to welcome him home.

"Accept the Masters, then, as holy brothers, as ministers of God, as agents of the eternal Presence, and know that whereas you may address the Presence and rise measurably toward the heights of cosmic glory, it remains for the Ascended Masters' consciousness to rise immeasurably in a cosmic sense to where God *is* in a more 'concentrated' form. Thus they are able to receive a greater concentration of blessings, which they in turn may pass on to those who aspire to reach him but have not yet done so."[2]

As Lady Master Leto says, "Most Westerners are able to

perceive in Christ Jesus an eye picture of an Ascended Master, whereas Orientals can more readily visualize the Buddha as such. Whatever personage may appeal to you from among the many religious figures who have arisen on the world scene, concentrate on the high spiritual attributes of that one—the loving qualities expressed in his or her countenance and in the vibratory action of his or her thought and feelings—and then strive to emulate those virtues that are apparent."[3]

Mastery

As we compare the joint services of Ascended Masters and unascended masters, let us define the term "mastery." Mastery is the state of having power of command, expert skill or proficiency in a given field, area of knowledge or discipline. Now, there are masters of science, of art, of music and of the professions. Yet these are not necessarily masters of life and death.

In our consideration of masters we are referring to those who have attained mastery over themselves. These are they who have learned to govern their energies and to discipline their thoughts and feelings. They have mastery over the cycles of life and are mastered by neither the tides of their returning karma nor the tides of the mass consciousness (with the exception, perhaps, of a narrow margin of their personal lives that may require the attention of the Master of masters). These are indeed unascended masters.

Serapis Bey says: "These masters have retained consciousness and a type of form in the unascended state because they are the guardians of certain lifestreams, because they recognize the heavy burden of this hour of the Kali Yuga."[4]

"There is a period prior to the ascension," Saint Germain says, "when the I AM Presence overshadows the Christed one, who then declares, 'I and my Father are one.'[5] During this period, which may last from several months to several years or even decades, the initiate walks the earth as an unascended Ascended Being, so called. This means that he has come into the closest proximity to the I AM Presence that unascended man can approach without actually going through the ritual of the ascension."[6]

Lanello adds: "These unascended masters speak of cycles. ... They speak of their coming and their going, entering into the world of form and maintaining the highest degrees of God-mastery prior to the ascension as they abide in etheric octaves."[7]

Many today consider Ramakrishna to have been an unascended master. Others consider the great master Babaji of the Himalayas and his sister, Mataji, to be unascended masters. Masters they are indeed, who have forgone the ritual of the ascension in order to serve what is known as the Bodhisattva ideal.

What the Chela Should Know about His Master

We turn now to the writings of the Ascended Master Saint Germain to examine the differences between Ascended Masters and the unascended masters of the Far East:

"The unascended masters are adepts who are called masters, yet they have not taken the ritual of the ascension. Some of these, after having entered nirvana or a lesser state of adeptship, return in consciousness to the physical form. Here they recharge their flesh forms in preparation for greater service; nonetheless, for various reasons, they do not go through the ascension process.

"A rare few among the unascended masters have been able to perpetuate life in the same body over long periods, thereby continuing the opportunity to balance a great deal of karma and becoming in the eyes of many as gods in the flesh.

"It is also true that some of these find it impossible to demonstrate the mastery of retaining life in one body. Therefore, they do reembody from time to time, while continuing to abide in the nirvanic state during intervals in their long journey toward higher mastership and the ascension.

"The powers that these unascended masters demonstrate are sometimes phenomenal, but this does not set them above those who are in the ascended state. All should know that soul progress is the real goal, not the exhibition of power in one or more of its forms (although such powers are often evidence of soul development). Also, seekers should beware of false adepts whose control of substance is used for self-aggrandizement and destructive intent. Often these put forth an appearance of good, but in reality they are self-oriented.

"It is true that by the exercise of their sovereign free will, men can elect to fulfill their evolution in any manner and by any means that they deem acceptable. But all should be apprised that we who have overcome the world point the way to the ascended state as the highest state to which anyone can aspire. From this state mankind do not fall back again into a form of lesser consciousness, and from this state a permanent entrance into nirvana and even higher aspects of God consciousness can be developed and retained as infinite progress is made.

"It is known that many of the Eastern masters do not summon enough of the Divine Will to enable them to pass all of the required initiations in order to transcend the flesh. Yet it cannot be denied that they frequently manifest high states of consciousness. To be associated with them as a disciple is not without responsibility, nor is it without limitation.

"It is understood by those who enter into the guru-chela relationship that there will be a certain involvement in karmic conditions that as an auric net surround all unascended mankind, whether they be advanced teachers or their pupils. For without karma no one can remain unascended without special dispensation from the Karmic Board.

"The benign aspects of their karma, which involve service, instruction and healing, enable unascended masters to confer definite benefits upon their chelas. These in turn can be relieved of varying amounts of their own negative karma as the master himself takes on (in part) the balancing of his disciples' karma.

"Let us also consider the benefits of becoming a chela of the Ascended Masters. The Ascended Masters may have a residue of karma that they must balance from the ascended octave, but being free from the karma-making round, they do not continue to make personal karma.

"It is true that Ascended Masters have at various times taken on mankind's karma and assisted them in working out their problems in the same manner as do those whom we have termed unascended masters. But the assistance that can be rendered to a chela of the Ascended Masters is always of the highest form. Never does it involve any form of danger whatsoever, except it be the danger of not accepting the opportunity for eternal life that the Master offers.

"Therefore, I would warn all students of light: you have a certain responsibility for the professions you make in the name of your teacher, whether he be ascended or unascended. For is it not written, 'By thy words thou shalt be justified, and by thy words thou shalt be condemned'?[8] That which is said incorrectly in the name of one vested with a high spiritual office carries the weight of karma for that office, which is always greater for the illumined than for the unillumined....

"In the same manner, if any teacher give out false doctrine, he is responsible to those who are injured by his error until they attain their ascension in the light. This is why Ascended Masters have karma. Many times just a few erroneous concepts that crept into an otherwise accurate spiritual document have caused the downfall of a sincere student. Thus, the Master who has gained his ascension for the good he has done must continue to assist those who have been hindered on their journey by the wrong he unwittingly committed while unascended.

"There are attached to the earth many great beings who are obliged to serve here until all imperfect markings that they made while unascended are erased. In the case of one who has served as a world figure, this may be until the last lifestreams win their freedom—or until another Ascended Being offers to hold his office and carry out his service while he goes on to still higher service in the cosmic reaches of infinity."[9]

The Bodhisattva Ideal

Some Ascended Masters have embraced the Bodhisattva ideal, vowing to serve the needs of humanity until the last soul is ascended. Kuan Yin, the Goddess of Mercy, has promised to keep the flame of forgiveness on behalf of the evolutions of this planet. Forgoing cosmic service and advancement in the hierarchical order, she will remain in the Temple of Mercy (located in the etheric plane over the city of Beijing) until all have returned to the heart of God. Such a commitment requires extraordinary dedication even in one who is ascended.

Kuan Yin says: "I am the instrument of judgment from the Lords of Karma to those who misuse the light of the violet flame in this age, perverting the cycles of mercy and the rituals of mercy whereby, through the path of initiation, the soul can indeed attain that soul liberation that is desired as the deep desiring of God within to be God....

"Understand, then, what it means to be as the instrument of mercy. This is why I am a Bodhisattva. For as I have looked on the suffering of earth's evolutions, I have said, 'Life to me is not worth living in the ascended octave while there is one soul on earth remaining who yet suffers. And so I am not willing to go on in cosmic service or cosmic consciousness. I must stay and stay.'

"And therefore, you can understand that my love for the God within the soul of the helpless victim remains that momentum of love which I sustain in the earth body—the counterpart of my love for God in the Great Central Sun. Because I know him in his glory, because I know Alpha and Omega in the fullness of the freedom of the rhythm of cosmos, I know what the God within the imprisoned soul can be. And I know that that God is the same God whom I adore in Father-Mother, Alpha and Omega. It is, therefore, my Father and my Mother who are suffering in my children whom I hold in my arms and rock in my arms in their finer bodies until you can come and tend to them in physical manifestation. Not your child alone but your Father-Mother God suffers the crucifixion this day."[10]

Kuan Yin's ministration is very real and as ancient as the hills. The Bodhisattvas have made a vow to serve God and the flame of freedom until every man, woman and child of Terra is ascended and free. This vow is a sacred calling. Kuan Yin cautions us, however, against taking this vow ourselves unless we thoroughly understand the service of these dedicated ones.

"Being one with all life," she says, "we are aware of all life in its manifestations from the highest to the lowest. This is part of the Bodhisattva ideal, which is a part of those who are standing with humanity. And there are quite a number upon this planet, although few compared to those who go their own way of riotous living. It is a very high and holy order, and I suggest that you think long and hard about this calling before you respond and say, 'I will do the same.'

"For when aeons pass and men are not moved by the

flame that you hold, remember that you might wish you had chosen another easier or more gratifying way. As the centuries pass—the thousands of years and the cycles—and the same individuals whom you have nourished by the power of your heart flame are involved in the same involvements in the world, you find that you cry out to God and say, 'O Lord, how long! How long will this wayward generation be in coming to the knowledge of the divinity and the love of the sacred fire that we have held for so long?' "[11]

Now, it is neither desirable nor proper that all should pursue this path. In most cases those who do so have earned their ascension but have bypassed it, to provide a focus or an anchor point upon the planet for the higher Mind of God. This is the role of the mahatma, the "great-souled one," who, out of his humble communion with the flame of life, has drawn forth and taken as his own identity the great solar awareness of the consciousness of God.

Such a one becomes a vehicle through whom the beautiful currents of divine grace may radiate daily into the world of form. Without such dedicated souls in their midst, millions would be deprived of the divine currents that are vital not only to their existence but also to the balance of forces on the planet. These Bodhisattvas are of great assistance to hierarchy in maintaining a vibrational contact upon the planetary body that is stabilizing to the planet.

The Fearless Compassion of the Bodhisattva

Lord Maitreya exemplifies the Bodhisattva's virtues of kindness, fearless compassion and *virya* (vigor). Helena Roerich, who released the teachings of El Morya through the Agni Yoga books, wrote of Maitreya and the path of the Bodhisattva in her book *Foundations of Buddhism:* "What qualities must a

Bodhisattva possess? In the Teaching of Gotama Buddha and in the Teaching of Bodhisattva Maitreya, ... the maximum development of energy, courage, patience, constancy of striving, and fearlessness was underlined first of all. Energy is the basis of everything, for it alone contains all possibilities.

"Buddhas are eternally in action; immovability is unknown to them; like the eternal motion in space the actions of the Sons of Conquerors manifest themselves in the worlds.

"Mighty, valiant, firm in his step, not rejecting the burden of an achievement for the General Good."

Helena Roerich continues: "There are three joys of Bodhisattvas: the joy of giving, the joy of helping, and the joy of eternal perception. Patience always, in all, and everywhere. The Sons of Buddhas, the Sons of Conquerors, Bodhisattvas in their active compassion are Mothers to All-Existence."[12]

This "active compassion" of the Bodhisattva, embracing both fearlessness and virya, finds its ultimate expression as forgiveness. For it is impossible to extend compassion to someone if you have not first forgiven him for his transgressions.

Kuan Yin describes fearless compassion as the epitome of a Bodhisattva's love: "I will tell you what has impelled us to reach beyond our ability, and I speak of all the ascended hosts. It is because we saw a need so great and had such compassion for the one who had that need, and we saw that none other stood by to help that one, none other would come if we did not extend the hand. In that moment, Love itself supplied the intensity, the sacred fire whereby we could leap to the rescue, to the side of one in distress, or enter some course of study so that we might become proficient in the knowledge that was needed.

"This response, then, this love that could forget itself and leap to save a life, this was the opening for the great fire of the Holy Spirit to enter the heart, to dissolve recalcitrance there, to melt the impediments to those twelve petals of the heart chakra and their unique vibration, to take from us hardness of heart, physical encrustations, disease, fear, doubt, records of death. All of these could vanish in the ardor of service."[13]

Saint Germain comments: "Think upon these words of the Bodhisattva vow: *fearless compassion!* Ah, what a state of mind to be in perpetually! Fearlessness to give of the fount of one's being, to extend compassion instead of criticism and backbiting, to give such flood tides of love as to fill in the chinks and cracks of another's shortcomings.

"Fearless compassion means one no longer fears to lose oneself or to loose oneself to become such a grid for the light to pass through that the Infinite One never ceases to be the Compassionate One through you."[14]

Sangharakshita, a Buddhist monk and scholar, writes in his book *The Three Jewels:* "Despite the emphasis on compassion the Bodhisattva is no mere sentimentalist. Nor, for all his tenderness, is he an effeminate weakling. He is the Great Hero, the embodiment not only of wisdom and compassion, but also of *virya*, or vigour, a word which like the etymologically equivalent 'virility' signifies both energy and masculine potency."[15]

Maitreya himself tells us how the challenge to embody the virtue of loving-kindness motivated him on the Path:

"Long ago I took my vow:

I will not leave thee, O my God!
I will not leave thee, O my God!

"And I saw my God imprisoned in flesh. I saw the Word imprisoned in hearts of stone. I saw my God interred in souls bound to the ways of the wicked. And I said again:

I will not leave thee, O my God!
I will tend that fire.
I will adore that flame.

And by and by some will aspire to be with me—
To be Maitreya.

"And one day I sat, my head in my hand, deep in thought, and Lord Gautama said to me, 'What are you thinking, my Son?' And I said, 'My Father, can we win them with kindness and with love? Will they respond to love?' And my Father said to me, 'If you hold within your heart, my Son, the full orchestration of love, 144,000 tones of love, if you yourself will come to know love, then, yes, you will win them with love.'

"My heart leaped for joy. My Father had given to me the challenge to know love, to be love, not for the sake of mere love and loving love, not for the sake of the mere bliss of the communion of love, but for the salvation of souls, for the reaching out unto my God in humanity."[16]

Appearances of the Masters

Ascended Beings can materialize and dematerialize a form that resembles in all aspects the fleshly body of other men but is in effect a spiritual body, a celestial body, not a terrestrial one. Unascended beings cannot.

Yet this is not an absolute criterion, for there are a few unascended masters who can also dematerialize and materialize the body. However, most of these operate through a projected consciousness whereby, rather than assembling and disassembling the atoms of a physical body, they create in consciousness a body form that may be projected anywhere in the world and may or may not be seen by others.

Saint Germain, following his ascension in 1684, was granted a dispensation by the Lords of Karma to return to the world as an Ascended Being who bore the appearance of an unascended being. In the eighteenth century he became known in Europe as Le Comte de Saint Germain, the Wonderman of Europe.

Inasmuch as Cosmic Law has allowed exceptions to the rule that Ascended Masters do not reembody, it is possible that the Ascended Master Maitreya, who has been referred to as "the Coming Buddha," will receive a similar dispensation. Lord Maitreya has said that five hundred years after the beginning of a true golden age, when stability has been reached, he may decide to come and embody with his Bodhisattvas.

But we also know that a Buddha, whether ascended or unascended, may choose to appear in a tangible form to selected lifestreams. Thus, without reincarnating, Maitreya might be seen walking and talking with his disciples in his Ascended Master light body, which he may precipitate to the etheric level for those who can see him at that level yet whose karma binds them to the physical octave.

Maitreya explains: "I AM Buddha. I AM Mother. I stand betwixt time and space, the Master of both. Yet I abide in neither but I abide in the heart of the chela and in the stupa of the Buddha. I come out of the Tushita heaven, where I have been discoursing this night with Bodhisattvas who have attained to that level of God Self-mastery and enlightenment that is required of those who abide in this realm. When you attain to that level you may also go there, for this is a plane of heaven that is reserved for those having the Bodhisattva attainment or greater.

"Thus, in many art forms you will see depicted the Buddha surrounded by many Bodhisattvas abiding in this Tushita heaven. These blessed unascended ones look to the day of my coming in the earth when they may reincarnate with me to be messengers of the dharma of the New Age. They are filled with wonder that intimations of this dharma and full cups of it are given through the dictations of the Ascended Masters through the Messengers, that those in embodiment who are also on the path of the Bodhisattva may be forerunners and indeed anchor the new age of Aquarius for our coming.

"I am here in the fullness of the Coming Buddha who has indeed come. But I may one day come with my Bodhisattvas to a certain level of incarnation if there shall be a golden age upon earth. Thus, many sweet smiling faces of these blessed ones look upon you as their point of hope for fulfillment of the long-awaited dream. It is their dharma to embody (whether or not I do), for they must fulfill their path of the ascension and in the process become teachers of the dharma."[17]

Unascended Masters

Unascended masters are subject to the ills of the flesh, to karma-making circumstances and to the ever-present possibility of being torn down just at the moment when they are ready to be raised up. However, the peril is not so great for these blessed servants as it might first appear, for they do have self-mastery and they are not likely to be caught off guard.

As long as men are embodied in the veil of flesh, there is the possibility that the devotee in an unguarded moment might open the door of his consciousness to inharmony of one kind or another. The karma that might be incurred would have to be balanced before he could once again be restored to the fullness of grace that he had held prior to becoming enmeshed in mortal thought and feeling.

As we discussed in the previous chapter, there are certain requirements that must be met by a candidate for the ascension. Some graduate from earth's school as valedictorians of their class, while others are grateful to be included even as "tail-end Charlie."[18] An unascended lifestream who has met these requirements may elect to remain in embodiment, forgoing the ascension in order to serve planetary needs. Such a one need not forfeit his right to progress in the cycles of initiation according to his own level of devotion and attainment. Indeed, he may accelerate the expansion of his solar consciousness while carrying out the assignments of the hierarchy from his unascended state.

Thus it may come to pass that unascended avatars realize a greater degree of spiritual advancement than some newly ascended Masters. An unascended Bodhisattva who has kept the flame on behalf of millions of lifestreams for thousands of years would certainly be ahead of one who has recently ascended with minimal requirements.

Of course, once ascended, even the least in the kingdom advance rapidly. Unfettered by the world and the density of human consciousness, Ascended Beings can rise to heights of mastery much more quickly than those who are burdened with the responsibilities of serving the needs of the planet from the unascended state. Nonetheless, the latter acknowledge with the Christ, "My burden is light."[19]

Lord Lanto has announced a dispensation whereby the Ascended Masters have determined to step through the veil and walk and talk with mankind through their chelas: "And so the decree went forth and became an Ascended Master fiat. And the determination was made that we would walk the earth through *you*, that we would move through your mind, that we would speak through your lips, that we would flash our concepts into the world through you!"[20]

This dispensation was a prelude to the time when if a certain quota of ascensions is met in a one-thousand-year period, many Ascended Masters will be given the dispensation to walk the earth in visible light bodies in order to preach to the mankind of earth who, up to that time, will have failed to make the choice between light and darkness.

Jesus challenges us to balance our karma and so become unascended masters: "Right on earth you can walk as ascended unascended beings. Would you not like to be an unascended Ascended Master? An unascended Ascended Lady Master? This means that you have the power and authority of an Ascended Being while you yet walk the earth in robes of flesh. This is possible in this age.

"Hasten, then, the balancing of your karma. Let not one opportunity pass to be Sons and Daughters of Dominion. And then watch. Watch the great opportunities that the Cosmic Lords and hierarchies shall present to you to be victors over hell and death, to have the all-power of heaven and earth, and to extend it unto the children of mankind. . . .

"And so the earth, a ball of golden light, shall ascend into the golden age."[21]

The Coming of the Avatars

The coming of unascended masters into embodiment is indeed a blessing to the evolutions of an entire planet, even though not all recognize that such an event is taking place. From time to time throughout the history of our planet, great souls of light have descended to raise the vibrations of earth and the consciousness of mankind: Enoch, Melchizedek, Abraham, Moses, the Old Testament prophets, Jesus the Christ, Mary his mother, and Saint Joseph (Saint Germain), as well as the Eastern adepts Confucius, Lao-tzu, Zarathustra (Zoroaster), Gautama Buddha, Maitreya, Krishna and Kuan Yin.

Nor has heaven ceased to bless the earth with avatars and their love. In the 1960s, for example, the earth received countless lifestreams who had pledged to stand, face and conquer with the mankind of earth every form of error that had been imposed upon the race.

On February 4, 1962, on the occasion of a conjunction of planets that astrologers around the world hailed as a cosmic moment, a great number of highly illumined souls were born. Lady Master Venus foretold that as these Christs "come to maturity they will assist the mankind of earth to find their way back to the heart of God." She said: "These beings are indeed masters. They are avatars in descent as was the Christ, and their mission is to guide the mankind of earth in the Ascended Master age—the Great Golden Age." The Lady Venus explained that the coming of these souls with their cosmic retinue "precedes the time when the Ascended Masters themselves shall step from octaves of light into visible form."[22]

In 1964 nine souls who had attained the Buddhic consciousness came into embodiment at strategic points on the globe. These had long ago met the requirements for the ascension, but they volunteered to return in the power of the three-times-three to blend their energies with the service of the holy Christ children born in February 1962.

The momentum of light that these Buddhas have magnetized in their auras may be felt for hundreds of miles. When they are in complete attunement with their God Presence (as in meditation or out of the body during sleep), their auras enfold the entire planet in the balancing power of the threefold flame sustained by Gautama Buddha in his etheric temple over the Gobi Desert.

Now, the attainment of a Buddha is greater than that of a Christ—that is, the office of Buddha is greater than the office of the Christ in the order of the spiritual hierarchy. Hence many Ascended Masters have not yet reached the Buddhic consciousness. Every Ascended Master would gladly pay homage to the light and mastery of these unascended lifestreams, even as the three Magi (themselves unascended masters) came to worship the Christ Child.

Not many months after the coming of the Buddhas, one of the nine passed from this world "as a flower cut from the vine,"[23] so lacking in purity were his surroundings. Dauntless in his mission, he volunteered to be born again so that the power of the three-times-three and the pact of the Holy Nine might not be broken.

Thus on April 7, 1969, the Master Jesus announced that this Buddha would return in the land of India, where he was to be born to a blessed couple who had volunteered at inner levels to sponsor and protect his precious lifestream. And so the mission of ascended and unascended masters working hand in hand with humanity moves on, and another chapter in the never-ending Book of Life has a happy ending that promises new beginnings for all.

In 1973 we received the dispensation for the descent of ten thousand and one avatars. These are Christed beings who have the cosmic consciousness and have attained great mastery in other systems of worlds. They are no longer required to reembody, and yet they have volunteered to be born of earthly parents in order to liberate the planet and prepare the way for the descent of the seventh root race.

The Order of the Prophets: The Drama of Elijah the Prophet

In our study of ascended and unascended masters, let us now consider the service of Elijah and his great devotion, which led to a most unusual dispensation granted by the Karmic Board in order that he might render further assistance to his beloved pupil Elisha. Chananda, Chief of the Indian Council of the Great White Brotherhood, refers to this dispensation in a letter to the Keepers of the Flame:

"In the drama of Elijah the prophet, who was caught up into heaven in a chariot of fire, one may learn how the victory of one man's trust and faith in God was able to give him his ascension in the light by the power of the sacred fire. In the case of Elijah the prophet, after his ascension he retained his higher vehicle (body) in the octaves of light but descended in part into the being of John the Baptist, who was truly one come 'in the Spirit and power of Elias [Elijah].'[24]

"His is perhaps the one exception, the one case in point, that will prove the divine rule. For in the main when individuals take the initiation of the ascension and are raised back to the heart of God from whence they came, they do not choose to reembody again upon the planet, nor are they chosen for such an activity.

"On the Mount of Transfiguration Moses and Elijah did appear with Jesus—which shows that after the decapitation of John the Baptist (which took place at the request of Salome), he did again proceed back to the heart of his ascended state to manifest as Elijah, the Ascended Master.[25]...

"The relationship between Elijah and Elisha was one of teacher and pupil. Thus Jesus had been initiated in this former embodiment under Elijah in preparation for his great mission in Galilee.

"It is the desire of every teacher to see his pupil excel and even surpass his own efforts, and therefore John said of Jesus, 'He must increase, but I must decrease.' So great was the love of the guru for the chela that he was willing to make the sacrifice of descending to earth from his ascended state to go before his pupil to 'prepare...the way of the Lord.'[26]

"It was the preaching and baptizing of John that paved the way for the coming of the Christ. His was the 'voice of one crying in the wilderness' (in the barrenness of human consciousness, devoid of the light of the Christ). It was John of whom Jesus said that he is 'more than a prophet, for this is he of whom it is written, Behold, I send my messenger before thy face, which shall prepare thy way before thee.'"[27]

Jesus describes his love for John the Baptist and recalls their life together as Elijah and Elisha:

"How well I remember when the disciples of John the Baptist came and told me that Herod's daughter had demanded his head and that the tetrarch, out of pride in his oath before men, had forsaken his oath to God and bowed to the will of the daughter of darkness. For a moment in eternity I, too, was seized with a sense of loss, even though I had been prepared for that hour—even though I knew that the work of the LORD's Messenger had been accomplished and that his time had come.

"This was indeed Elias come again,[28] the great prophet of old who had stood on Mount Carmel to challenge the workers of iniquity and the devils they invoked,[29] whom the LORD sent to the widow of Zarephath and promised her by the word of the LORD God of Israel that her barrel of meal should not waste, neither the cruse of oil fail, until the day that the LORD sent rain upon the earth.[30] And it was so.

"This was Elijah, the same who cast his mantle upon me when I was embodied as Elisha. He came upon me as I was plowing with twelve yoke of oxen in the field, and immediately I followed him.[31] And I vowed to him, my teacher, 'As the LORD liveth, and as thy soul liveth, I will not leave thee.' I saw him take his mantle and wrap it together and smite the waters so that we two might walk over the Jordan on dry ground.

"He taught me the laws of alchemy and to smite the waters of the human consciousness with its astral nightmares and the defenses of the Antichrist sent forth against the light of the prophets of Israel—the same elements of the carnal mind that would challenge us again in another era, but in the same place in time and space. And he promised me that if I learned my lessons well and if my mind would become congruent with his own—'if thou see me when I am taken from thee'—that a double portion of his spirit would be upon me.

"And so when I heard of the beheading of John the Baptist, I thought upon those days of our togetherness when as the disciple of the great Master, I had seen him challenge the wickedness of the prophets of Baal, of Ahab and Jezebel, and then how I had seen him ascend in a chariot of fire in the glory of the ascension.[32] And I remembered how he had promised to go before me to prepare the way for the lowering of the Christ consciousness into its rightful preeminence among the sons and daughters of Israel and among all who would choose to follow that which *is real*.

"By special dispensation from the hierarchy, John the Baptist came forth from the ascended state to set the stage for the coming of the Christ, for the descent of the fire of the Logos, and to initiate the spiral whereby all mankind might attain Christhood according to the example that the Father had given me to exemplify on earth as it truly is in heaven.

"And so I explained to my disciples, 'Among them that are born of women there hath not risen a greater than John the Baptist.'[33] For not in ten thousand years had the dispensation been given for an Ascended Being of his level of attainment to take on physical form in a mission for the hierarchy. And thus he truly walked the earth as the greatest of Masters, a karma-free being who laid down his life not only that I might live to fulfill the mission of the Christ, but that all who followed after might have the momentum of his mantle of purity and self-sacrifice. He lived that we might leave testimony upon the sands of time, an indelible mark in akasha of the unspeakable love that exists between Guru and chela, Master and disciple."[34]

Techniques of Self-Realization: Soul Expansion through Love

Devotees of the light who have desired a closer union with God have used various techniques through the ages. These practices have differed from East to West, but always the goal has been the same: the spiritualization of consciousness and the reunion of the soul with the Spirit.

Saint Germain gives further instruction on this subject: "Through various yogic practices individuals enter the state called samadhi. In this state the outer consciousness is suspended in its contact with the senses, and interior bliss is invoked by sustaining contact with the mighty light of God and his inner radiance within man's being.

"Many forms of control are developed over both body and mind through engaging in this practice. The ultimate end thereof is, of course, the attainment of nirvana or the nirvanic state.

"The state of nirvana is one in which the soul, having progressed through the orderly series of initiations available to man upon this planet, enters that cosmic rest whereby she becomes so completely absorbed in her individual I AM Presence that she maintains no contact whatsoever with the outer personality or form.

"Without waiting for the process of the ascension, some individuals pass through various forms of yogic trance into the higher realms. They leave behind the body temple and even the consciousness itself to enter straightway into the highly vibrating center of the Godhead, where all is so still that it seems to be in a state of perpetual rest.

"Dwelling in the peace of the Godhead, some are inclined to remain aloof from the warp and woof of creation. They find complete contentment in God and have no desire to go out from the sun center of his radiance. Thus the nirvanic state, for all practical purposes, becomes the cessation of three-dimensional action.

"I would call to your attention that although Lord Buddha reached this state, he did not permit himself to lose contact with reality as it exists in the denser spheres. Rather, because of the greatness of his love for the world and its people, he responded when he was called back from his nirvanic rest, and he once again descended out of this high initiatic mode into the world of form. There he became the hierarch of Shamballa or Lord of the World, enabling Sanat Kumara to return from his long exile upon earth to his planetary home, Venus.[35] (It should be pointed out, however, that Lord Buddha had attained his ascension before entering the state of nirvana and that he did choose to enter that state after his ascension.)

"It is definitely possible for individuals who are unascended masters, by reason of their high degree of spiritual attunement, to enter into the nirvanic state and still maintain a body in physical form. In some cases, they cast off the physical form, electing to remain in a state of bliss in the haven of nirvana.

"I would like to point out here that there are in the land of India and other parts of the world a few unascended beings who have attained such a degree of mastery over form and substance as to remain in one body temple for thousands of years. Some of these are not expected to relinquish their forms until the last individual upon earth has attained his God-victory.

"Such as these have even forsworn the bliss and peace of nirvana in order to serve the holy causes of freedom. They remain alternately in samadhic states or states of bliss and in periods of contact with mankind whereby they bring about wondrous blessings, conferred upon both nations and individuals by their service to life and their very presence upon earth.

"Contrasted to the aforementioned practices and teachings

is the goal of the ascension. As we have seen, the ascension has a different connotation than (1) the state of nirvana, or (2) the state of samadhi that is attained through the techniques of yoga, or (3) the state of mastership whereby the holy light of God is conferred upon embodied man in such a manner as to make him almost immortalized in form."[36]

Saint Germain teaches further: "In the attainment of nirvana, that fragment of the infinite which has been involuted in form becomes spiritually evolved to a certain high point in the manifest spectrum of the divine consciousness. But often the individual monad bypasses many of the lower steps of the ladder of attainment and moves directly, from whatever level he may have reached through self-effort, to the very apex of the Creator's consciousness of being. Entering the center of the Mind of God, the soul finds that realm known as the Sabbath or seventh day of conscious rest. This is quiescence—the consciousness of peace and wholeness. . . .

"Whereas the lower self must be raised to the realization of God Self–awareness that is native both to the nirvanic and the ascended states, the higher being of man always knows that 'I AM that I AM.' And it holds constant conscious contact with the many levels of divine consciousness. This is the Divine Presence who bypasses the personality consciousness of the monad and abides continuously in the nirvanic consciousness of rest. Here in the quiet glory of God, the Presence magnifies the eternal stillness that manifests unceasingly.

"Through the ritual of the ascension, man is able to raise not only his individual consciousness, as in nirvana, but also his lower vehicles, including the four lower bodies, retaining the transmuted faculties thereof. Through the ascension he redeems his substance from error, according to the promise of God that was heard in the heart of David as he expressed it in his wondrous Psalm: 'My flesh also shall rest in hope; for thou wilt not leave my soul in hell, neither wilt thou suffer thine holy one to see corruption.'[37]...

"Now, there are people who, through meditation and various spiritual exercises, have entered the nirvanic state prior to their demise—but for them this condition of nirvana must be temporary. I will explain why this is so: The consciousness of man before he is embodied in form is derived directly from the consciousness of God; the purpose of his identification with form and substance is in order that he might earn his vestments of consciously attained God-mastery. This comes about through his experiments in handling energy in denser spheres and his exercise of the creative faculty known as free will.

"When individuals who are seeking the light continue to express the imperfections of mortality and they exhibit an unwillingness to serve the Great Law of God in all of its requirements (which service is the basis for the expansion of all life and Truth), it follows that they will sometimes leap into the nirvanic state without having climbed the stairway of attainment. In the state of nirvana, man is as he was 'in the beginning,' before he entered the world of form. His consciousness is one with the consciousness of God; but, because his untransmuted self remains ensnared below, he is merely a transient guest in the house of the LORD, unworthy of peerage, disqualified as a candidate for the office of Divine Sonship.

"That grace which is attained mechanically cannot be substituted for the immortal grace of God that maketh all things right by light and Truth. Hence, it is in the world of form that victory must be won; for if the body dies while the consciousness is in nirvana, the consciousness must yet reembody in order to raise its vehicles. The good in man is indeed a part of the Causal Body of man, but that which is interred with his bones are the records of human infamy. These must be transmuted by light, and freedom must be won fairly according to the rules of the game if it is to be permanently retained. . . .

"Nirvana literally means to blow out or to extinguish the conscious identity—but nirvana is not nihilism! It is but the blowing out of the dense sense consciousness, that part of the human consciousness that feels separation from God because of its involvement in the pride of the ego. It is essential, then, in the attainment of nirvana and of the ascension, to offer all human qualities upon the altar of God. This is done in order that the fires of transmutation may bring the individual to that state of consciousness where, as the pure in heart, he can readily see God and, in seeing him, enter into fellowship with him.

"Saint Paul said, 'Now we see through a glass, darkly.'[38] All that has contributed to the lesser states of man's consciousness, all that has manifested imperfectly beneath nirvanic levels identifies with the lower vehicles and the unredeemed substance of mankind. This is the veil that must be rent before he can see 'face to face.' For above him shines the perfect temple of the divine archetype, and it is this temple of consciousness that he must contact and with which he must remain in touch. . . .

"When a house is built and the labor is performed, while there is joy in the ring of the hammer, in the hum of the saw, and in the finishing of the roughhewn timber, there is also joy in the stillness of completion. This is nirvana. And yet, after the divine energies have gone out and returned to the Godhead and the *pralaya** is ended, the eternal desire to create goes forth and this desire is inherent in the creation.

"It can be said that you rise with the sun and gather with the harvest. But as a Son of God you are no longer an unconscious part of all that lives in form, for through spiritual

---

**Pralaya* (Sanskrit): The dissolution and reabsorption of the universe at the end of a cycle. This is the transcendental phase of consciousness, the passive phase, the period when all manifestation is dormant.

evolution you have become a conscious part of life. You hold an awareness of the entire universe, and the universe is tangibly felt within yourself as you identify with God.

"There is, then, no actual extinguishing of the candle of being, but only an intensifying of its flame. Now the flame of soul-substance and reality within your heart identifies with the ocean of God's flaming identity, the real identity of your own mighty I AM Presence and of the Great Central Sun Magnet. This realization of one's True Self portends the wonder of the resurrection and the ascension.

"As you obtain entrée into the consciousness of God and find therein complete liberation from the pull of the senses, you become wholly godlike. This permanent state of nirvana is, of course, subject to the will of God—but in this case you *are* the will of God, for you have become one with it. The realization of one's own perfection in the heart of God is the fulfillment of the injunction of Jesus 'Be ye therefore perfect, even as your Father which is in heaven is perfect.'[39] The state of perfection is possible of attainment, regardless of human opinion to the contrary, even as heaven is the goal of those who do not even realize the height thereof....

"Those who attain nirvana temporarily, those who reach out for higher spiritual states through yogic practices or through the light and sound rays should be made aware of the fact that only that attainment which is tied to a progressive initiatic ladder is fulfilled by the crown of the ascension. Remember this in that connection: mankind may ascend or descend the ladder rapidly or at a turtle's pace, but the fact remains that to bypass any of the rungs will necessitate a return to take the lesson over again.

"Nirvana is best won by each soul when all of the rounds of experience prescribed as curriculum by the Ascended Masters are accepted and utilized by unascended man in complete obedience to the divine plan.

"Then let men enter nirvana. Then let them call for an end to all human sensation. If they will, let them terminate individual sight and sound, turning it on or off as they please—for those who identify with reality need no longer rely upon the senses to establish that which is real. They will have become reality. The ugly duckling of the human self will have become the Divine Swan, the *Paramahansa.** As he swims in the sea of spirituality and omnipresence, he is a part of divine awareness. He senses every storm and ripple in the universe of human consciousness; yet he bears the tranquility of the great depths at the very apex of God's consciousness.

"There is no need for man to leap across the initiatic span and leave behind a part of himself—a very important part. For after all, the four lower bodies that you have used are the platform upon which you have gained experience and thereby evolved your individuality. Herein are stored the very atoms of your life and your devotion—literal universes in action. It can be said that these systems evolving within you await your own conscious resurrection in order that the atoms within the orbit of your identity may also be raised into their freedom."[40]

The Translation of Enoch

Saint Germain tells us: "It is necessary that we consider the wonderful phenomenon that took place in the life of Enoch, 'the seventh from Adam,'[41] who was translated that he should not see death. For the fear of death has caused many individuals to recoil from passing through this change and to desire to retain their life forever in one physical form. Unless man were able, however, to escape from the restrictions of the finite form at will, he would find this state to be somewhat of a prison as

_____

*Paramahansa (Sanskrit): Divine swan, great-souled being.

he advanced in progressive cosmic states.

"Now, the translation of Enoch was somewhat different than the other states of attainment I have named, and yet it bore a marked resemblance to the nirvanic state. Enoch became so involved in consciousness with the Presence of God that all outer conditions lost their hold upon him. Hence, he 'walked with God: and he was not; for God took him.'[42] This was both literal and figurative. For he moved in a constant state of higher consciousness until the light rays that penetrated his body and form became so intense in their action that they concealed him from human sight. Thus he was translated or transformed, and he vanished from the eyes of men.

"In later periods Apollonius of Tyana and others performed similar feats to that of Enoch. Some (such as Apollonius) were subsequently reborn; therefore, this was not an identical action to that of the Master Enoch. Enoch elected after his translation to ascend completely into the Godhead by continuing the light action of 'mobile elevation' that carried him into his own God Presence. Therefore, the first translation of Enoch was not the final ritual of the ascension, for the ascension is the highest initiatic conferment that the mankind of earth can possibly receive."[43]

The Highest and Most Revered Guru: The I AM Presence and the Christ Self

All Masters, teachers and experiences are meant to lead the individual to the feet of his own guru. But one ought to be careful in accepting the claims of self-styled masters. For unless there be absolute certainty about the qualifications of the teacher, there is always the possibility that such a one will unwittingly misguide his pupils. The safest route to finding God is through attunement with one's own Divine Presence, or the I AM consciousness of each individual, which hovers ever near the aspiring soul. (See the Chart of Your Divine Self facing page 44 and pages 315–16.)

Through the crystal cord, the stream of life called the "lifestream," the energy pulsating from one's own individualized God Presence (I AM) descends into the domain of the Christ Self of each individual, where this great Mediator can translate into straight knowledge the requirements of each hour. Thus divine instruction can be conveyed personally to each aspirant through his own Christ Self.

Sometimes those who attach themselves to unascended masters tend to idolize their gurus. But often the chelas are not able to sustain their own exalted opinions of them. Then too, the dark forces of the planet are always looking to destroy men's faith in one another. These do not hesitate to use gossip, circumstantial evidence, and the students' own momentums of fear and doubt to tear down the idol they have fashioned. And so, because the image was not the One Most Holy but an idol to adorn the egos of its makers, it is easily dashed to the ground.

The unknowing chela sometimes places the idol of the guru so far above himself that it becomes absolutely necessary for him to topple the image in order to regain a sense of his own personal worth and independence. If he only knew that a truly spiritual leader teaches by example, always sees the Christ in his pupils, and never attempts to dominate their lives or their beliefs, he would not feel the need to become involved in this seesaw consciousness.

Wise is the devotee who will guard himself from such extremes of thought and feeling. Let him hold to the immaculate concept for all men—both rich and poor, bond and free, wise and ignorant, exalted and abased. Then he will not so easily be taken from the light by the dark arrows of destruction that will surely be sent his way, nor will he become a disillusioned victim just when he is beginning to gather greater light into his being.

Long ago, the prophet Jeremiah foretold that the LORD would make a new covenant with the house of Israel: "I will put my law in their inward parts, and write it in their hearts; and will be their God, and they shall be my people. And they shall teach no more every man his neighbor, and every man his brother, saying, Know the LORD: for they shall all know me, from the least of them unto the greatest."[44]

Isaiah also saw that the time would come when "thy teachers [shall not] be removed into a corner any more, but thine eyes shall see thy teachers: And thine ears shall hear a word behind thee, saying, This is the way, walk ye in it."[45] In fulfillment of these inspired sayings, the sure word of prophecy comes to each individual from his God Presence through the mediation of his Christ Self. And this Word that framed the universe will illumine all who will heed the call from on high.

Guides along the Homeward Path: Guardians of the Sacred Guru

The primary function of the ascended and unascended masters is to help each man unfold his own latent divinity—but never to do it for him. Their purpose is to help the soul reestablish her communion with God; with her own threefold flame; with life, Truth and love.

In the service of the light that is the life of men, the masters ascended and unascended bring to the evolutions of this planet illumination, clarification of the laws of God, and verification of ancient knowledge that has been handed down from generation to generation (yet not always in its original form). The courageous stand that they have taken in defense of Truth (even to the point of death) has enabled the many who have followed in their footsteps to be conquerors, both in the world and of the world.

There is neither desecration nor delay in the initiatic process whereby the more highly evolved consciousness imparts to the lesser evolved consciousness a portion of itself. For in the final analysis, the identity of the master under whom one serves and takes one's training is not as important as the fact that one has become God-identified and Christ-centered in one's own individual manifestation of the divine consciousness.

And regardless of who the guru may be, it is always the God Presence and the Christ Self of the chela who, through the guru, imparts the gnosis of spiritual wisdom once the chela has committed his being to the disciplines of hierarchy.

The one God and Father of all employs his many manifestations to lead his children along the way that reaches up to him. Sometimes seekers are fooled by the erroneous concept that they have no need of a teacher, either ascended or unascended. They are led to believe by spirits of seduction that they can and should go directly to God and his Christ.

There is nothing wrong with this idea if one can make it work. But to bypass the experience of the Ascended Masters, who know every step of the way, is like setting out upon a jungle expedition without the help of native guides. To ignore the disciplines of the Brotherhood simply to assert one's independence—or even out of a sense of misguided loyalty to God—is wrong. For God himself glories in those servant Sons and Daughters of his heart, who serve only that they may express their love for him.

To deprive men of the blessing of giving themselves in service to less evolved souls or to refuse to receive the ministrations of ascended and ascending beings is to deny the giving of self in service to life. This is the road that leads to nihilism, for one cannot deny another without ultimately denying oneself.

The truly wise and humble are always receptive to those who are well qualified in their field of specialization and to those in the educational systems of the world who can capably direct and encourage their students. In fact, corroboration among scholars and scientists is a means of avoiding repetitious error and unnecessary research.

Only by accepting the findings of their predecessors can those who pick up the torch of knowledge advance a particular branch of learning in one brief lifetime. Often these return to continue their investigations right where they left off in a former embodiment.

Wouldn't it be an unfortunate turn of events if these men of discovery were to reject the platform of knowledge that they themselves had served to build, simply because they subsequently refused to come under the tutelage of the acknowledged heads of their specialized fields? Likewise, are spiritual climbers not wise to refresh themselves on their journey by tarrying at the feet of the Masters?

Among the solitary climbers upon the mountain, there have been a few who have made it alone. But the many have been broken upon the rocks of limited personal experience, and they have suffered setback after setback. If these solitary climbers would leave the peaks of pride and associate with the groups that the hierarchy has established, receiving their instructions from the Ascended Masters or even a true unascended master, they would more quickly and more safely find their way back to the Father's house.

El Morya says that the mountain crevasses are filled with the bones of solitary climbers who have sought to find out the divine mysteries by themselves. "Spurning help, spurning the aid of heaven or the assistance of those more experienced among mankind, these individuals proceed on their own. The jagged peaks present a challenge to them, and they are determined to pursue that challenge."[46]

The role of the spiritual order is, in actuality, choosing not to separate yourself as a solitary climber upon the mountain, but rather instead to determine that you will link yourself to that sherpa, that guide, who carries you into the Himalayas because he has been there before. And in the manner and role of spiritual God-seeking, the Master is one who has been over the road. The Master has seen, the Master knows and the Master has chosen to tarry within the precincts of the world order for the Brotherhood and on behalf of mankind. Wise are they who establish themselves in the Brotherhood consciousness and are willing to receive that sacred trust which is ever dedicated to the raising of mankind into that native God-image in which they were originally made.

Men must also exercise care in their selection of companions on the Path, lest they become enmeshed in the trivia of the plains. But on the other hand, they might well become the instrument that will draw the souls of fellow seekers into the foothills leading to the summits of self-mastery.

"Unto them that are defiled and unbelieving is nothing pure; but even their mind and conscience is defiled."[47] Yet contamination works both ways, and the true disciples who will follow the Christ are not afraid to move among "sinners" in order that they might infect them with righteousness. As James says, "The wisdom that is from above is first pure, then peaceable, gentle, and easy to be intreated, full of mercy and good fruits, without partiality, and without hypocrisy."[48]

No Competition between Ascended Masters

In serving under the Ascended Masters, men have had extended to them the greatest assistance possible on the homeward path. The Ascended Master Jesus and the Ascended

Master Saint Germain are both well known to many.

Let it be clear that, since Ascended Masters have become wholly one with God through the ritual of the ascension, there is and can be absolutely no competition between them. For they are truly all one, all one in God. Therefore, no struggle on the part of one Master to subvert the students of another is conceivable. Neither would the Ascended Masters at any time create a feeling of disrespect for one another.

Therefore, those individuals or organizations that attempt to malign or discredit the service of one or more of the Masters can easily be identified as mouthpieces of the false hierarchy. Those who pay allegiance to only one Ascended Master and fail to acknowledge the panoply of Ascended Beings who represent the consciousness of God in its many jewel-like facets are only cutting themselves off from the universal magnification of the Body of God that fulfills the promise of Jesus: "Verily, verily, I say unto you, he that believeth on me, the works that I do shall he do also; and greater works than these shall he do; because I go unto my Father."[49]

Each lifestream who wins his victory embellishes the entire universe. By cutting himself off from any one of the Ascended Masters or by speaking disparagingly of him, an individual denies to himself the blessing of the Master's personal momentum of God-victory and its manifestation in his own world.

Universality is universality; it is all-inclusive. The harmony of all the Masters of Wisdom, both ascended and unascended, is beautiful to behold. This harmony is a symphony of unity that comprises the total outreach upon this planet of the representatives of God who make up the entire Spirit of the Great White Brotherhood.

The existence of these Sons and Daughters of God can never be refuted by human logic. Those who deny the plan of God only deny themselves and their own opportunity to become illustrious servant Sons and Daughters. As the rays of the sun mellow the essence of the solar fires that would consume mere mortals, so do the Sons and Daughters of God temper the light that no man can touch except he too become that light.

Let all feel free to open the doorway of the heart to the eternal God as he expresses himself in the victorious service to life of every Ascended Master. The Ascended Masters are the safest guides anyone can have. They know every step of the way. They have mastered life, and they long to assist the aspiring disciple in finding his own freedom. They have no axes of a personal nature to grind; they serve only the cause of heaven, and the infinite love that they express is freely given to every part of the Body of God on earth and in heaven.

Fortunate is the man who can open his heart to his own destiny, to his own reality, and learn to abide therein by sitting at the feet of the Ascended Masters. By using the great flames of freedom, by obeying Cosmic Law and by giving strict attention to the guidance of the Ascended Masters, he will more quickly come under the dominion of his own I AM Presence, his great winged God Self, the magnet of pure love. This love will lift him out of the socket of mortal thought and feeling into the deathless, birthless realms of infinite adoration to the one universal God.

Yet an adoration that is not practical, that does not enhance one's service to one's fellowman, is in no way worthy of one's energy. The energies of God are not only for the exaltation of God in man but also for the implementation of his most practical cosmic service to life.

By following in the footsteps of the great Masters who have walked the earth bearing the torch of divine illumination, each one can add the momentum of his life's victory to the universe—as all move onward in the grand halls of the cosmic galaxies toward that perfection which originally came forth as the Divine Image.

The I AM Presence of each one is the Master Instructor who will show the budding consciousness how to manifest the perfection of his divine identity, just as Jesus did. It is the plan of the Creator that each one shall outpicture within himself all that God is. Thus there is established in the life of every soul that order which is heaven's first law.

Saint Germain leaves us with this closing word: "We have sought here to clarify some of the differences existing between Eastern and Western schools of thought. We have sought to alleviate human distress stemming from those who felt that a great dichotomy existed between the practices of embodied masters and the practices of Ascended Beings. In our desire to clarify, our love has been expressed—yet the infinite way that looms ahead contains numerous floral offerings of spiritual thought and beauty that await your discovery. This pathway leads to your own mighty I AM Presence and to your eventual ascension in the light, even as we have experienced it." [50]

Chapter 4

Hierarchy

When I consider thy heavens, the work
of thy fingers, the moon and the stars, which
thou hast ordained; what is man, that thou
art mindful of him? and the son of man,
that thou visitest him?

For thou hast made him a little lower
than the angels, and hast crowned him with
glory and honour. Thou madest him to have
dominion over the works of thy hands;
thou hast put all things under his feet. . . .

O LORD our Lord, how excellent is
thy name in all the earth!

PSALMS

Hierarchy

SECTION ONE

Microcosm and Macrocosm

"AND I BEHELD THE GREAT ELECTRONIC fire ring of the Central Sun. I saw the surface thereof as of molten gold, blending with an azure blue. The sky became a sea and, behold, the soft glow as of pale pink roses of living flame bubbling upon the surface beneath, translucent and then transparent; a white fire core that pulsed and rose and fell with a holy radiance inundated my soul. My eyes I sought to shield from the glorious wonder, which I knew to be reality, infinity and love without end.

"All knowledge, all power, all love—going on forever and having neither beginning nor ending—were before me. And I saw the naturalness of home, of friends, of family, of all that ever was and is or is to come. Ribbons of interconnecting glory from this gigantic orb spread into space from galaxy to galaxy, from star system to star system; and the song of the music of the spheres moved upon the strings of my heart as a lute of fire.

"I heard the turning of the seemingly silent spheres and the tones of the cosmic fires, of dead and dying worlds, blended with the nova, the eternally new, the children of space, interstellar systems moving outward into the far-flung deserts where the fractional margins spread apart—yet they were engulfed in the love of the Center."[1]

Such is the description of the center of the universe, from the perspective of the seraphim.

The Eternal Logos

Man takes a great deal for granted in his concepts about nature and the natural order of things. Without thinking through for himself the logic of reality and the workings of the universe, he all too quickly accepts the traditions that are handed down to him. He does not question the miracle of the cosmic order of the stars and planets traveling on their appointed course, beckoned by some unknown objective, governed by an invisible principle, an unseen hand that is at once the Framer and the framework of the vast design.

Where and how does man fit into a scheme so bold that seems to mock his very world—speck of dust that he is, tumbling with other specks of dust?

The eternal Logos, the power of the spoken Word that in the beginning of cycles issued the Great Command, is the key to reality and to hierarchy. Therefore, let us explore the origin of the Word in God and the evolution of its meaning to man.

The word *logic* is related to the word *logos,* from the Greek for speech, word or reason. Ancient Greek philosophy considered the Logos to be the controlling principle of the universe. *Logos* has been defined as "the divine wisdom manifest in the creation, government, and redemption of the world and often identified with the second person of the Trinity [the Christ]."[2]

The scriptures record that in the beginning was the Logos

and the Logos was with God and the Logos was God.[3] This Logos—this Reason, this Word of God—is the power behind all physical manifestations. They are phenomena—the Word is noumenon.

Bearing the imprint of the Divine Mind, this potential of being is found in the heart of the atom and in the heart of man, evolving there the creative energies with which the Creator has endowed each of his servant-suns.

Let us consider, then, the scientific reality of that which lies within the domain of nature as an inherent intelligence. For the power of the Logos functions independently of man and requires no assistance from any exterior source, save the one Source of all Being.

Operating within a framework of laws and cycles preordained by the Mind of God, a spark of the eternal Logos is locked within the seed atom of every son and daughter of God. Carrying the stamp of man's fiery destiny, the seed atom is the receptacle of the Word of God that went forth to define the identity of each individual.

In a universe where man can easily lose himself among dead and dying worlds, where is that rock of Truth upon which he can plant the banner of his soul? Where is that changeless change which is the center of all Being?

Man searches for the ultimate he hopes he will not find— for in finding it the hope of new worlds to conquer would be lost, and with it his raison d'être. How can he resolve the conflict of his desire for security within the Law and his soul's need for freedom beyond its confines?

Saint Germain explains the marvelous duality of the divine nature and therein provides us with the foundation of our understanding of hierarchy:

"One of the great mysteries involving the concept of the changeless nature of being is that whereas the aspects of Deity do not undergo change in the sense of deterioration, they do undergo transforming change 'from glory to glory, even as by the Spirit of the Lord.'[4]

"This must be understood: From the human standpoint, the laws of God remain inviolate and cannot be changed as they apply to human conditions. At the same time, the very nature of the infinite is to transcend itself, to rise ever higher in consciousness into that realm of God-bliss, whose vibrations are pulsating in transforming spirals of divine awareness. As the curve of the infinite appears to be a straight line to mortal eye, so the transcendent nature of God appears changeless to unascended souls."[5]

This seed of life will unfold the mysteries of the universe to all who will let themselves be taught the communion of the Holy Spirit.

We propose here no faith that is not verifiable through science, when that science is wedded to the reason of God and dedicated to the demonstration of his laws. We propose no science that is not grounded in the law of the eternal cycles, in Cosmic Truth, and in that faith which is "the substance of things hoped for, the evidence of things not seen."[6]

In this chapter we shall disclose the relationship between the spiritual and the material universe, which in the past have not been correlated by either scientists or religionists. The entire cosmo-conception contained herein was explained to us by the Master Saint Germain, who also provided the charts to give a visual presentation of the grand mysteries unveiled.

The Indivisible Particle

In the light of what scientists now know about the atom, it is difficult to imagine that the concept of the atom as a solid, indivisible particle went unchallenged from the fourth century

B.C. until almost the twentieth century A.D. The Greek philosopher Democritus was the first to envision the universe as composed of countless infinitesimal balls, which he called "atomoi." (*Atomos* is a Greek word meaning "indivisible.")

In the early nineteenth century, the ideas of Democritus about the building blocks of the universe found experimental confirmation in the work of John Dalton, who drew up sketches of molecular structure and developed the first table of atomic weights.

Scientific understanding of Dalton's atomic theory began in earnest in the late 1890s, when J. J. Thomson experimentally determined some of the properties of the electron, the first subatomic particle to be discovered. He theorized that atoms were made up of a large number of negatively charged electrons (which he called "corpuscles") contained in a ball-shaped positive field.

In 1903 Philipp Lenard put forth the hypothesis that the atom was made up of "dynamids," pairs of negative and positive charges floating in space. The very next year Hantaro Nagaoka proposed a model of the atom as a circuit of electrons revolving around a heavy center, which he compared to the ringed planet Saturn.

In 1911 Ernest Rutherford determined that the positive charge of the atom was concentrated in its center, with the negatively charged electrons swarming around the nucleus. And in 1913 Niels Bohr theorized that electrons moved within distinct spherical shells.

Thus, once challenged by the scientific community, it took only fifteen years to disprove the theory of the indivisible atom and to discover much about its internal structure. The faith of the ancients was replaced by the discoveries of modern man. A new world of scientific discovery opened up, leading to the splitting of the atom in the 1930s and the release of tremendous energy—energy that mankind are at liberty to use for the bane or blessing of the race.

Would that religionists approached their explorations of the spiritual world with the same objectivity and dedication that we have witnessed in the fields of science! If such were the case, man might bring his concepts of the spiritual universe to a par with his understanding of the material universe. Setting aside dogma and our fears of hellfire and eternal damnation, let us approach the throne of grace with scientific reverence. Let science and religion come together as handmaids of salvation before the Divine Theosophia.

Units of Hierarchy

For many centuries the object of mankind's worship has been one God, one universal presence who functions throughout cosmos to meet the needs of his creation at every level of his Self-awareness. The teaching concerning hierarchy does not refute this conception; it only adds to it the understanding that wherever God is in the universe, he individualizes himself for the purposes of creative expansion.

In the beginning, God called this individualization "man." Man, then, is the basic unit of hierarchy, and hierarchy is the orderly progression of the individualization of the God Flame from the lowest to the highest expression of the Almighty One.

Saint Paul understood the division-of-labor principle operative in the Father's vineyard, which is the foundation of hierarchy. He explained it to the followers of Christ at Corinth in this wise:

> Now there are diversities of gifts, but the same Spirit.
> And there are differences of administrations, but the same Lord.

And there are diversities of operations, but it is the same God which worketh all in all.

But the manifestation of the Spirit is given to every man to profit withal.

For to one is given by the Spirit the word of wisdom; to another the word of knowledge by the same Spirit;

To another faith by the same Spirit; to another the gifts of healing by the same Spirit;

To another the working of miracles; to another prophecy; to another discerning of spirits; to another divers kinds of tongues; to another the interpretation of tongues:

But all these worketh that one and the selfsame Spirit, dividing to every man severally as he will.

For as the body is one, and hath many members, and all the members of that one body, being many, are one body: so also is Christ. . . .

For the body is not one member, but many.[7]

As First Cause, God is one; as ultimate effect, he is the individed whole. As the breath of life, he enters into facets of identity without number, a diversity in oneness so splendid that it is beyond the reckoning of minds confined to time and space—a design so vast that the parts lose sight of their oneness and of their integration in the whole.

The revelation of the concept of hierarchy is heaven-shattering, just as the discovery and splitting of the atom was earth-shattering. But when we see that in fact they are one and the same mystery—that Matter is nothing less than the stepping-down of Spirit—it is altogether logical to suppose that we would find in the invisible world a system of components or hierarchical offices just as complex as those in the "simple" atom.

The atom is not solid as Democritus thought, and God in all of his wondrous Self-expression is not a simple monad.

The process of inductive reasoning, which Saint Germain set forth in his embodiment as Francis Bacon, has been used to solve many of the riddles involving the atom. Let us apply this method to our study of hierarchy. Proceeding from Matter to Spirit, let us look—with confidence in the supreme ordering of all levels of the conscious manifestation of life—and expect to find a diagram of heaven that will be just as satisfying as the beauty of the atom, if not more so.

"Now, at a time when the world wanders in a dizzy whirl, the wisdom of far-off stars is invoked and the heavenly hierarchies are called upon by embodied men. We read, 'Then began men to call upon the name of the Lord.'[8] The holy ingredient of the divine image dominates the fabric of the divine seed and creates the tendencies for the unfoldment of his beauty."[9]

The individualization of the God Flame over and over again, worlds without end—this is hierarchy. God's love fulfilling itself through the seed of Abraham, the sand of the seashore, and the stars without number—this, too, is hierarchy. The serpent swallowing his tail, the self becoming the not-self* so that the Self might appear—this is hierarchy.

Man first perceives hierarchy when he peers beyond the masks of mortal men and beholds in their place the Christ in radiant manifestation. The assimilation of hierarchy begins with the ritual of Holy Communion, for "he that eateth my flesh, and drinketh my blood, dwelleth in me, and I in him." The assimilation of hierarchy ends in Christ, whose body is "broken for you."[10] The breaking up of the divine Logos into light particles without number and the scattering of the

---

Not-self as used in this chapter refers to the antimatter self, the anti-body, not to the unreal or synthetic self, as the Ascended Masters more commonly use the term.—Ed.

Lord's Body throughout cosmos—this was and is hierarchy.

Hierarchy is composed of points of light, knowing who I AM and expanding the potential of that I AM according to design. Man first loves hierarchy when he loves the Christ in all whom he meets, and his love is increased when he adores the fire breath of God that comes forth as a fragrance of light from the heart of the atom.

Hierarchy is billions of star clusters, spiral nebulae, sun galaxies, planets and constellations swimming in the sea of God's love. Hierarchy begins and ends in the heart of the atom and in the heart of the Great Central Sun Galaxy. Man is a unit of hierarchy, even as every sun and star and system of worlds is a unit of hierarchy.

Hierarchy begins within the White Fire Body of the Father-Mother God, called the Sun behind the sun, whose focus of individualization in the heart of cosmos is sustained by the brooding flames of Alpha and Omega. These Most Holy Ones are referred to as the Beginning and the End[11]—because their consciousness of the Godhead embraces the beginning and the ending of universal cycles.

When the Spirit of God desires to send forth a portion of itself into expression in the microcosmic-Macrocosmic wonder, it issues the command "Let there be light!"[12] Obediently, particles of energy, light atoms and starry bodies shoot from the Center of Being and go forth into orbit around the heart of the Father-Mother God—and there is light.

Worlds are born; cycles are begun; the void is filled with fiery whirlpools endowed and endowing with light, surging with the joy of the Great Command. "Let there be light! Let there be light! Let there be light!" echoes across the corridors of cosmos. Universes expand, flaming suns breathe in and out the sacred breath. There is life! There is life! There is life! And in that life is the potential of eternal renewal. "Except ye be born again ye cannot enter in!"[13] cries the Mediator of our true being. "I AM born again! I AM born again! I AM born again!" replies the electron that has gone forth—and once more the progression of infinite spirals has begun.

Reminding us of this cosmic moment of the Great Outbreath, Alpha says:

"Expand, then, our light without limit! Accept our blessing today, and know that the powers in the Great Central Sun are no different from the powers in the sun of your system of worlds. For there is a duplication of the light from our light present there, and that which Helios and Vesta manifest is a duplication of our radiance.

"It has been our wish from the beginning to share with all the creation all the goodness that we have, and to hold back nothing of our radiance from the smallest atom on the smallest system of worlds. Therefore, the permanent atom within each of your hearts is a replica of the crystal atom of my own Being."[14]

The going out and the coming in of planets, of suns, of solar and star systems from the center of our galaxy is comparable to the release of electrons through the fission and fusion of atoms. The earth we live on is an "electron" that leaped from the heart of the sun in response to the Great Command. Our solar system is an "atom" whose sun-nucleus came forth from the center of our galaxy. This center, referred to as "the Flaming Yod," is another focus where Spirit becomes Matter and Matter becomes Spirit by the process that scientists describe as nuclear transformation.

The energy released in this process is called the divine Logos, or the Word of God that "was made flesh and dwelt among us."[15] This is the Christ, whose impetus is the Holy Spirit.

The Christ stands at the center of the cross where Spirit and Matter meet. The Christ, as the transformer of the sacred fire, personifies Spirit in Matter and Matter in Spirit. The Holy Spirit is the action of Alpha and Omega within the nucleus; it is the formless aspect of the Christ, the invisible counterpart of the visible manifestation of the Son of God, whose likeness is found in the heart of an electron, a planet, a star or a sun.

If we can conceive of the earth as being an electron that has gone forth from the center of our solar system, then we can also understand that our sun is an electron that has gone forth from the nucleus of the Flaming Yod. Going one step further, we shall see that even our galaxy is an electron that went forth from the very center of life along with billions of other galaxies now revolving around the core of cosmos, the very heart of God Self-expression.

This flaming center of God's Being is most reverently called "the Hub." The Hub is that point in the Macrocosm which received the original fiat "Let there be light!" At that instant the mighty electrons separated from the neutrons and went into orbit, leaving the protons to hold the balance in the nucleus. The neutrons that remained intact are those which are destined to retain the consciousness of God in the formless state, which men call Spirit, while those that separated into protons and electrons are destined to manifest God's nature in form, or in Matter.*

This pattern persists all the way from the Great Central Sun to a single atom within the body of man. The Masters have told us that even the electron itself is as complex a system as the entire atom.

Assigning the components of the atom to their hierarchical offices, we note that the neutron is the focus of the White Fire

---

*For the purposes of our discussion, we shall define matter as a structure of electrons that surround a nucleus and are related to it in the time-space sequence. Time is determined by the rotational speed of the electron as well as its orbital velocity, while space is measured by the distance maintained between the electron and the nucleus.

Body within the white fire core or nucleus. The White Fire Body is the vortex of light behind the core of all creation. It is the sphere of the Father-Mother God out of which proceed the positive and negative polarities (called twin flames) of each monadic expression of the Godhead.

Just as there are an infinite number of drops in the ocean of God's Being, so there are an infinite number of atoms in the Body of God we call the Macrocosm. The nucleus of each of these monads contains qualitatively (but not quantitatively) the full potential of the Deity.

Within the nucleus are thirty-three different types of particles, along with a host of much shorter-lived particles called resonances. The most important of these particles are the neutron, the proton, the neutrino and the pion. The neutrons represent complete manifestations of the Deity, whose components in that particular cycle have elected not to separate for the purposes of expansion in the world of form.

Out of the neutron proceed the proton (the I AM Presence) and the electron (the lower self). The neutrino represents the Christ Self, and the pion represents the Holy Spirit.

The protons, representing the Father aspect or the I AM Presence, are the positively charged particles that remain in the nucleus to hold the focus for that part of the Deity which has gone forth into form. In turn, the electrons (the negatively charged particles) hold the balance for the protons in the world of time and space; they represent the Mother aspect of God.

The protons retain the image of perfection in the world of Spirit in order that the electrons might fulfill their destiny in Matter. Although the God Presence represented by the proton is androgynous, in relation to the negative electron the proton is the positive pole. Through the polarity established when the electron separates from the center, the abundance of the Godhead is increased.

Both the masculine and feminine aspects of the Deity are also found within the negative polarity of the electron. Some electrons have a "plus" spin and others have a "minus" spin. These correspond to twin flames who have elected to enter the world of form simultaneously. Representing the masculine and feminine polarities of the Deity, both are on the negative pole because they are in the form world; yet they maintain an opposite polarity toward each other.

When the electrons have completed their round in the world of form, they return to the heart of the atom. The reunion of the electron with the proton produces the neutron, or the manifestation of the androgynous nature of the Godhead. In this return of the electron to its source, the prophecy is fulfilled: "That which thou sowest [the electron] is not quickened [is not made whole] except it die [unless it return to the proton]." [16]

The Nucleus of Life

The nucleus of every atom, planet, sun, star or galaxy has the same basic design, called the white fire core. It is neither Matter nor Spirit, but the essence of the twain. This is the focus of God in the planes of Spirit and Matter—of God who is forever transcending himself as the alchemical transformations between Spirit and Matter take place.

This essence that is neither Matter nor Spirit is called fire. Fire (and each flaming sun that has come forth from the heart of God) is the bridge between Matter and Spirit. Fire is perhaps best described as flowing Spirit-Matter. (The action of flow has been shown to us as the continual movement of the electrons to and from the heart of the sun, sustaining the permanent creations of God.) Scientists refer to fire as a plasma, which is defined as nuclei stripped of their electrons. Thus both the nuclei and the electrons are in a state of flow.

Matter, then, is seen as a state in which the electrons are tethered in orbit around nuclei suns in a stable pattern. That which we call Spirit retains the same pattern, but at a much higher frequency and in a dimension that is in polarity with Matter, hence invisible to those living in Matter.

Nuclei that have been stripped of their electrons do not fall into the category of dense matter. Lacking the negative charge of the electron, such nuclei will not coalesce as matter. The nuclei that have been stripped of their electrons represent the positive or Spirit-formless aspect of Deity. The wandering electrons, unattached to the nuclei, represent the negative or Matter-formless aspect of Deity. Because these electrons are unattached and freely flowing, we cannot say that fire is Matter-form, but that it is Matter-formless.

Natural fire serves a purpose in the world of form that is parallel to the action of the sacred fire. Natural fire breaks down the matrix of substance by heating the fuel molecules to the point where the electrons are no longer bound to the nuclei. This produces a plasma (a flame) and reduces the components to a simpler form. In like manner, the sacred fire removes the human matrix superimposed upon God's energy and returns that energy to the Causal Body in its primal or purified state.

Hydrogen, Helium and the Holy Spirit

Hydrogen is the first element to be formed in the transition from Spirit to Matter. This gas is found in abundance throughout the galaxy as the first step-down from the white fire core. The sun and stars are almost pure hydrogen. Highly flammable, hydrogen is the least dense element (that is, the closest to Spirit), having only one electron revolving around its nucleus and one proton in the center.

Hydrogen atoms seek to join in molecules containing two atoms, because each electron seeks its other half, even as twin flames are magnetized to each other. (The components of atoms do not have an individual identity as does man; therefore, electrons can reunite with any proton or enter the orbital shell of any atom capable of accepting them.) This desire for completion, which results in the formation of molecules, is seen in all atoms whose outer shells are not complete.

The helium atom, having two protons, two neutrons and two electrons, is the next to be formed in the chain of materialization. (Scientists say that the intense light of the sun is the fire produced by the nuclear conversion of hydrogen into helium.) This atom demonstrates the principle of the union of twin flames. In the first shell of the helium atom there are two electrons, one having a plus spin and the other a minus spin. These electrons are comparable to twin flames coming forth from the I AM Presence in the nucleus, each twin (each electron) having its own individualized God Presence (the proton).

Any atom like helium whose electron shells are complete (meaning that the orbital paths contain the maximum number of electrons) will not combine naturally with other atoms. This is because the electrons are in pairs, one member of the pair having a plus and the other a minus spin. Therefore, the electrons are not seeking union with electrons in another atom in order to complete their pairs. Their pattern being complete, they need only gather enough of the Christ light to return to the nucleus. This gathering is accelerated both as the speed of the electrons in their orbital paths is accelerated and as their individual spin is maximized.

The reason that the two electrons in the helium atom with a plus and minus spin do not unite while in orbit is that they have not magnetized enough of the Christ light, whose impetus or binding force is the Holy Spirit. When they do magnetize a sufficient quantity of the Christ, they first attract their anti-matter particles and then return to the protons and simultaneously unite with one another.

This, then, is the purpose of materialization, whether of twin electrons or of twin flames: to gather that amount of the Christ light through the action of spin (experience in form) which is needed to produce the alchemical marriage between the lower self (the electron) and the Higher Self (the proton).

When there is nuclear transformation, such as (a) when electrons come forth from or return to the nucleus or (b) when there is a fusion or fission of atoms, there is a release of the Christ light, which scientists call binding energy. This energy is a necessary part of nuclear transformation, whether exothermic or endothermic (whether there is a release or an absorption of energy), and without it such transformations cannot occur.

Whether God's energy is going from Spirit to Matter or returning from Matter to Spirit, the Christ light is the necessary agent of its transformation. Whether the purpose of the Creator is to materialize or to dematerialize, the power of the Logos—the Word of God, the only begotten Son—stands as the Mediator between the formed and the unformed.

This Christ is the fire of Aton, the one God worshiped by Ikhnaton and acknowledged as the fire of the atom by those who through science have contacted the sacred essence of life.

For many years scientists have asked the vital question "What holds the particles in the nucleus together? Why don't their mutually repellent positive charges cause them to fly apart?" The search for a mechanical explanation of a spiritual noumenon has not been without fruit, but the mastery of both mass and energy can only come when the relationship between the material phenomenon and the spiritual cause is discovered.

In reality, it is the action of the Holy Spirit that holds the nucleus of the atom together. The Holy Spirit is the power behind the atom that unites the energies of Alpha and Omega. It is the power behind the enormous potential of the atom, and it is responsible for the release of the Christ light that occurs in fission and fusion. It is indeed the cohesive power of man and the universe, and it permeates all life—for without it nothing in the Cosmic Egg would have orientation, integration or organization. The particles that focus this great energy are elusive and short-lived, because the charge of the Holy Spirit is so powerful that form cannot contain it. They dissolve and give birth to new forms that take over their function of holding the flame of life for a brief span.

Antimatter and the Ascension of Noble Electrons

That which scientists refer to as antimatter plays an important role in the ascension of electrons and of sons of God. Antimatter is the reverse pattern of Matter as you would see it in a mirror. It is the relationship of the self and the not-self—of "me and my shadow." It is a magnetic forcefield* that is in polarity with Matter. Antimatter is the mirrored image of that which descends into form. It is neither Spirit nor Matter, but an outline upon the ethers of that which has been ordained to expand the power of the Logos in the planes of Matter.

Every light body externalized in form has an "anti-body." Like a shadow that is always there but is perceived only in contrast to the light, the anti-body is a characteristic of every body that has gone forth from the White Fire Core of Being. The story of Peter Pan, who lost his shadow and came back to find it, illustrates the point that no manifestation in Matter is complete without its antimatter.

---

*Some of the terms used here may have an esoteric significance that is different from the usage in physics. The Messengers are faced with the difficulty of expressing spiritual and physical truths that have not yet been discovered by scientists, and thus the ideal words are not available.—Ed.

When the raison d'être of Spirit's descent into Matter is fulfilled—that is, when the evolution of the particles has resulted in their expansion to the limit of their preordained potential—the particles of Matter retain a magnetism identical to that held by their anti-bodies. At the moment of congruency, polarity is achieved and they rush toward each other, canceling each other out upon contact.

The burst of light observed when an electron and a positron (the corresponding antimatter particle) unite is the net gain of that particular round of manifestation. This is the "light harvest" that ascends into the Causal Body as the yield of the atomic manvantara. Congruency is thus the key to the ascension or the return to the White Fire Core. It is the key to the transformation of Matter in Spirit and Spirit in Matter.

Each of the thirty-three particles of atomic nuclei has an antiparticle. These thirty-three components within the atom represent the thirty-three initiations or planes of God's consciousness through which the Monad must pass in going out and returning to the Hub of Life.

The ascension of the electron takes place only when all of the thirty-three particles have fulfilled their destiny in form by gathering the light necessary for congruency with the seed image held in the antiparticles.

Matter and antimatter cannot come together until their cycle in form is complete (unless, of course, their coming together is induced in the course of a scientific experiment). Thus the union of the electron and the positron under natural conditions takes place simultaneously as all thirty-three particles collide with their anti-bodies, return to the center of the atom and then ascend into the White Fire Body. (See figure 2.)

The release of energy that occurs when particles meet their antiparticles is the conversion of Matter to Spirit, which we call the ascension. The conversion of Matter to Spirit takes place

FIGURE 2: The evolution and involution of Matter.

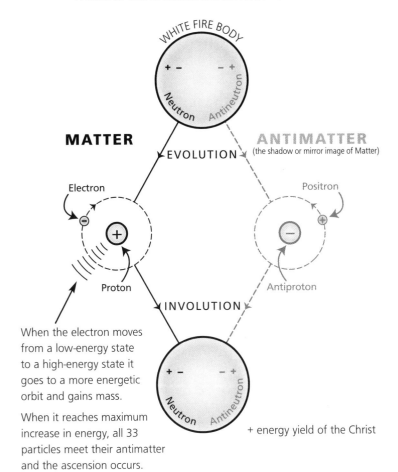

When the electron moves from a low-energy state to a high-energy state it goes to a more energetic orbit and gains mass.

When it reaches maximum increase in energy, all 33 particles meet their antimatter and the ascension occurs.

through the ritual of sublimation.[17] This release of energy is an example of the conversion of mass into energy described by Einstein's equation $E=mc^2$ (energy equals mass multiplied by the square of the speed of light). The mass, or atomic weight, is equal to the power of the Logos that originally infused the atom with the potential of its creative cycle.

The ionization potential is the maximum energy that an

electron can obtain without losing its identity (its tie to the nucleus). It is the maximum multiplication possible of the talents placed by God within the mass.

In man, this multiplication takes place by the intelligent use of free will. At the atomic level, it takes place automatically by the action of the particles within a framework of preordained laws and cycles. The energy yield when an atom of Matter ascends (i.e., unites with Spirit) is always greater than that which was originally used to create the atom. Otherwise creation would have no purpose, the universe would not be expanding, and God and man would not be continually transcending their former state.

The womb of the Macrocosm is a cosmic forcefield filled with the essence of the Holy Spirit. It is a sea of ether in which Matter, as a whirlpool of energy in motion, is suspended. The particles of the atom are projections of Spirit or light into this ether. The circumstance of these particles—their life and motion in ether, known as time and space—produces the effect we see and touch, called Matter. Thus the whirlpool of Matter is nothing more than the coordinate of the light particles projected into the ether of the Holy Spirit.

The energies gathered by the electron in its orbital whirl are the energies of the Holy Spirit—the universal essence in which all life (both Spirit and Matter) is suspended. When misqualified by man, instead of being magnetized to the electron as an accelerating momentum of Christ-power, this essence lodges between the electrons as that density, that substance of sin which prevents the fulfillment of the life plan of men and electrons. Thus all sin, technically speaking, is a sin against the Holy Spirit.[18]

While the proton represents the I AM Presence, the nucleus taken as a whole represents the Causal Body and the electron represents the physical body. In man, the physical body is the temple of the living God Presence, the etheric body is the sheath of the Holy Spirit, the mental body is the instrument of the Christ, and the emotional body is the forcefield of the World Mother.

All we see of man in the time-space dimension is the physical aspect. So, too, we see only the physical "quarter" of the atom. Planets, suns and stars all have etheric, mental and emotional envelopes. These must not be discounted in our attempts to fathom the mysteries of man and the universe of atoms all around us.

The dual view of Matter as both particles and waves must also be considered. Every son of God—every particle of the whole that has come forth from the White Fire Core of the Great Central Sun—emits light by the very nature of its origin in light, the eternal fount of Being. Emitting light, it creates waves in its movement through the essence of the Holy Spirit that permeates the Macrocosm. We observe the electron as both a particle and a wave as it orbits the nucleus of the atom. Man too is a point of light even as he emits light, and the stars that shine are suns of righteousness ensouled by Sons of God.

Whereas God expands through the planes of Spirit and Matter, man expands through the focuses of Spirit in Matter. Therefore, God created the spiritual-material universes whereby the cycles of creation might be externalized first as Spirit-formless (fire), then as Spirit-form (air), then as Matter-formless (water) and finally as Matter-form (earth). (See figure 3.)

The step-up in the electron's velocity and rate of spin is accomplished through spiritual evolution or through the application of the ascension current to the electrons. By Cosmic Law the full power of this current may be applied only to those particles of creation that have already attracted enough of the Christ to retain their identity when reuniting first with their anti-bodies and then with the center of Being.

200

FIGURE 3: Externalization of the cycles of creation. (Genesis 1:3–10)

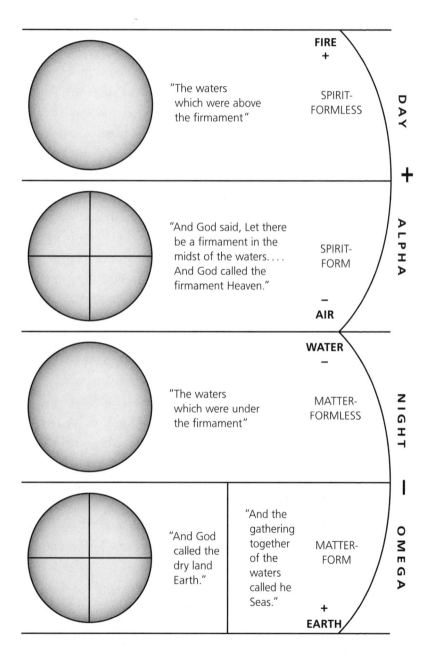

Unascended beings can invoke the ascension flame, but it is never released from the Godhead in a greater measure than that which can be safely absorbed. The intensity of the focus of the ascension flame guarded by the seraphim in the retreat at Luxor is great enough to disintegrate any form.

Thus only those who have earned the ascension are allowed to step upon the dais in the flame room. If one who is not ready for reunion with his God Presence were to come into direct contact with this powerful focus, he would be instantaneously dissolved. This is one more reason that man must not attempt to reproduce the ascension through mechanical means.

The function of the ascension current is to accelerate the electron and all of the particles within the nucleus to the point of congruency with their anti-bodies. When all thirty-three particles unite with their anti-bodies, symbolizing the completion of the thirty-three alchemical initiations through which the soul must pass, they ascend into the White Fire Body.

This phenomenon was beheld by those who witnessed Jesus' disappearance from their sight into a cloud of glory.[19] Jesus was the electron who came forth from the heart of the nucleus of the I AM Presence. Leaving behind the proton, he descended into the world of form by the power of the eternal Logos.

Having fulfilled his mission on earth, Jesus attained congruency with his reflected image. The forcefield of energy that held him bound to earth and apart from the not-self* was therefore dissolved. At the moment of congruency, he disappeared from the sight of mortal men. He demonstrated the ascension into the heart of the atom, the I AM Presence, where his permanent identity is preserved forevermore.

When the electron goes forth from the heart of the atom,

---
*See note, page 186.

when man descends to do the will of God, he comes forth with
the speed of light—destined to multiply the talents of God in
the world of form by the squaring of the circle, by making
practical the threefold aspect of the threefold flame of the
Christ consciousness through the implementation of the four
elements.

When the time comes for his return to Spirit, he ascends by
the action of the Christ-power, the impetus of the squaring of
the speed of light. Without that impetus, dematerialization cannot take place.

The dematerialization process has been observed only as
an effect of matter and antimatter coming together for mutual
annihilation. This is all that scientists can observe because they,
too, are "electrons" in the world of effect. The cause behind this
phenomenon is not seen except by the "seer-scientist," whose
explorations in Matter are only the beginning of his probings
of the spiritual world. These probings will one day lead him
into all Truth if he will but let them.

Yes, there are anti-planets, anti-suns and anti-galaxies—
and even an anti-cosmos! But as long as there is a magnetic
field, these anti-bodies will not collide with their corresponding
bodies. This magnetic field exists until the electron or the light
body has completed its reason for being in the planes of Matter.

If we will remember that the purpose of Spirit's materialization is the expansion and development of the potential of
the Logos, then we will not grieve when Matter and Spirit
unite at the completion of a cycle. Instead we will rejoice,
because the return can take place only when the electron has
perfected all phases of its existence and fulfilled its role of
expression in the planes of God's consciousness.

The Song of the Atom

The excellent name of God, I AM, is truly manifest in all the earth![20]

Let us hear the song of the atom. It is the hum of the electrons in their orbits, responding to the keynote sent forth from the protons in the nucleus. The eye or "I" is spoken by the proton (the God Presence) and the "AM" is the response from the electron, its extension in form. Across the vast distances of the atom, the cosmic love song echoes: "I...AM, I...AM, I...AM."

It is the chanting of the name of God at the speed of light that sustains the forcefield of the atom, magnetizing the power from within to fulfill the destiny without. When the charge released by the power of the spoken Word reaches a certain intensity, a sufficient momentum of the Christ light is magnetized by the electron, causing it to merge with the positron and to return to the flaming heart center of Being.

The neutrons in the center of the nucleus also repeat the name of God. But being whole, theirs is the song of the Great Amen (the AUM), meaning "We are one.... we are one.... we are one." Therefore, meditations for the purpose of drawing forth the creative potential of the Godhead into Spirit-form and Matter-form necessarily contain the "I AM" affirmation, whereas meditations used for the cycle of return, first to Matter-formless and then to Spirit-formless, concentrate on the AUM (or OM).

At this point in cosmic history, the hierarchy has instructed us to emphasize the use of the "I AM" in order to bring the kingdom of God, the golden age, into manifestation on earth from the planes of Spirit-form to the planes of Matter-form. The AUM may be used prior to giving decrees in one's personal meditations to establish that contact with the center of Being which is necessary to draw forth the fires of the atom. Each period of meditation thus represents a cycling of energies to and from the God Presence.

The AUM is intoned to send love and devotion to the Almighty, preceding the release of cycles from the Great I AM. Upon the tone of the AUM one's consciousness ascends to the Hub in preparation for those dynamic "I AM" invocations so needed to work change in worlds still in a state of becoming.

Cause and Effect in Spirit and in Matter

The natural chemical elements that are found in the physical universe are the materializations of the 144 flames of God. The Maha Chohan, the representative of the Holy Spirit to the evolutions of the earth, has told us that oxygen is a condensation of the flame of the Holy Spirit. Without the Holy Spirit, which is the Fire Breath of God, man cannot live, nor can life go on. The same is true of oxygen.

There is at least one corresponding element for each of the 144 flames of God that come forth from the twelve rays. Physicists working hand in hand with the Ascended Masters in their university will discover this correlation of the elements to the flames of God. The time will come when there will be no limit to the alchemical experiments that will be performed, releasing Christ-powers not seen on this planet since the first three golden ages.

One of the more important discoveries to be made will be the true operation of the law of cause and effect. Whereas scientists have isolated many causal relationships on the physical plane, most have not yet observed the causal relationships that exist within and between the other planes of God's conscious manifestation and the Four Cosmic Forces. Future research will reveal certain points or spirals in each plane, wherein the cause and effect sequence transcends the boundaries of the plane and continues into and through the next plane.

The entire process of precipitation is based on this knowledge of the law of cause and effect. Once scientists are able to produce their "first cause" in the realm of Spirit and then to lower it through the etheric, mental, astral and physical ranges of vibration, they will have found the key to universal manifestation.

The role of the spiritual scientist, then, is to correlate the cause-effect relationship on each of the four planes. When they master this art and the four sacred rituals of creation, preservation, disintegration and sublimation,[21] their creations will be endowed with immortality. As long as men attempt to create on the physical plane alone or refuse to acknowledge the natural order of precipitation, they are ignoring the laws of God—and they will find that their efforts are subject to decay.

At this point it would be well for us to reiterate the warning of the hierarchy that "mere mechanics are not the prime requisite in the knowledge of God, but the pure power of love is the perception of the Infinite."[22]

Let all who undertake the study of the sacred sciences remember that the kingdom of heaven cannot be taken by force, the secrets of the universe cannot be mechanically mastered nor can the mysteries of life be applied by rote. Total surrender of the lower self to the Higher Self and complete identification with the Godhead are the only means whereby man can find the Truth that shall make him free.

In all fields there is danger in trying to provide a mechanical explanation for those spiritual functions that originate beyond the planes of Matter. We must be prepared to accept the limitations inherent in our frame of reference. There are dimensions, hence processes, that exist as pure Spirit. These we shall never be able to explain until we become a part of that world. Nevertheless, we may be the beneficiaries of the light released in these spiritual processes, whatever our level of conscious awareness.

The secondary cause that is observable within the plane of effect can, of course, be discovered. But the ultimate Cause behind the lesser cause-effect relationships we experience can never be fully known until we rise to that Cause and become a part of it.

The prophet's role is to break the ground for new discovery in all fields. It is our hope that our discussions in this chapter will provide keys whereby trained scientists will press on in their respective fields to open new avenues of discovery for the blessing of humanity.

Stones in the Holy Arch

With the emanation of life from the Great Central Sun to the periphery of infinite-finite existence come the individualizations of the universal intelligence in hierarchical order: Cosmic Beings, angelic hosts, interplanetary and intergalactic servant-Suns, Ascended Masters, and elemental phases of life representing the Four Cosmic Forces.*

Coming forth to do their perfect work are these particles of the grand atom that we call our universe and of the galaxy that is our home. Functioning throughout cosmos, these atoms in the Body of God are first of all the manifestation of order— for order is heaven's first law.

Hierarchy is the holy arch of spiritual beings who serve under the Godhead. They act as transmitters and transformers

*The reference to the four beasts in Revelation 4:6 and following is the symbology used for the Four Cosmic Forces and their representation at every level of hierarchy, including the four lower bodies of man. The word *beast* means *be*ing in *A*lpha focusing *S*un-power from Spirit to Matter (*t*). *T* always stands for the place where Spirit and Matter meet.

of the will of God into the many planes of existence, from the highest to the lowest and from the lowest to the highest—from Spirit to Matter and from Matter to Spirit. Just as in all nations there is a government responsible for running the affairs of state, so all representatives of hierarchy have and hold the portion of God's consciousness that spans their own specific charge and responsibility.

In man we observe a government that organizes and directs the functions of the physical body. And in the nucleus of the atom, we observe the government of the most fantastic energy system ever devised. There also exists a government behind the natural order. For the most part invisible to mankind, yet charged by God with the responsibility of administering to all life, the offices of this heavenly government (this "higher archy") are as necessary to the function of the Macrocosm as are atomic particles to the function of the microcosm.

Just as a man standing in the center of a brilliant light does not distinguish objects therein until he becomes accustomed to the intensity, so man living midst the wonders of hierarchy does not perceive these components of existence until he adjusts the lens of his consciousness to a higher level. Invoking the Spirit of God, man is able to penetrate the veil and to perceive these servants of God, who have positioned in the denser manifestations of the microcosmic world beautiful focuses of divine intelligence charged with the responsibilities of governing the nature kingdom.

Free will, within the boundaries of God's laws, gives spontaneity to hierarchy at every level of manifestation. Without free will there would be no hierarchy, for the foundation of hierarchy is free will—God's free will reflected in the free will of his sons and daughters. Free will is the soul of creativity. It is the joy and enthusiasm that make life endearing and full of hope in the universe of God's consciousness that is forever transcending itself.

The evolutions of Matter mirror the evolutions of Spirit. In the Macrocosm, Christed beings ordained by God freely administer his energy laws. And in the microcosm the mighty electrons (suns of flame) have a free will of their own, enabling them to function within a framework of law and order that lends purpose to their existence.* Reflecting on the joy of this cosmic freedom, Saint Germain has paraphrased Sir Walter Scott: "Breathes there the man, with soul so dead, / Who never to himself hath said, / This is my own, my native universe!"

Divine Creativity Released to the World

It is the supreme purpose of hierarchy to make the light patterns and cosmic rays released from the fount of God's Being and consciousness readily assimilable by every part of life, no matter what its level of awareness.

Inasmuch as the human monad, existing as the natural man without the correct use of his spiritual faculties, does not operate with awareness of the higher octaves of life, he seldom makes direct contact with the spiritual hierarchy. Yet many of the advanced thinkers of the world occasionally do come face to face with the consciousness of one or more of these great beings, the result being the unfoldment of many creative ideas and ingenious inventions considered to be far ahead of their time.

---

*The concept of the electron having free will is reflected in scientific theory. Most physicists have abandoned the classical view of matter as particles whose exact movements can be known and predicted with certainty. Through quantum mechanics they view matter as "probability" waves—the rising and falling probability that a particle will be at a given place at a given time. The peaks of the waves surrounding the nucleus of an atom coincide with the most probable positions of an electron's path.

Indeed, sometimes fifty or more years may pass before a release of the Brotherhood to a dedicated scientist becomes the common knowledge of the world. These lively stones in the larger temple of life provide the cosmic impetus of God's intelligence and power, together with the quality of internal love that fashions all after the Divine Image.

It has been said that man proposes and God disposes. The truth of this saying, not only in the basic sense of creation but also in the more finalizing aspects of manifestation, will become apparent to everyone who can split the atom of the mortal self and come face to face with the wonderful "constellations of reality." These fragments of light stand side by side with the striving ones holding the great scientific treasures of the ages.

God creates and man creates. God proposes and disposes; but when unascended man proposes, Ascended Man disposes! Thus in reality, that which man supposes to be the result of his own noble efforts is simply the result of his contact with the higher spiritual world and with those beings who stand just above him in the hierarchical order. These beings step down to his level the energy and intelligence from higher spheres, making them practical to his state of evolution.

God in hierarchy sheds abroad throughout the universe fragments of his omniscience. This release of divine intelligence, together with the power and the love that coalesce it into form, is the stimulus for creativity at all levels and the source of man's happiness. The drama of the cosmo-conception is enhanced by the unveiling of progressively brighter worlds, as man scales the initiatic heights and earns the right to probe greater mysteries by his greater dominion.

Free Will

Although the assistance of hierarchy is everywhere apparent, from time to time man dares to defy the integrity and justice of God by citing examples of his seeming negligence with
regard to accidents, natural disturbances, wars, sickness and
untimely death. Some argue that because God has all knowledge, all power and all wisdom, he should permit the hierarchy
to interfere in human affairs to protect each individual's person
and property. The fact that he does not leads them to curse his
name or deny his existence.

In the natural order of cosmos outpictured through hierarchy, man has demanded and received of the Father his freedom from the control of the Godhead. Like the prodigal son,[23]
man has asked for his portion of life and the opportunity to
live as he will. Therefore, the principle of noninterference
must be regarded as protective of the sovereignty of individual
free will.

By Cosmic Law, the Ascended Masters are not permitted
to enter into the affairs of mankind unless they are invoked
through prayer, affirmation or decree. If mankind desire continued assistance, they must repeat this ritual within each
twenty-four-hour cycle. "Ask, and ye shall receive."[24] This is
the order of hierarchy, and nothing can change it.

Being aware of the components of the atom and their
behavior patterns gives the mind a greater ability to attune with
the spirit of nature and to control the elements. Likewise, being
aware of hierarchy is a means of attuning with highly evolved
spiritual beings and of implementing the fantastic spiritual
power that God has placed at the disposal of Ascended Man.

Millions of souls throughout the planet are oblivious to the
order of hierarchy and to the role they themselves play in it.
For every part of life, ascended and unascended, is a monad in

the great chain of being. Finding one's niche in hierarchy, then, is one of the great challenges of existence that makes life meaningful. Man must be aware not only of hierarchy but also of the need to cooperate with their service in order to bring himself into attunement with cosmos and to discover his cosmic raison d'être.

It is fruitless to deny the existence of hierarchy, to say that one will go directly to God, bypassing his appointed officers and their divinely ordained ministrations. For although one may desire to do this, one is seldom capable of such a feat. Man must rise step by step upon the stairs of heaven, evolving through the planes of God's consciousness, which are ensouled by Cosmic Beings of such magnitude as to include entire galaxies within their God Self-awareness.

The enemy would tempt the Son of God, saying, "If thou be the Son of God, cast thyself down: for it is written, He shall give his angels charge concerning thee: and in their hands they shall bear thee up, lest at any time thou dash thy foot against a stone."[25] But he who was fully apprised of Cosmic Law would not bypass even the laws of physics, placing himself above the hierarchical order. He would not tempt his God by asking him to do that which he must do for himself.

Hierarchy is based upon the cosmic responsibility of keeping the flame of life—not only for oneself and one's family but also for the atoms and electrons descending and ascending from the heart of God, for nations and planets and solar systems, for star clusters, galaxies and universes.

Hierarchy is cosmic responsibility in the fullest sense of the word. It means that we shall respond to our cosmic ability to keep the flame of life burning within the entire Body of God.

In a *Pearl of Wisdom* addressed to "All Who Yearn to See," El Morya says: "If the outer world lies in shambles, is it a reflection of the inner world? What is the limit of individual responsibility? Is man responsible for the universe or only for himself? If I am my brother's keeper,[26] who is my brother?

"The enormous power within the individual, if it were unleashed, would give universal control even to the monad. Is it any wonder that hierarchy has prescribed the initiatic process as a ladder leading to God? Is it any wonder that laws govern the appointed rounds of man's adventures? What, then, are the limits to which man should aspire?

"Let men understand the tertiary divisions. Let them understand how body, soul and spirit, when functioning as one, must also yield to the prescribed limitations. Let them realize that power is intensified within the cube of reasonability."[27]

Hierarchy is the product of the system of cosmic reward: "Be thou faithful over a few things and I will make thee ruler over many things: enter thou into the joy of thy Lord."[28] Every word that proceedeth out of the mouth of God represents a step of spiritual initiation and cosmic evolution. Every cosmic glyph unfolding his wisdom and his love is a step in the hierarchical order.

The Christ consciousness is the mark of one who attains to hierarchical office. The new name that such a one receives is the key to the electronic pattern of his I AM Presence. Every Christed one who ascends, who reunites immortally with the I AM Presence, becomes a white stone, a purified cube of substance, in the Everlasting Temple of the City Foursquare.

The new name is not given until one ascends or holds the office of an unascended master or member of the Great White Brotherhood. The new name is never given by another but is spoken from within the heart by the voice of the I AM Presence at the moment when the soul attains God consciousness.[29] "To him that overcometh will I give to eat of the hidden manna, and will give him a white stone, and in the stone a new name written, which no man knoweth saving he that receiveth it."[30]

Hierarchical Roles

The role of the spiritual hierarchy serving this planet is manifold. They organize and direct constructive endeavor in every field; they are patrons of the arts and sciences; and they sponsor God-government in the nations of the world, seeking to improve social conditions and to advance world culture and education.

They stand behind the scenes, waiting to give assistance wherever it is invoked and wherever men and women espouse noble causes and are receptive to higher guidance. They keep the flame of life for millions who know not that they even have a threefold flame that must be daily nourished and expanded.

They act as step-down transformers for the cosmic energies required to sustain life on this planet, energies that mankind are incapable of absorbing directly because of the accumulation of density in their four lower bodies.

They hold the balance of the Four Cosmic Forces in man and nature and in animal life, compensating for the discord thrown off by mankind and adjusting the magnetic field of the planet whenever destructive vibrations, either from within or without, threaten its equilibrium as it rotates on its axis and journeys around the sun. They adjust the alignment of the four lower bodies of the earth whenever necessary. Without their intervention it would not be long before mankind would destroy himself, as he has done in past ages.

Members of the hierarchy maintain retreats where they enshrine the flames of God for the purpose of anchoring a particular momentum and virtue of the Great Central Sun within the forcefield of the earth, thus making the qualities of the flame more directly available to humanity's evolving consciousness. Disciples of the Masters are invited to study in these retreats after they have passed certain initiations in focuses maintained by representatives of the hierarchy on the physical plane. Later in this chapter we shall describe certain key offices of hierarchy, the qualifications for the offices and those who presently hold them.

Hierarchy continues to uphold the banner "Man, know thyself." El Morya comments: "Let us begin with the monad of self and feel no need to enlarge that monad, but only to enlarge our concept of unity that reaches out to serve the God-harmony of a universe."[31]

Hierarchy and the Cosmo-Conception: The Egg and the I

> *When I consider thy heavens, the work of thy fingers, the moon and the stars, which thou hast ordained;*
>
> *What is man, that thou art mindful of him? and the son of man, that thou visitest him?*[32]

As we rise in consciousness upon the words of the Psalmist of old, gazing upon the starry wonder overhead, let us consider the map of the universe as the map of hierarchy and our key in the understanding of the cosmo-conception.

We live in a giant Egg. And all that we can see or know or imagine lives with us in this Egg. Far-off worlds, seen and unseen, are confined within the Cosmic Ovoid. Cell mates are we—our prison walls measured by billions of light-years.

Beholding the heights and depths in which our small world is suspended, we find it hard to realize that there is a point beyond which we cannot go, a line we dare not cross. Within this infinite Egg, this cosmic incubator, man is free to make or destroy himself. Within the boundaries of his playpen, man's freedom is total. But no matter what his outlook, no matter how many dimensions he may scan or how many universes he may conquer, man cannot refute the fact that his home is the Cosmic Egg.

How many other Eggs are held within God's hand we do not know. We ponder the mysteries of life and of the Cosmic Egg itself, aware that as long as we are what we are, we shall never really be able to discover all there is to know about our place in the sun, nor shall we wrest from God's heart the secret—how many Eggs have come forth from the White Fire Body?

We lose ourselves in our imaginings until our finite minds would break—and then, the calculus of our search too wearying, we retreat to the habitation he has envisioned for us. We resume our everyday lives and continue our musings within the track of those progressive cycles over which we can gain some degree of mastery, hence perspective of reality.

But once the mind, limited and self-limiting, has glimpsed that which is beyond the gloria in the highest, it is nevermore content with its surroundings nor can it remain attached to self. There is a cosmic hunger that must be filled, for the mind has fingered the Limitless One; it has contacted the Infinite.

The courage to forsake old and dying worlds overtakes the soul. The insatiable quest for life commences and it shall never end. Man breaks the chains of his bondage; the ball that once hung about his neck lies at his feet. His ego is no more. He does not fear to let go of ancient relics, for his soul has seen at last the other side of life and consciousness and being. The ways of the ego, reminders of spirals of self-annihilation, are no longer relevant. The challenge of the highest mountain beckons. All else is expendable. Unfettered and free, the soul exclaims:

"I AM the All-in-all! I AM all One, and all life is One in me!"

The Holy Trinity in the Cosmic Egg

The diagram of the Macrocosm in figure 4 illustrates the interaction of the planes of Spirit and Matter within the Cosmic Egg. The yolk represents the planes of Spirit-form and Matter-form, and the white represents the planes of Spirit-formless and Matter-formless.

Our universe is a cross section of this giant Ovoid, an externalization of Spirit suspended in Matter and Matter suspended in Spirit. Universes without number revolve around the Great Hub of Life interpenetrating one another, each within another dimension—each a slice, a verse, of the Great Central Sun Galaxy.

This galaxy is the all and everything of the Cosmic Egg, the entire contents thereof—yolk and white put together as spheres within spheres. In figure 5, we see the Hub in relation to these spheres, which form a trinity of Causal Bodies within the Cosmic Egg. Surrounding the Hub are the three great Causal Bodies: the Great Central Sun and the Great Causal Body forming the yolk and the Great Central Sun Galaxy forming the white, their relationship to one another being that of the ratio of the golden mean.

Thus the Cosmic Egg is composed of the Trinity in actualization of Father, Son and Holy Spirit. The Great Central Sun (the Pink Causal Body) is the focus of the Father; the Great Causal Body (the Yellow Causal Body) is the focus of the Son, the eternal Logos; and the Great Central Sun Galaxy (the Blue Causal Body), embracing all three, is the focus of the Holy Spirit.

The Father is the Fount of Love that framed the universes; the Son is the Fount of Wisdom that makes plain the Father's love; and the Holy Spirit is the Fount of Action that brings both into universal manifestation, worlds without end.

FIGURE 4: The Cosmic Egg. Diagram of the Macrocosm.

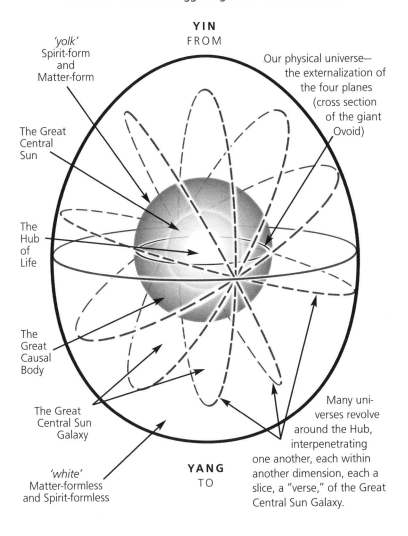

YIN
FROM

'yolk'
Spirit-form
and
Matter-form

Our physical universe—
the externalization of
the four planes
(cross section
of the giant
Ovoid)

The Great
Central
Sun

The
Hub
of
Life

The
Great
Causal
Body

The Great
Central Sun
Galaxy

Many uni-
verses revolve
around the Hub,
interpenetrating
one another, each within
another dimension, each a
slice, a "verse," of the Great
Central Sun Galaxy.

'white'
Matter-formless
and Spirit-formless

YANG
TO

Issuing from the Sun behind the sun—the White Fire Body
behind the Hub—the three Causal Bodies expanded from the
center of the Egg at the Great Outbreath, and worlds within
worlds were born. As these moved progressively away from the
Hub, it was like the expanding of a great balloon.

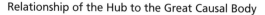

FIGURE 5: Diagram of the hierarchical spheres.
The trinity of Causal Bodies.

Relationship of the Hub to the Great Causal Body

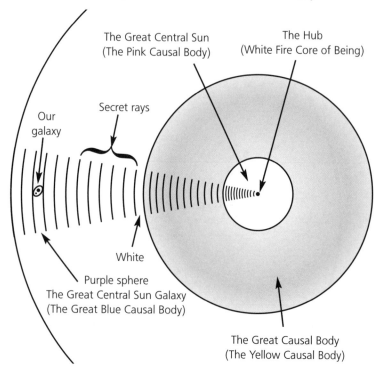

The space between heavenly bodies in the outer spheres makes the Blue Causal Body appear to be greater in size, and so it is. For time and space are characteristics of the yin aspect of God—of the materialization of universes within the white of the Egg. The diminishing of these factors as one travels from the periphery to the center and their total absence within the Hub characterizes the yang aspect of God and the spiritualization of universes within the yolk.

The concentration of light bodies within the Great Central Sun produces the quality of God we call Spirit; their diffusion in the Great Central Sun Galaxy produces the quality we call Matter; while the combination in the Great Causal Body produces the illumination of the eternal Logos, the Word made flesh, the Christ incarnate.

We see that in the white of the Egg, Matter is suspended in the formless aspects of Spirit and Matter; whereas in the yolk, Spirit is suspended in the form aspects of Spirit and Matter.

Because it is impossible to know God directly or to define his Being, we speak of him in allegory and metaphor so that our finite minds can gain a co-measurement of the infinite. The story of God is the story of the mother hen that lays the Cosmic Egg and broods o'er it with sheltering wing. The story of man is the story of the chick that is warmed inside the egg during the period of incubation. Having eaten the yolk and the white and grown to fill the egg, it breaks the shell and emerges into a new world.

Likewise, when man eats the yolk and the white of the Cosmic Egg, digesting the four aspects of God's Being, he becomes that which God is. When the microcosm absorbs the Macrocosm, it is no longer the microcosm. When man swallows the Cosmic Egg, he can no longer be called man; therefore he is called God.

In this metaphor we learn the ritual of Holy Communion, and we understand the mystery of eating the Body of Christ. When Jesus gave this teaching, he said: "I AM the living bread which came down from heaven: if any man eat of this bread, he shall live for ever: and the bread that I will give is my flesh, which I will give for the life of the world." Many understood not his saying: "Except ye eat the flesh of the Son of man, and drink his blood, ye have no life in you. Whoso eateth my flesh, and drinketh my blood, hath eternal life; and I will raise him up at the last day."

It is recorded that "from that time many of his disciples

went back, and walked no more with him. Then said Jesus unto the twelve, Will ye also go away? Then Simon Peter answered him, Lord, to whom shall we go? thou hast the words of eternal life."[33]

Beholding the Macrocosm as a giant Ovoid that God has made, we understand that God himself does not enter the Macrocosm, even as the hen does not enter the egg. Nevertheless, the Cosmic Egg is composed of the LORD's body, even as the egg issues from the hen. Hence, in a very real sense, God is in his Egg; but he is not confined to it as is man, the *man*ifestation of himself.

We begin to see that Spirit and Matter are but the yang and yin of him who is the Source of all and is still beyond our all. We cannot say, then, that God is confined to Spirit and that his externalization is confined to Matter, but only that Spirit and Matter are the dual expression of God, both being found in the form and formless aspects of creation.

Because we live in Matter and identify with it, we relate Spirit to our divinity. But it is when Matter and Spirit merge as one—when the electron returns to the heart of the Sun—that man is closest to his God.

In our diagram of the hierarchical spheres (figure 5), we observe the White Fire Core—which appears transparent like a crystal sphere—surrounded by the Great Central Sun, composed first of a white band followed by five iridescent bands and then by six color bands. These twelve bands are spheres within spheres surrounding the Great Hub. They are the crystallization of the twelve planes of God's consciousness through the action of the twelve rays—five secret rays and seven color rays.

In each of the three Causal Bodies (identical in pattern to the Causal Body of man), the five iridescent bands represent the aspect of God's consciousness that has remained in the formless state during a given cycle of creation. The five secret rays are the coordinates, in the planes of Spirit-formless and Matter-formless, of the seven color rays that coalesce in the planes of Spirit-form and Matter-form.

These five phases of God's consciousness are represented in the atom by the undivided neutrons, whose electrons have not separated for the purposes of expansion in the world of form. The six color bands that follow, together with the white band surrounding the White Fire Core, represent those neutrons that have divided into protons and electrons. These are the seven aspects of God that have come forth from the center of life to expand the kingdom of God, to multiply his talents, and to return the light yield to the Lord of the Harvest at the end of the cycle.

When the command "Let there be light!" went forth from the heart of God, there was light—because the Elohim (mighty electrons from the White Fire Core of God's own Being) separated from the neutrons and leaped into orbit in the Great Central Sun.

The writer of the book of Job records the voice of the LORD that spoke to Job "out of the whirlwind" (out of the flaming center of Being), asking him, "Where wast thou... when the morning stars sang together and all the Sons of God shouted for joy?"[34] These morning stars, these Sons of God shouting for joy, are the mighty electrons that come forth from the Hub to project the glory of life into the four planes of the creation according to the design of God's Causal Body. Let us see, then, just how the morning stars and the Sons of God are born.

Rotation at the Hub of Life

The two general classifications of the creation are the formed and the unformed. These exist within both Spirit and Matter as planes of God's consciousness: Spirit-formless and

Spirit-form, Matter-formless and Matter-form. In addition, we find in the heart of every atom that plane which is neither Spirit nor Matter, but the bridge between the two. This plane is called the "White Fire Core."

We have, then, in addition to the four divisions within Spirit and Matter, the Spirit-Matter category composing the nucleus of every monad. Here energy is in a permanent state of transformation between the unformed and the formed. The White Fire Core of the Great Central Sun is the Source of all life. It is the focus of the Electronic Presence of God and his Christ; it is the fire of the Holy Spirit out of which proceed the twelve spheres of the Great Causal Body.

This White Fire Core is the hub of the spiritual-material universe. From it proceed the children of the sun—the form and formless aspects of innumerable galaxies spiraling through the Body of God, giving birth to suns and stars, planets and solar systems. A veritable focus of the Holy of holies, the White Fire Core of every particle of being is the integrating factor between Spirit and Matter, between the flaming presence of God in manifestation and the God Presence in the Sun behind the sun.

The Hub of the Great Central Sun may be visualized as an immense diamond, for it truly is the focus of the diamond-shining Mind of God. (The word *diamond* means *d*eity *i*ndividualized in *a*ction in the world—French, *le monde*—of form.) This is the seat of the one Mind out of whom all creation sprang. The thought-action of the Universal Mind produces rotation at the very Hub of Life, and out of rotation come forth the energy patterns that we interpret as the rays of God.

Infinite in number, these light waves are focalized as the twelve aspects of the Creator's consciousness. As the diamond rotates, we see these rays shooting forth as giant beacons, criss-crossing the facets of God's Mind, weaving the deathless solar body of the universe.

In figure 6, the diagram of the Hub, we see that in the center is the City Foursquare, the City of the Sun, suspended within the cosmic cube. Encircling the cube is the Sphere of the Twelve Conceptions, the sundial of hierarchy that turns in a clockwise direction.

The cube within the sphere is the throne of the Four Cosmic Forces who ensoul the cardinal points (north, south, east and west) and the four levels of consciousness (earth, air, fire and water) in Spirit and Matter at the eight corners of the cube. The Solar Beings who fill these positions in hierarchy are the

FIGURE 6: Diagram of the Hub.

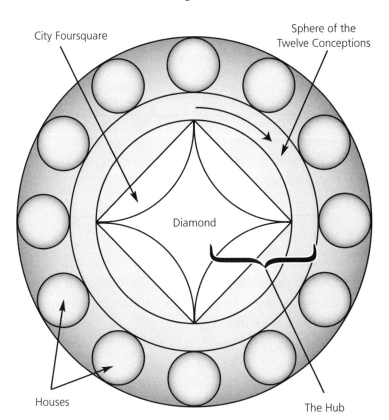

Four Pillars in the temple of God's Being, who make possible the crystallization of the God Flame throughout the Macrocosm.

Surrounding the Hub are twelve temples over which the Twelve Hierarchies of the Sun preside. These twelve temples, positioned on a giant "beltway," revolve around the diamond-shining Mind of God in a counterclockwise direction.

The twelve o'clock line of the diamond is the open door of God's consciousness that no man can shut. This is the birthplace of all cycles, sons and galaxies that come forth during the manvantaras of the creation. As the diamond revolves in a clockwise direction, creation comes forth through the open door and enters one of the Twelve Temples of the Sun.

After the Divine Monad comes forth from the twelve o'clock line of the sundial and enters the house that is opposite the open door at the moment of birth, it begins to spiral around the Hub, entering each of the twelve temples in clockwise order.

Thus the Divine Monad of everyone born of the Spirit passes through and comes under the influence of each of the twelve hierarchies within the White Fire Core before it is sent through the twelve spheres of the Pink Causal Body of the Great Central Sun.

Signs in the Heavens

As the earth revolves around the sun of our solar system, it appears that the sun "enters" (comes under the influence of) twelve constellations. Long ago the Chaldeans gave to these star formations the names that have since been used by both astronomers and astrologers.

For the purposes of identification, we, too, shall use these names for the Twelve Hierarchies of the Sun, who focus their God-power through these constellations. Let it be noted, however, that the human qualities ascribed to these so-called signs of the zodiac should not be confused with the divine attributes that the Almighty has charged the twelve hierarchies to guard.

These twelve hierarchies transform, or step down, the tremendous concentration of light-energy focused by the Four Pillars and make this light assimilable for the sons and daughters of God dwelling throughout the spiritual-material universe. Within their respective quadrants, the Four Pillars anchor the threefold flame action that issues from the White Fire Core.

The blending of the Trinity in the Hub brings into focus not only the power of the Four Cosmic Forces but also that of the twelve rays as these relate to precipitation in the planes of Spirit and Matter.

Each of the Twelve Hierarchies of the Sun is responsible for projecting and maintaining one ray in manifestation in Spirit and in Matter. Within the tri-unity (the threefold flame action) of each of the twelve rays are to be found twelve flames that coalesce as the twelve thousand virtues of the particular attribute of the Deity embodied within the ray.

Thus, together the twelve hierarchies are responsible for focusing the twelve rays, the 144 flames, and the 144,000 virtues of the Godhead that are destined to be externalized in the spiritual-material universes of cosmos.

The Temples of the Sun at the twelve o'clock, three o'clock, six o'clock and nine o'clock lines are under the hierarchies of Capricorn, Aries, Cancer and Libra. The mission of these cardinal signs (who serve on the blue plume) is to project the will of God into the universe and to endow the creation with the godly attributes of the twelve rays.

They are assisted by the hierarchies of the fixed and mutable signs: those who serve on the pink plume (Aquarius, Taurus, Leo and Scorpio) and those on the yellow plume (Pisces,

Gemini, Virgo and Sagittarius). Let us now trace the cycle of precipitation that the Monad follows through the Twelve Temples of the Sun within the White Fire Core. (See figure 7.)

FIGURE 7: Cycles of precipitation followed by the Monad through the twelve Temples of the Sun within the White Fire Core.

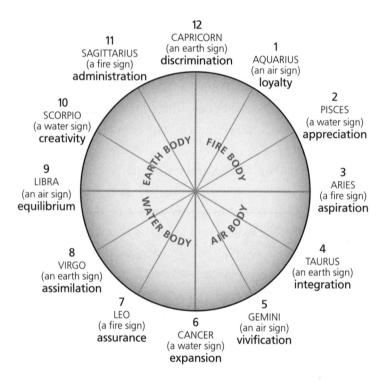

Cycles of the Son within the Sun

Beginning at the twelve o'clock line, the origin of cycles where earth becomes fire, it is the responsibility of the hierarchy of Capricorn to draw forth from the consciousness of God, by the power of the Logos, the perception and the *discrimination* of the design of the Monad that is to take form.

The hierarchies of Aquarius and Pisces then implement the divine blueprint through devotion and *loyalty* to the immaculate design. The hierarchy of Aquarius sustains that which is aborning and nourishes it by the power of the love plume. The hierarchs of Pisces adorn it, in turn, with the *appreciation* of the wisdom of God.

These three hierarchies are responsible for sustaining the etheric pattern, or fiery destiny, of the Monads that come forth from the heart of God. Sons and daughters of flame descending into form are nourished by their power, wisdom and love. The etheric bodies of planets and incoming souls are established, thanks to their devotion to the divine plan.

Here, then, in the first three Temples of the Sun, the hierarchs of Capricorn, Aquarius and Pisces bring forth from the world of the formless to the world of form the patterns of God-realization. This fire phase of the creation is a most important cycle, for it sets the pattern that must be followed by the remaining nine hierarchies.

At the three o'clock line where fire and air meet, the hierarchs of Aries receive the etheric pattern and begin to weave its design in the mental quadrant. Enfired with the will of God, these hierarchs aspire to capture the perfect pattern and to make it tangible through the Mind of Christ. *Aspiration* is the keynote through which they inspire the Monad with the mental fire that makes the vision of the creative plan intelligible in the planes of Spirit-form, Matter-formless and Matter-form.

Astrologers correctly assign to Aries the first position in the zodiac, for it is only when the etheric fire pattern reaches the mental plane that it is recognized in the world of form. And so it appears that the cycle of creation begins in Aries. We do not see the daffodils until their tiny green shoots emerge from the earth in spring. Yet germination, stimulated by the fires of the sun through Capricorn, Aquarius and Pisces, marked their true beginning in the plane of Spirit-formless.

Assisting the hierarchs of Aries to coalesce the divine ideation in the plane of Spirit-form, the hierarchs of Taurus serve by the power of the Holy Spirit to effect the *integration* of the design that has come forth from the heart of the Father. Using the love ray, they are most practical as they mold the design out of the earth element, making it available to every level of God's conscious manifestation throughout the universe.

When the torch is passed to the hierarchs of Gemini, these invoke the flame of illumination to lend the air of *vivification* to the idea as it meshes with the thoughtforms of the universe. This concludes the service of the hierarchies governing the air quadrant.

Where air and water meet, the hierarchs of Cancer invoke in the plane of Matter-formless the blue plume of the will of God for the *expansion* of the etheric and mental patterns through the emotional body. The hierarchs of Leo give the *assurance* by the fire of the love plume that the idea which has come forth from the diamond-shining Mind of God will live to fulfill its fiery destiny.

The hierarchs of Virgo, through reverence for the wisdom of God and mastery over the earth element, protect the *assimilation* of the idea in the feeling world.

As these hierarchies lend the pressure of their momentum of precipitation to the externalization of the God-idea, the plane of Matter-formless is saturated with the power, love and wisdom of the waters of eternal life.

The hierarchs of Libra infuse the idea with the will of God where water and earth meet. Here in the plane of Matter-form, the matrix is destined to materialize by the perfect balance of the Alpha and Omega spirals—the twin flames of Spirit and Matter.

In the house of Libra where dominion over air in earth is taught, the Monad finds that *equilibrium* of love-wisdom, held in the scales of the will of God, which is necessary for the final descent into form. The torch is then passed to the hierarchies of Scorpio and Sagittarius, whose mastery over water and fire in the plane of Matter-form and whose love of *creativity* and wisdom of *administration* completes the ritual of creation.

In summary, the hierarchies of Capricorn, Aquarius and Pisces teach the precipitation of the fire body (the etheric body) through the mastery of the fire element; they use earth, air and water as the essential elements of their creation. The hierarchies of Aries, Taurus and Gemini teach the precipitation of the air body (the mental body) through the mastery of the air element, using the elements of fire, earth and air as keys.

The hierarchies of Cancer, Leo and Virgo teach the precipitation of the water body (the emotional body) through the mastery of water, using the elements of water, fire and earth. Finally, the hierarchies of Libra, Scorpio and Sagittarius teach the precipitation of the earth body (the physical body) and the mastery over the earth element through the use of air, water and fire.

This cycling of the Monad through the Four Cosmic Forces in the four planes, under the Twelve Hierarchies of the Sun and the twelve rays of God that they focus, fulfills the mandate "Let there be light!" and effects the transformation from Spirit to Matter of every idea born in the Mind of God. (See figure 8.)

This is the true teaching of the law of precipitation. With this knowledge, alchemists of the Spirit, together with scientists of Matter, may bring forth the beauty of creation with the assistance of the Twelve Hierarchies of the Sun and those elder brothers of the race appointed to serve under them on behalf of the evolutions of earth.

FIGURE 8: Cycles of the Four Cosmic Forces in the four planes.

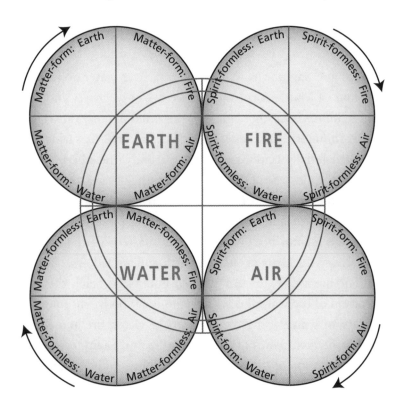

The clocks of the twelve hierarchies govern the cycles of precipitation that take place within each of the twelve houses. Thus, each house is divided into the twelve phases of the larger clock that must be studied under the ray of that house. In addition to all of these cycles, each band of the Causal Body is also divided into twelve sub-spheres, thereby focusing the twelve bands of the Causal Body within each sphere.

These cycles within cycles are infinite, and they govern precipitation at every level of God Self-awareness. Centuries, decades, years, months, weeks, days, hours, minutes, seconds and microseconds are examples of the wheels within wheels that clock the energy spirals that descend from the heart of the Hub to the heart of embodied man. The time required for the revolution of a heavenly body around each of the twelve spheres may be millions of years, according to our reckoning. The frequencies of these spirals are stepped down according to the law of cycles until they become assimilable to the lifewaves evolving at the farthest periphery of the spiritual-material universes.

The cycle of the electron in its orbit around the white fire core of the atom governs the cycles of time and space. Since the orbital and rotational speed of the electron varies according to the light of the soul, the cycles of time and space also vary among individuals, planets, suns and stars. When scientists discover how to clock the speed of the electron, they will discover vital information concerning the law of cycles that governs every aspect of life.

The Vesting of the Monad with the Spheres of Reality

Let us follow the course of the Monad through the Great Central Sun (the Pink Causal Body) after its birth in the White Fire Core. (See figure 9.)

As we have said, all heavenly bodies come forth through the open door at the twelve o'clock line of the diamond in the Hub. But at what point they come forth, into which house, and under which ray within that house is determined by the position of the diamond in relation to the beltway at the moment of birth, which is preordained by the immaculate conception of the Monad within the Mind of God.

Let us take, for example, a heavenly body that comes forth when the open door is at the five o'clock line of the outer circle. Having been born into the house of Gemini, the body

FIGURE 9: The spheres of the Causal Body.

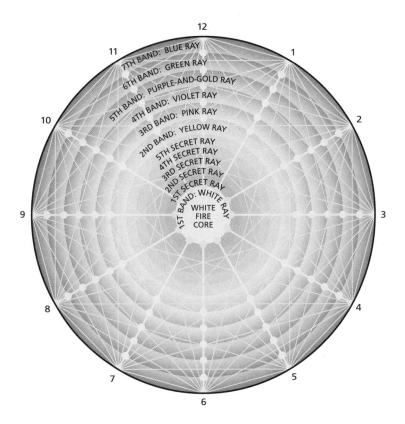

immediately begins its spiral within the first band. Moving in a clockwise direction, the body enters the twelve houses within the white sphere, each house having its own wheel or clock within the great wheel. Here the Monad puts on the white sphere and receives the armour of God-purity.

When the body returns to the five o'clock line, after having passed through the twelve houses, it enters the first sphere of the secret rays. During its spirals through the five spheres of the formless world, the Monad gathers unto itself the flames of God anchored there as it forms these spheres within its own

Causal Body and magnetizes the potential of the Godhead within.

The sojourn within the bands of the five secret rays is one of inner spiritual development that will set the pattern for that which is to be externalized in the world of form. The secret rays play a most important role in precipitation, for all that is to follow will come forth from the potential sealed in the White Fire Core, the first sphere and the planes of the secret rays.

Within the second band, the yellow sphere of the Great Central Sun, the Monad attains the first color of awareness "that I AM" in the plane of Spirit-form. Here the soul evolving within the Monad gains an identity separate and distinct from that God-awareness of the universal I AM in which the Monad was immersed in the flaming center of God's Being and with which it continued to identify within the white sphere and the spheres of the five secret rays.

Thus, after the period of gestation in the White Fire Core and its geometrization during its first six cycles around the Central Sun, the Monad is "born anew" in the second band, where it experiences the cycle of illumination. Here the soul beholding the Monad exclaims, "I AM THAT I AM!" During the twelve phases of the evolution of the heavenly body within the yellow band, the soul consciousness is illumined with the wisdom of the creative intent, and the plan of God is sealed in the folds of the yellow robe with which the Monad is vested.

The power to expand the plan is not accorded the soul until the knowledge of how to use that power is thoroughly digested. Beginning in the yellow sphere and continuing through the remaining color bands, the soul must learn how to precipitate in form. It must understand the laws of cosmos and the energy framework of adhesion and cohesion that define its creative potential and domain. Not until the soul has passed all initiations pertaining thereto in the next four spheres does it enter the blue sphere of the Monad, where it is given the power and the authority to create.

Each of the twelve houses of the sun has important lessons to teach the soul concerning the application of God's love as the cohesive power that holds together the creation that is aborning. During the cycle of the Monad in the pink sphere, the soul is expected to develop such love for the Creator and for his consciousness that it shall never depart from the original blueprint held within the purity of the White Fire Core. This is the meaning of the mantle of love: one who wears it never loses sight of the purposes of God.

In the fourth band the Monad gains the violet sphere of freedom and the soul learns the responsibilities of free will. She is taught how she may bring forth the creations of God in the planes of Spirit-form and Matter-form according to the original divine plan through the wisdom and the love of God. The substance of freedom gathered here can transmute anything extraneous to the divine plan that the soul may encounter in its evolution. Here the soul learns the ritual of precipitation as the knowledge of divine alchemy, and the sacred science is anchored in the Causal Body.

In the fifth sphere the Monad gathers the purple-and-gold weavings of Cosmic Christ devotion to principle in God and man. The soul learns how to minister unto the needs of the creation and how to restore in them the image of perfection. With the momentum of all that has gone before, the twelve hierarchies in the Temples of the Sun now teach the soul how to define brotherhood, practicality and cooperation with all of the evolutions that proceed from the heart of God—each facet fulfilling an aspect of the Deity, complementing one another and the whole.

The design of hierarchy as the manifestation of the brotherhood of man under the Father-Mother God is found in the purple sphere. In this sphere the atoms form molecules to diversify the Creator's manifestation in form, and mankind learn how to work together and how to cooperate with angels, elementals and cosmic hosts.

In the sixth band the Monad puts on the green sphere, which balances the precipitation in the fourfold aspects of fire, air, water and earth. The healing green focuses through the All-Seeing Eye of God the formulas for creation in the realms of form. It shows man how to retain singleness of vision and constancy of purpose in the world of form, and it contains the science of the *ideation* ("idea-action") of God. This abundance of God's consciousness is awarded to man when he has successfully fulfilled the preceding cycles. As in all things, past attainment determines present and future accomplishment.

Entering the seventh sphere of God's consciousness, the action of the will of God and of his cosmic faith and power seals the creation in its immortal design. Only after having drawn sufficient momentum of the blue ray will the Monad be adorned with peace and permanence in the heart of God.

Man must earn the right to wield the power of God's creative energies. These are received only when the soul has proved through all previous cycles that she can sustain the divine matrix that was originally bequeathed to her—no matter how far she may journey from the center of the Godhead.

Having completed the spirals in the Great Central Sun where it has developed its own God consciousness or God Self-awareness, the Monad now enters the Yellow Causal Body. Here it will go through the same twelve-cycle ritual in order to attain the Christ consciousness and its own Christ Self-awareness.

When the Monad enters the Blue Causal Body, the soul descends into embodiment, the Word becomes flesh and a heavenly orb takes on dimension in the physical universe.

Here, while the Monad performs the same ritual on high, the soul will attain its solar consciousness and the awareness of Self in the planes of Matter-form as the outpicturing of the Holy Spirit.

This is the magnificent consummation of all the cycles that have gone before. Here every step of initiation taken by the Monad in the twelve houses is intended to be matched by one of precipitation in form—as Above, so below. Truly, this is the externalization of the expanding universe and God's kingdom come.

The Return Cycle

The many universes within the Cosmic Egg came forth from light seeds projected into the White Fire Core of the Central Sun. With the great outbreathing of the Holy Spirit, they spiraled forth, first through the Great Central Sun, then through the Great Causal Body and finally through the Great Central Sun Galaxy.

With the Great Inbreath, the cycles of manifestation in both Spirit and Matter will return to the center of the Hub. All that is electronically balanced by the power of the Logos will retain its identity when the Cosmic Egg unites with its antibody. Then the Lord of the Vineyard will bring the fruits of the harvest into the great storehouse—into the Causal Body of the Cosmic Egg. Universes that have not attained the divine polarity will lose their form and individual consciousness. The energy potential originally invested in them will be returned, neither multiplied nor lost.

When the Monad fulfills the twelve spirals in the Blue Causal Body, it commences the cycle of return to the heart of God through each of the twelve spheres of the Blue, Yellow and Pink Causal Bodies. The power of God that comes forth through the blue ray in the seventh sphere provides not only the final impetus for the fulfillment of the law of cycles in Matter-form but also the momentum needed for its return to the flaming center of God's Being.

The reverse process of precipitation is sublimation, or the ascension. Having fulfilled the going-out (yang) phase of the divine plan in the spiritual-material universe, the Monad cycles from the house of its birth in a counterclockwise direction on the return to the Hub. This is the coming-in (yin) phase of the divine plan. Just as the initiation of cycles in the plane of Spirit is on the twelve o'clock line, so their fulfillment is generated by the focus of the World Mother on the six o'clock line.

The return cycle of the Monad may commence while the soul is still unascended, precipitating good works in Matter-form. However, on the inbreath (the coming in) the soul must reap the karma, both good and bad, that it has sown in the outbreath (the going out).

Having fulfilled the requirements of the Great Law, the soul can ascend any time during the return cycle of the Monad through the Blue Causal Body. For according to the Great Law, anywhere that the individualization of God has realized the allness of God, it can ascend into that allness. Thereafter, the Monad, having drawn the soul into itself, continues to spiral on the pathway back to the Great Hub of Life.

If, while the Monad is spiraling through the Blue Causal Body, the embodied soul does not take full advantage of the momentums of the spheres and the teachings of the twelve hierarchies released from the heart of the I AM Presence, it must take these lessons over when the Monad passes through their houses on the return cycle. The prodigal sons who have squandered their inheritance during the outbreath must redeem it during the inbreath. This, then, is the action of karma in its universal implication.

On the return cycle the Monad enhances the glory of God in each sphere by blending its momentum with that of all who have ever gone before in the rituals of creation, preservation and consummation.

The momentums gathered in the three Causal Bodies are available to all who follow in the footsteps of the ascending ones. This is the law of the expanding universe, which makes possible the greater works that are intended to be accomplished by each succeeding individualization of the God Flame. Since the three Causal Bodies are constantly expanding (through the expanding Causal Bodies of each Monad), the greater power of the divine Logos thus externalized becomes available to evolving souls. Therefore, when his time is come, the disciple is expected to do greater works than his Master.

Unless the soul has externalized the God consciousness, Christ consciousness and solar consciousness in the Blue Causal Body, she cannot ascend and her identity will not be preserved when the Monad enters the Yellow and Pink Causal Bodies.

The I AM Presence—the individualization of the God Flame—always comes forth from the White Fire Core of the Great Central Sun. But the lower vehicles the soul uses for her evolution in the Blue Causal Body are formed under the direction of the Solar Logoi in charge of the planetary chain in which she is to evolve.

While the soul is unwinding karmic cycles created in the course of her involvements in Matter-form, the I AM Presence continues on its appointed course, cycling through the spheres of the Blue Causal Body. Thus, every day people are sowing and reaping karma, all in different cycles. While some evolutions are going forth from Spirit to Matter, others are returning from Matter to Spirit.

The Flaming Yod, the White Fire Core of our galaxy, is a son of the Hub that has spiraled through the Great Central Sun

Galaxy to the position it now holds in the tenth house of the blue band of the purple sphere passing through cosmic initiations under the hierarchy of Scorpio. Our galaxy is among many son galaxies that have come forth from the flaming universe of God's heart, all moving in a clockwise direction and located at various positions within the twelve spheres of the Blue Causal Body.

The Flaming Yod is itself the focal point of another trinity of Causal Bodies giving birth to the suns, stars and planets within the galaxy in the same manner as the larger bodies come forth from the Hub. Thus our galaxy and all evolving within it are in one cycle of the Great Central Sun Galaxy, while the members of our galactic family are in different cycles within its Causal Bodies, each in a different house in a different band.

We would leave you with one immense thought before terminating our analogies of the creation: The Macrocosm, the giant Egg, including within its "shell" an infinite number of universes, has a twin flame. With the first outbreathing of God, two noble electrons went forth from the nucleus of his heart, one with a plus and the other with a minus spin. Such relativity only the Mind of God can encompass.

Destined one day to return to the I AM God Presence, these cosmic lovers will begin moving toward one another at the moment of the inbreath. And after all of their children have been drawn into the flaming Hub of their respective centers, final reunion in their androgynous sphere will take place through the victory of their ascension into the light.

Interplanetary and Intergalactic Energy Veils

Due to the fact that man has been given free will, the presence of *evil* (the *e*nergy *veil*) is not confined to our planet or to our solar system. Wherever sons and daughters of God have entered the Blue Causal Body and gone forth on the journey into form through the cycles of God's solar consciousness, they have had the opportunity to misqualify the energies of the Holy Spirit while the Monad has cycled through the twelve houses of initiation.

Some of the floating gases and debris that obscure the light of the suns in the six outer rings of the Great Central Sun Galaxy are the remnants of the misuse of God's energy. This density obscures the light of entire sections of the heavens. Scientists tell us that if they were not there, we could read at night by the light of the Milky Way.

If the transmutation of these astral islands is not accomplished before the Great Inbreath, the patterns that sustain them will be cancelled out when the cosmos is drawn into the Hub.

The advantage of transmuting all intergalactic and intragalactic misqualifications before the inbreath is that through transmutation the energy, as talents, is multiplied and then used to glorify and expand the kingdom. Energies that remain imprisoned in an imperfect matrix until the end of the manvantara are like the buried talent of the profitless servant. As the Lord has said, those who fail in their opportunity to embellish the universe are cast into outer darkness[35]—the darkness that they themselves have created by their misuse of the sacred gift of free will.

No one who truly observes life can escape the conclusion that science and religion must go hand in hand. As Saint Germain released the information in this chapter, he said:

"Write. It is time that man should truly understand his environment, that through this knowledge, religion and science might become pillars in the temple of the golden-age civilization, equal in right and authority, one complementing the other, two halves of the spectrum of human knowledge, both receiving the inspiration of the Christ.

"For science comes down to man from the Mother aspect of God, and religion from the Father aspect. The Christ, as the Mediator between the two, brings forth those inspirations and revelations that lead men of empirical faith and intuitive reason onward in their quest for greater and greater knowledge of our expanding universe."

The mysteries of life, in all of its fantastic wonder, are not intended to be contained within the mind of man, ascended or unascended. Only God is totally aware of himself. Often the Masters have told us that even they do not really know who God is, but only the "I AM THAT I AM"—that portion of himself which he has deigned to externalize. However, the Masters are not limited in any sense of the word; for with the knowledge of the I AM, they can continue to explore and expand for millions of aeons and still not come to the realization of who God is.

Having briefly examined the structure and operation of universes within the Cosmic Egg, let us turn our attention to the offices of hierarchy with a view to discovering how God has assigned his flaming Sons to minister unto the needs of those evolving in the Great Central Sun Galaxy.

Founts of Hierarchy

> *I AM Alpha and Omega, the begin-*
> *ning and the end. I will give unto him*
> *that is athirst of the fountain of the water*
> *of life freely. He that overcometh shall*
> *inherit all things; and I will be his God,*
> *and he shall be my son.*[36]

Fount of Unity: Twin Flames over All

> *And the* LORD *God said, It is not good that the*
> *man should be alone; I will make him an help meet for*
> *him.*[37]

The first office of hierarchy we shall discuss is that of twin flames. Born of the androgynous sphere of the Father-Mother God in the Sun behind the sun, twin flames represent the wholeness of individualized being. Each flame is the nucleus of a Divine Monad, one half of the whole.

It is not good for man (*man*ifestation) to be alone. Serving in pairs that can never be divided, these individualizations of the Divine Father and the Divine Mother oversee the creation at every level of conscious being.

Throughout the Cosmic Egg, God has ordained twin flames of the Holy Spirit to do his will, to focus his wisdom and to expand his love. Over every physical sun, whether it be an atom, a planet, a star, a Flaming Yod or the Great Hub itself, there are twin flames appointed by God as the Sun God and Goddess for that system of worlds.

The highest representatives of the Godhead in the Cosmic Egg are Alpha and Omega, who abide in the City Foursquare in the Great Central Sun. There they hold the focus of the Father-Mother God on behalf of the lifewaves of the universes within the Egg who are the externalization of their God Self-realization. Maximus (meaning "God is great") is the authority in the Sun behind the sun for the Great Maxim Light, which is the first cause behind the effect that we have called the Cosmic Egg.

Each star in our galaxy and in the millions of galaxies revolving about the Hub has twin flames who hold the focus of God's identity. These twin flames keep the flame for billions of Spirit-sparks and lend their momentum of light and service to that star and to all evolving within its system. Helios and Vesta serve in this capacity in our own solar system.

Each one reading this book should pause to consider that he and his twin flame are destined to become the God and Goddess of a system of worlds. This is the destiny to which the Father-Mother God created twin flames. All who have ever gone forth from the Great Hub have vowed to fulfill their responsibilities to the Father-Mother God under the loving direction of Alpha and Omega.

As Alpha teaches: "The Christ consciousness—stainless, pure white, white fire substance—has gone forth. The beautiful orb of the Buddha, the transcendent love of the Christ—all these come from the bosom of the Beginning and stretch forth, radiant poles of identity, unto the Ending.

"I AM Alpha and Omega, the Beginning and the Ending of thyself. And in the entering in to the heart of the Mother, Omega, in the entering in to the fullness of her heart, there is signified the end of thyself and the birth of thy new beginning. For the serpent has swallowed his own tail, and all endings are new beginnings.

"With the vanishing from the screen of identity of all that is false in the self, all that is true comes to birth. And so Vesta, in the sun of your system of worlds, is the Mother who invests her energies in you; and Helios is the God of that sun.

"'Be thou faithful over a few things, and I will make thee ruler over many things'[38] is the Great Law that came down, pulsating through the ethers from on high, from our octave. This is the sacred Sun teaching released to Helios and Vesta. It is the God-promise to every son in every system of worlds whatsoever.

"And if ye would one day fulfill thy destiny, know, then, that spiral nebulae shall flow from thy heart with greater ease than a spider spinning a web. The radiance of the light shall flow out from thy chakras, and thou shalt find, each one, that in this unlimited universal creativity without beginning and without end, without father and without mother, thou hast been blest with a victory over all unwieldy desires and that there has been bestowed upon thee here in the schoolrooms of earth the necessary training in humility that makes thee worthy to be a God of thine own universe. And then thou shalt know the meaning of that which tonight seems but dim to thy perceptions when I say unto thee:

"In my house are many mansions.[39] In my house are many man's sons. Then thou shalt know that thy destiny lay not in the consummation of substance and the acquirement of wealth or of fame, but of God's qualities; that those given into thy charge and keeping in the shepherd-kingdom sector of the universal consciousness were given to thy charge and keeping that they, in hearing thy voice, might hear my voice, and that perfection might live, and that sin might not exist in our octave to spoil and to destroy.

"And so the cherubim that keep the way of the Tree of Life[40] keep the way unto my house, and no man can enter here and abide except he come clothed with my flame. When ye rise from your physical being, clothed and robed in my flame, ye may ascend so far and no farther, for the Angel of thy Presence knoweth how far ye may go and not be consumed by our light."[41]

The sun god and goddess must represent to the evolutions within their system the complete complement of the divine polarity. Thus, around each flaming Sun Center of Being are focuses of the Twelve Hierarchies of the Sun, tended by twelve sets of twin flames who ensoul the 144,000 Christed virtues externalized in the twelve bands of the three Great Causal Bodies.

In the God Star Sirius, which is the focus of the Central Sun for this sector of our galaxy, the twelve hierarchies focus their flames at the Court of the Sacred Fire through the Four and Twenty Elders.[42] These twelve sets of twin flames preside over the twelve temples or outer courts surrounding the central court.

Surrounding Helios and Vesta are twelve Temples of the Sun presided over by twelve sets of twin flames. As the earth revolves in its orbit during the twelve-month cycle of the year, her evolutions pass through and come under the benign influence of each of these twelve houses. Through their joint service with Helios and Vesta of stepping down the radiation of the hierarchies of Sirius, of the Flaming Yod and of the Hub, mankind are able to receive and assimilate a portion of the great momentum generated in the center of the diamond-shining Mind of God.

Fount of the All-Seeing Eye: The Silent Watchers

> *The Lamb which is in the midst of the throne*
> *shall feed them, and shall lead them unto living foun-*
> *tains of waters.*[43]

Abiding within the White Fire Core of God's Being is the Great Silent Watcher, the beholder of the fiery destiny of all the son galaxies and their evolutions that have ever proceeded from the Great Hub of Life. This office of hierarchy is essential to every level of God's Self-conscious awareness throughout the universe of his individualization, both in and out of form.

Focusing the purity of the immaculate design of all who have gone forth in an identity pattern apart from God with or without the gift of free will, the Great Silent Watcher is the beacon of the eye of God. When trained upon any being or segment of the universe, this beacon "squares the matrix"—that is, realigns the energies with the original blueprint, the image most holy that is stamped upon the seed atom when the I AM Presence is born in the heart of the Hub.

Every beloved son and daughter begotten of the Father-Mother God is overshadowed by a Silent Watcher who guards the flame of the All-Seeing Eye, who nourishes and expands the matrix of its destiny—that portion of the Deity which is to be established within the Monad, first as cause in Spirit and then as effect in Matter.

Wherever they serve throughout cosmos, the Silent Watchers hold the network of the cosmic antahkarana. As pillars of fire, they stand in the Temples of the Sun—magnets of perfection, mirrors of Cosmic Truth. Filigree threads of light connect the energies of their service, creating the lines of force that hold galaxies in orbit around the center of God's Being.

Not the pull of gravity, which is man's explanation for this attraction between heavenly bodies, but the magnetism of the Holy Spirit—the intense love of the Creator's plan held in the heart of the Silent Watchers—keeps the flaming sons and daughters of God upon their appointed rounds.

The Great Central Sun Magnet, the center of flaming love-purity within the Hub, is the focus of the Holy Spirit of God. It energizes the momentums of unity that make all of the universes of God's conscious manifestation an individed whole, an integrated network of galaxies evolving from one dimension to the next. The Great Central Sun Magnet is the energy source for the flame of life wherever it manifests. The Silent Watchers are the keepers of that flame. With the assistance of innumerable helpers, they guard its purity and power, its wisdom and love.

The Great Silent Watcher in the Great Central Sun, whom we know as the Elohim Cyclopea, is encircled by 144 God Flames, each of whom is over countless legions who have but one goal in life: the bringing forth of the image of the Christ throughout the Macrocosm and the microcosm of God's Being.

Every individualization of the God Flame from the center to the periphery of the Cosmic Egg is guarded by a Silent Watcher. God has left no manifestation of himself without a guardian spirit to supervise the correct outpicturing of the Christed plan for its manifestation.

In man the Silent Watcher is the Mediator known as the Christ Self. In nature the Silent Watchers serving under Cyclopea are the devas who hold the Christ-pattern for the blessed elementals. In angelic realms the mighty seraphim and the covering cherubim are entrusted with the responsibility of guarding the immaculate conception of life.

The cherubim guard the flame of the ark of the covenant between God and man, focused in the Great Central Sun. They keep the way of the Tree of Life, both in the City Foursquare and in every son and daughter of God. "And they rest not day and night, saying, Holy, holy, holy, LORD God Almighty, which was, and is, and is to come."[44]

The seraphim tend the focus of the Electronic Presence of the Almighty—the greatest Silent Watcher of all—in the flaming sea of crystal in the very heart of the Hub. Merging with the crystal and the flame, they dance before the throne in a twenty-four-"hour" or twenty-four-phase cycle.

Every "hour" a new band of seraphim arrives from the far reaches of cosmos to assume their place on the platform that revolves around the Great Flame of Life, focus of the Most High God. As these arrive, another band leaves, and so on in each twenty-four-"hour" cycle. Thus the bands of seraphim, each in multiples of 144,000, stand in the presence of God twenty-three "hours" and serve in the world of form one "hour." Being saturated with the crystal fire radiance of God himself, the seraphim can never be contaminated by unascended evolutions (as were the angels who fell with Lucifer), for it is literally impossible to slow down the frequency of their holy auras.

The seraphim receive the great solar "heat" generated by the fires of God's heart over a figure-eight pattern used to step down the tremendous velocity of the Christ light released from the center of God's Being through the "wings" of the seraphim and thence to the periphery of universal manifestation. The seraphim assist the Great Silent Watchers to radiate this light through the universes of the Macrocosm, where the Christ Self of stars, planets and sons serves to step down the energies conveyed by the seraphim to the level of individual need.

Thus it is the service of the Silent Watchers to act as agents of the Great Central Sun Magnet to step down from one level of God's Self-awareness to the next the energies of God's potential, so that these might be useful and relevant to each successive stage of evolving life.

The antahkarana (the web of life) is composed of the

filigree threads that connect the Silent Watchers serving throughout the Macrocosm. This antahkarana is the conductor of the energies of the Great Central Sun Magnet. The crystal cord that connects the God Self and the Christ Self with the Great Central Sun Magnet is part of this antahkarana. Think of how many suns and son galaxies, how many step-downs or transformations this web must pass through before the energy of God becomes assimilable for our use!

Threefold Flame Fount: Kingdoms of Power, Love and Wisdom

> *When the poor and needy seek water, and there is none, and their tongue faileth for thirst, I the* LORD *will hear them, I the God of Israel will not forsake them. I will open rivers in high places, and fountains in the midst of the valleys: I will make the wilderness a pool of water, and the dry land springs of water.... That they may see, and know, and consider, and understand together, that the hand of the* LORD *hath done this, and the Holy One of Israel hath created it.*[45]

The threefold flame of life focuses the Trinity of the Godhead in the White Fire Core of all Being. This Trinity manifests in hierarchy as a threefold division of cosmic service. Thus all of the hosts of light serve within one of these three divisions, known as kingdoms: the kingdom of the elementals, the kingdom of the angels and the kingdom of the Gods.

Embodying the qualities of God-power, God-love and God-wisdom respectively, these kingdoms represent the circling of the square of the Four Cosmic Forces for the purpose of their precipitation in form. The threefold flame in the center of the City Foursquare manifests first in the four quadrants of the sundial. Then, through the rituals and ministrations of the Twelve Solar Hierarchies, the outer circle becomes the square, and ideas take form in the planes of Spirit and Matter.

In the stepping down of the cosmic threefold flame through the kingdoms of elementals, angels and Gods, the hierarchies of the sun are assisted by the Elohim, the Archangels, and the Chohans of the Seven Rays. The names of the hierarchs serving in these offices are included in figure 10. Let us review their functions.

The Elemental Kingdom

To the builders of form was given the important task of bringing into Spirit-form and Matter-form the designs of God and man. As transformers of the Four Cosmic Forces, the beings of fire, air, water and earth serve to nourish God-ideas as they spiral through the three Causal Bodies. They also serve to balance and align the four lower bodies of men and planets. Laborers in the Father's vineyard, harvesters of his sowings, the fiery salamanders, sylphs, undines and gnomes occupy a key position in the threefold action of God in manifestation.

The hierarchs of this kingdom are the twelve Elohim. Representing the Father aspect of the Trinity, they implement the blue plume of his consciousness. As Cosmic Beings in charge of the precipitation of form, they wield the power of the Great Central Sun Magnet throughout the Great Central Sun Galaxy.

The Elohim endow creation with the power of the Creator, his will and his divine direction as it is lowered from the planes of Spirit-formless to Matter-form. Under them serve the directors of the elements—the planetary hierarchs of earth, air, fire and water—and the elementals in their command. (See figure 11.)

Although the Seven Mighty Elohim who serve on the seven color rays are known to some students of hierarchy, the

FIGURE 10: The rays and their hierarchs in the three kingdoms.

Seven Rays of God Focused on the Days of the Week	God-Qualities Amplified	Representing the Cosmic Hierarchy in the Elemental and Angelic Kingdoms		Representing the Interplanetary Hierarchy in the Kingdom of the Gods	
		Elohim and Divine Complements	Archangels and Divine Complements	Lords of Karma	The Chohans and their Retreats
1st ray (Tuesday) Power of God Blue	Faith, protection, desire to do the will of God	Hercules Amazonia	Michael Faith	The Great Divine Director	El Morya Darjeeling, India
2nd ray (Sunday) Wisdom of God Yellow	Wisdom, intelligence, understanding, desire to know God through the Mind of Christ	Apollo Lumina	Jophiel Christine	The Goddess of Liberty	Lanto The Grand Teton, Wyoming, U.S.A.
3rd ray (Monday) Love of God Pink	Compassion, charity, desire to be the love of God in action	Heros Amora	Chamuel Charity	Nada	Paul the Venetian Southern France; focuses in the Statue of Liberty and the Washington Monument, U.S.A.
4th ray (Friday) Purity of God White	Purity, wholeness, desire to see God through purity of heart, motive and deed	Purity Astrea	Gabriel Hope	Cyclopea	Serapis Bey Luxor, Egypt
5th ray (Wednesday) Truth of God Green	Constancy, science, healing, desire to precipitate the abundance of God	Cyclopea Virginia	Raphael Mother Mary	Pallas Athena, Goddess of Truth	Hilarion Crete, Greece
6th ray (Thursday) Peace of God Purple and gold	Devotion, service, ministration of the Christ, desire to be in the service of God and man	Peace Aloha	Uriel Aurora	Portia, Goddess of Justice	Nada Saudi Arabia
7th ray (Saturday) Freedom of God Violet	Freedom, ritual, order, transcendency, desire to make all things new by God's power of transmutation	Arcturus Victoria	Zadkiel Amethyst	Kuan Yin, Goddess of Mercy	Saint Germain Transylvania, Romania, and Table Mountain, Wyoming U.S.A.

FIGURE 11: Hierarchs vested with the authority
of the Four Cosmic Forces for the planet Earth.

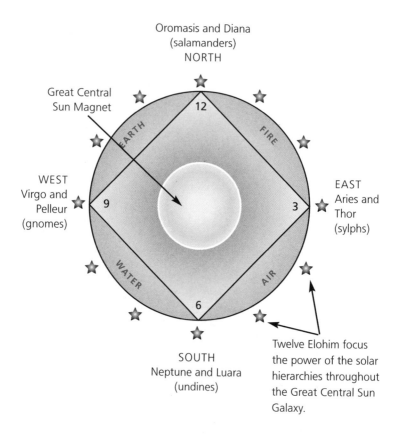

Oromasis and Diana
(salamanders)
NORTH

Great Central
Sun Magnet

WEST
Virgo and
Pelleur
(gnomes)

EAST
Aries and
Thor
(sylphs)

SOUTH
Neptune and Luara
(undines)

Twelve Elohim focus
the power of the solar
hierarchies throughout
the Great Central Sun
Galaxy.

identity of the five who serve in the Great Silence (in the five
inner bands of the Great Central Sun and in the same bands of
the Yellow and Blue Causal Bodies) is not generally known.
These five will come forth when mankind have demonstrated a
greater degree of mastery over the energies now available for
their spiritual evolution through the seven "active" rays.

The Elohim who came forth from the heart of God in
response to the Great Command are comparable to the electrons that go forth from the nucleus of the atom. Just as

without the electrons that create an energy whirl of time and space there would be no Matter, so without the Elohim there would be no world of form.

The five Elohim serving on the secret rays correspond to the neutrons that remain in the heart of the atom. Their power and authority can be invoked by addressing "the Elohim of the five secret rays." Their momentum can be used to develop the bands of the secret rays in the Causal Body of man and to magnetize the flaming potential of the White Fire Core of each atom of being.

The Angelic Kingdom

Serving on the pink plume of God's love and representing the third person of the Trinity are the angelic hosts of light—agents of the Holy Spirit—to whom was given the holy ordination of ministering to the needs of both men and elementals. Under the direction of the Archangels and their divine complements, called Archeiai, the angels respond instantaneously to the decrees of the Father-Mother God.

These transformers of God's love were designed to infuse the creation with the cohesive force of the Holy Spirit—the binding energy released in all creative action, which brings into focus the power of the spoken Word.

The angels were created out of Spirit's own essence to sustain the magnificent feelings of the Creator throughout the universe. Their assignment is to infuse men and elementals with the qualities necessary for planning and executing the will and wisdom of God in form: faith, hope and charity; peace, understanding and compassion; purity, comfort and healing; mercy, forgiveness and such praise of eternal life as would unite men and elementals in service to their Creator and in love to one another.

As messengers of God, the angelic hosts, the mighty Archangels, the cherubim and the seraphim descend on pinions of the sacred fire, bearing rainbow hues of joy, beauty and delight. Aureoles of the dawn, they portend the advent of the Christ in every man.

Their love and unfailing direction is a clarion call that integrates the lower self and the Higher Self in unity and purpose, in plan and action. Their love is a balm of friendship, an unguent of healing and the oil of heavenly inspiration. Their love is a divine magnet that keeps the stars on their appointed rounds, each Monad in his rightful place, and the atoms of our beings inclined to do the heavenly will. Their love is a sacred tone, the music of the spheres, the Spirit that animates nature and all things beautiful. It is their love that nurtures the sweet influences of the Pleiades, that strengthens the bands of Orion, that adorns Arcturus with his Sons.

The Kingdom of the Gods

When he bringeth in the firstbegotten into the world, he saith, And let all the angels of God worship him.

And of the angels he saith, Who maketh his angels spirits [referring to the angelic kingdom] and his ministers a flame of fire [referring to the elemental kingdom].

But unto the Son he saith, Thy throne, O God, is for ever and ever: a scepter of righteousness is the scepter of thy kingdom [referring to the kingdom of the Gods].

Thou hast loved righteousness, and hated iniquity; therefore God, even thy God, hath anointed thee with the oil of gladness above thy fellows.[46]

Representing the Christ, the second person of the Trinity, are the hierarchs of the kingdom of Ascended Masters, Cosmic Beings, and men becoming Gods. To the *man*ifestation of God destined to become cocreator with him was given the responsibility of overseeing the creation and of working with God to plan, to design, to invent and to direct.

Before man went forth from the center of God's Being, he asked, "Father, might I not be given the freedom to choose the way, the plan and the action of my life?" In his great heart of love, the Father knew what pain might come upon a creation that would be free to go against his will; but he also saw the great opportunity for expansion and rejoicing that would come to those who would choose to follow his plan.

And so, out of his infinite wisdom came the fiat: "Man shall have the gift of free will; and whosoever shall prove in thought and word and deed that he can choose wisely and well in all things, to him will I give glory and honor and power and dominion; he shall sit upon my right hand, and he shall preside over the kingdoms of heaven and earth (over the angelic and elemental kingdoms)."

Angelic ministrants and elemental servants of earth, air, fire and water accompanied man as he descended into form, trailing clouds of glory and vowing, "Lo, I AM come to do thy will, O God!"[47] During three golden ages man talked freely with his God and associated intimately with angels and elementals. Communion with all life was unrestrained, and cooperation among the three kingdoms was unspoiled.

Herein was the outpicturing, yet to be recaptured on this planet, of the plan of God for his creation. Man's portion was to become the Christ and to sustain on earth the illuminating radiance of God's Mind. The beings of the elements were to build the temple to grace his wisdom, stone on stone of measured will—the Architect's designs. The angelic hosts, inspired by the plan, were to bring to both man and nature coals of inspiration, still glowing from the Father's hearth.

To assist man in his responsibility, God created the hierarchical office of Chohan, the Lord or "Law," of the ray. As representatives of the Twelve Hierarchies of the Sun, the seven Chohans of our own planet are the chosen ones, divinely appointed by the cosmic hierarchy to serve under the Maha Chohan, the representative of the Holy Spirit. In his service each Chohan administers on behalf of mankind all of the qualitative aspects of his own specific ray, while harmonizing his administration with that of the Chohans of the other rays.

Thus, the Chohan of the First Ray administers to statesmen, leaders and organizers, whose activities come under the first ray of God's will, of God's power. The Chohan of the Second Ray of wisdom and illumination assists educators and all who strive to raise the cultural levels of the world.

Artists, designers, beauticians and all those of a creative nature serve under the Chohan of the Third Ray of love and beauty. Those who are dedicated to the purity and discipline of any undertaking serve with the Chohan of the Fourth Ray of ascendancy and purity.

The Chohan of the Fifth Ray of healing, truth, science and precipitation administers to doctors, scientists, healers, musicians, mathematicians and those consecrated to the abundant life.

Ministers, nurses and all who administer to mankind's needs assist the Chohan of the Sixth Ray of ministration and service. Diplomats, priests of the sacred fire, actors, writers and defenders of freedom serve with the Chohan of the Seventh Ray of freedom, transmutation and diplomacy.

The Chohans are selected from among the most qualified Ascended Beings who have arisen from earth's schoolroom. They are assisted in their task by legions of angels, elementals and other Ascended Brethren who carry out the plan of God for the most complete expression of the seven rays that is possible for the mankind of earth. The Chohans always obey Cosmic Law; yet they are given certain latitude, in keeping with their individual evolutions, capacities and endowments, to direct mankind in the most adroit manner, giving such loving assistance and spiritual direction as may be the requirement of the hour.

All of the offices of hierarchy come within the framework of one of these three categories of the sacred fire. All are necessary to precipitation, each one complementing the other. Man, "who was made a little lower than the angels" (having been given free will and the opportunity to descend into form), is thus "crowned with glory and honour"[48] as he overcomes the world and gains self-mastery through the correct use of his free will.

When man reaches a certain level of initiation, the hierarchy of Elohim and of Archangels must obey his commands. Like the Chohans, he is given legions of angels and of elemental builders of form who serve the office in hierarchy to which he has been appointed by qualification. Only to the Christed ones (to those who have attained the Christ consciousness) is given this power over the form and feeling aspects of the Godhead. It is the responsibility of hierarchy to train life's evolutions (the children of God) to rise in the order of hierarchy that they might be found worthy to be called God's sons and daughters. Having been found faithful servants, they are made rulers over the elemental and angelic kingdoms.

The LORD in his infinite love has also provided for the initiation of angels and elementals, that they too might rise in the order of hierarchy. Through centuries of allegiance to the Creator and unswerving devotion to his creation, angels may be given the sacred gift of free will and the opportunity to enter the portals of birth. Once they descend into form in this manner, angels begin evolving through the kingdom of the Gods, subject to the same tests, initiations and karmic laws that apply to the sons and daughters of God. When they have met all of these requirements, the angels may pass through the ritual of the ascension and may then qualify to fill the office of Archangel or Archeia for a system of worlds.

The elementals, too, may evolve through the kingdom of the Gods on their way to become directors of the elements and servants of the Elohim. This opportunity may be opened to them and to their complements after they have proved their ability to sustain simple and then more complex patterns in nature—first a drop of rain, then a blade of grass, a rose, a mighty oak, a giant redwood. They are then endowed with a threefold flame and serve under the disciplines of an Ascended Master before taking physical embodiment. While in embodiment, the elemental must progress through the same rituals and initiations outlined by the hierarchy for men and angels.

All of life (hence, all of God) is in the process of ascending when it follows the divinely natural process of spiritual evolution. It is, therefore, through the ascension that angels, elementals and men find their way back to the heart of God and the eternal life they knew before the morning stars sang together.

Fount of Power: The Sacred Manus

> *Blessing, and honour, and glory, and power, be unto him that sitteth upon the throne, and unto the Lamb for ever and ever.*[49]

Emissaries of the will of God on behalf of billions of souls, beholders of perfection, hovering flames of comfort and Truth rocking the cradle of life, the sacred Manus come to nurture a planet gone astray and lifestreams whose blessed feet have never touched the earth. Arbiters of our destiny, these blessed keepers of the flame will not forsake their trust until every man, woman and child is ascended.

Everyone who comes forth from the heart of God is placed in the charge of a cosmic mother and father. In addition to being under the watchful eye of the sun god and goddess of the solar system, we are all part of a family—a unit of hierarchy called a mandala—sent to externalize a perfect plan of God. This mandala is as detailed as a flower or a tree and includes billions of facets, each one a Spirit-spark reflecting a slightly different aspect of the Mind of God, enhancing the facets of his neighbors.

The Manu guardians of our "race family" act as our Father and our Mother. Tenderly caressing each individual God Flame, they blend our talents like the petals of a lily, showing us through brotherly love how to magnify the virtues of the Christ in one another.

The office of the Manu is held by twin flames representing the Father-Mother God for an entire lifewave, called a root race. In every system of worlds and on every planet where life is evolving, seven root races come forth to fulfill their divine plan in seven fourteen-thousand-year dispensations, usually succeeding one another so that only one root race occupies the planet during a given dispensation.

According to the divine plan, twin flames are given the opportunity to exercise free will through fourteen cycles of incarnation—seven masculine and seven feminine. That is, the one who incarnates under the masculine polarity of the Causal Body first as male will pass through seven incarnations in a male body, and seven incarnations in a female body. Ultimately the soul who began as the male ascends as the female, and vice versa.

On the earth, the first three root races (representing the first, second and third rays) came forth, fulfilled their divine plan and returned to the heart of God through the ritual of the ascension. The remaining fourth, fifth, sixth and seventh root races that are to complete their evolution here are under the sponsorship of the following Manus: the fourth root race, Lord Himalaya and his twin flame (whose focus is in the Himalayas); the fifth root race, Lord Vaivasvata and his twin flame (whose focus is also in the Himalayas); the sixth root race, the God and Goddess Meru (whose focus is centered over the Island of the Sun in Lake Titicaca, Peru); and the seventh root race, the Great Divine Director and his twin flame (whose focuses are in the retreat of the House of Rakoczy, Transylvania, and the Cave of Light in India).

These root races are evolving on the fourth, fifth, sixth and seventh rays respectively. Within each root race are seven sub-root races, each of these serving on one of the seven rays within the main ray.

The focus of the masculine ray of the Godhead for the earth is held in the retreat of Lord Himalaya, and the focus of the feminine ray is held in the retreat of the God and Goddess Meru.

Coming forth into embodiment with their root races, the Manus serve as world teachers to establish the archetypal pattern of the Christ for the race. The Manus usually ascend when their children have completed their rounds in embodiment. Hence, the Manus of the first three root races are engaged in cosmic service with the ascended evolutions of their cosmic family.

Because the fourth and fifth root races have tarried on earth longer than intended (due to the infiltration of Luciferians and laggard evolutions from other planets), the Lords Himalaya and Vaivasvata have taken their ascension. Their divine complements remain in embodiment to anchor their twin flames in form. The twin flame of the Great Divine Director, who is sponsoring the incoming seventh root race from higher octaves, remains unascended, holding the focus for the golden-age culture from her home in Europe. The God and Goddess Meru have both chosen to ascend prior to the evolutions of their root race, preferring to serve them from the ascended state.

Fount of Wisdom: Lord of the World
Planetary Buddha
World Teacher

> *With thee is the fountain of life: in thy light shall we see light.*[50]

The hierarchical office of Lord of the World is vested with the highest authority of the Godhead on behalf of a planet and its evolutions. Upon the recommendation of the Lords of Karma, the one who holds this office is selected by the Solar Logoi from among those who have passed the Buddhic initiations and qualified under the laws of hierarchy as the most advanced initiates on a particular world.

The Lord of the World receives the divine blueprint for the world from the planetary Silent Watcher and guards the three-fold flame on behalf of angels, elementals and men, serving to externalize the flame of the Christ in the planes of Spirit and Matter. He also focuses all of the planes of God's consciousness, including those of the five secret rays. Having mastery in both the inner planes (the planes of the five secret or passive rays) and the outer planes (the planes of the seven color or active rays) of the Great Causal Body, he holds the balance of peace in the four lower bodies of the planet.

Sanat Kumara, hierarch of Venus, kept the flame as Lord of the World for thousands of years. (Sri Magra, now in cosmic service, held the office of Lord of the World prior to Sanat Kumara.) Known as the Ancient of Days,[51] Sanat Kumara volunteered to hold the balance of light for the earth at a time when cosmic councils had voted for its dissolution because humanity was not contributing enough light to warrant its existence in the solar system.

When Sanat Kumara came from Venus to make the earth his temporary home, he was accompanied by a retinue of many great beings of light, including his daughter (the Lady Master Meta) and three of the Seven Holy Kumaras (Lords of Flame who represent the seven rays on Venus). They established the retreat known as Shamballa on an island in the sea where the Gobi ("Go be") Desert is today. Now the retreat of Gautama Buddha, Shamballa is the focus where the Lord of the World, assisted by the four hierarchs of the elements, holds the balance of the threefold flame on behalf of the earth.

In a ceremony held in the Royal Teton Retreat on January 1, 1956, Lord Gautama Buddha was anointed by God to serve the evolutions of earth in the office of Lord of the World. He assumed this position from his teacher, Sanat Kumara. The hierarch of Venus was then awarded the honorary title of Regent Lord of the World.

Gautama sustains an individual light-tie (a thread of light) from his heart flame to the heart of every lifestream evolving upon earth, whether in or out of embodiment. This tie is not withdrawn until the lifestream ascends or goes through the second death.

Lord Gautama is a native of Venus, but he has served the people of this planet through many embodiments. During the Lemurian epoch he experienced great illumination. Reembodied in northern India in about 563 B.C. as Prince Siddhartha, he became convinced at an early age of the futility of worldly life and sought earnestly for a higher way.

Relinquishing his earthly kingdom and severing all human ties, he raised the cup of his consciousness until he became one with his own God Source. Merging with divine Truth, he passed initiations leading to his attainment of nirvana and the Buddhic level of God Self-awareness. Returning to the human form transfigured, he came to be known among his people as Buddha—that is, "Enlightened One." He remained in his physical body and became the Teacher of teachers, expounding the Middle Way that had been revealed to him as the Eightfold Path of attainment.

Gautama passed through the ritual of the ascension in the month of May at the close of that embodiment and remained in the planes of nirvana until he returned to active service in answer to the calls of his followers.

Each year in May on a plateau on the northern slope of the Himalayas, the Wesak festival is held to commemorate Lord Gautama's birth, his attainment of Buddhahood and his ascension in the light. At that time the radiation of the Buddha is anchored in the world of form through his Electronic Presence, which is both seen and felt by many pilgrims who gather for the ceremony.

Lord Gautama has twelve initiates serving under him, nine of whom have recently elected to embody to serve mankind at the unascended level and to set the example of the Buddhic consciousness that all are destined one day to attain. The remaining three Buddhas are Ascended Masters.

One of these three, Lord Maitreya, serves directly under Lord Gautama in the position of Cosmic Christ and Planetary Buddha. The responsibility of the office of Planetary Buddha includes keeping the flame of the Cosmic Christ on behalf of the lifewaves of the planet.

A native of Venus, Lord Maitreya succeeded Lord Gautama in the office of Planetary Buddha in the January 1956 ceremony. These two initiates of the sacred fire were the first to respond to the call of Sanat Kumara to come out and be separate from worldly spirals and to keep the flame of the Christ. A close and long associate of Lord Gautama, Lord Maitreya was also a chela of Lord Himalaya. Lord Maitreya now has his own focus of illumination in the Himalayas.

As Cosmic Christ and Planetary Buddha, Lord Maitreya oversees the office of World Teacher, presently held jointly by Jesus and Kuthumi. The three, together with Gautama and others serving the wisdom ray, bring to mankind—no matter what the level of their Christ Self-awareness—the understanding of how each one might live the life of the Christ through the practical application of the laws of God.

It is the responsibility of the World Teacher to bring to the outer consciousness of embodied mankind the knowledge of the indwelling Spirit of God and of the Christ Self, the very personal presence of the Christ within each one, fashioned in the image of the only begotten Son of God, the archetypal pattern for all of his sons and daughters.

Every two-thousand-year cycle is under one of the seven rays. During each period the hierarchy instructs humanity to attain the Christ consciousness under the corresponding ray. Moses focused the emphasis of the fifth dispensation under his guru, a great Cosmic Being.

As the fifth dispensation was drawing to a close, a survey was made at inner levels to determine the requirements for mankind's evolution during the next two-thousand-year cycle. Jesus became the Christ incarnate for the sixth dispensation, which drew to a close in the mid-twentieth century. (Saint Germain is presently guiding humanity under the seventh dispensation.)

At inner levels the World Teacher outlines the spiritual instruction to be given to humanity for each two-thousand-year cycle. Acting through readied and willing instruments, he releases the teachings of the Christ at every educational level and in all fields of human endeavor, sponsoring the divine plan for a golden-age culture.

Jesus assumed the position of World Teacher after serving as Chohan of the Sixth Ray. A native of Venus, he came to the earth as an advocate and guardian of the divine principle in man. Throughout his many embodiments—including those as Abel, Joseph the son of Jacob, Joshua, David and Elisha—Jesus was prepared by God under the tutelage of Lord Maitreya for his final embodiment of service.

Born almost karma-free, Jesus as a small child felt the overshadowing presence of Lord Maitreya and knew, even then, that "I and my Father are one." [52] His years between the ages of twelve and thirty were spent in research and application of the sacred mysteries in Egypt and the Far East.

Jesus' three-year ministry of teaching, healing and demonstrating the science of precipitation was accomplished through his oneness with his own God-reality and his mastery of the Christ consciousness, manifest in a perfectly balanced threefold flame. Thus he became the example for the age of what is required of every son and daughter of God. He proved what can be done when the son, beholding his own I AM Presence, affirms, "Not my will, but thine, be done." [53]

Jesus recounts for us one of his earliest experiences in hierarchy, when God showed him the flowers below and the stars above as hopeful expressions of the Most High:

"Consider the flowers of the field as I recount for you a tale of my own Galilean embodiment. It was at the age of seventeen that one eventide I passed into a certain field. It was moonless, and the stars shone their splendor above.

"I was alone with God, and around me the grass commingled with myriad daisylike flowers whose upturned faces seemed to take hope from my gaze. . . . And in my buoyancy of heart and blitheness of spirit—feeling the dew upon my feet, which were bare upon the grass, and smelling the odor and scent of joy in the floral release—I communed with God and sent my love to the flowers below my feet.

"Suddenly they were transformed, and I saw them no more as flowers but as the faces of men. I saw them as though they were shining with hope, and they became majestic—tiny, but majestic. I mused and meditated upon them and I spake unto my Father—unto my God and unto your God—and I said, 'Can I raise them up? Can I give them the hope of a greater magnitude?'

"The Father spake unto me and said, 'Come see ye.' And suddenly I was transported beyond that field, and the cosmos was before me. My feet were placed as upon a rock in outer space, and all around me I saw the stars that they did shine— worlds of hope and worlds without.

"And I felt as though I were a shepherd of planetary significance and as though each face of the flowers that had been below me in the field were indeed now a planet—teeming with multitudes of people and requiring the hope and the release of God's energy that came through me then in that experience.

"I was transformed. I was electrified! My soul did rejoice and as David of old, I sang a hymn unto God. And I said in the quietness of my youth: 'O God, thy majesty is great to behold. In the numberless luminous orbs of the heavens are the sheep of thy pasture and the flowers of thy sky—immortelles, shining ones full of hope, believing in thy grace and wondrous loveliness. How can any, then, ever cease to believe in thy greatness?'

"And I mused upon Abraham of old—I, who was of the

seed of David, mused upon Abraham and his faith. And I recalled, then, in my thoughts how that God had spake unto him saying, 'I shall make thy seed as the sand beside the sea, innumerable. I am the LORD thy God that made the heavens and the earth, and I shall make thy seed as the stars innumerable and without number.'[54] And my heart was glad and I did rejoice.

"I found myself after this experience wandering in the pasture and upon the meadow there. And for a moment I was dazed at the experience and I reeled as one drunken. Then out of the soft folds of the night stepped beloved Holy Amethyst, and she enfolded me in the love of Lord Zadkiel and her own. And I knew her comfort then for the first time in that embodiment. And the angels became nearer and dearer to me as the years passed and I communed with them as with men."[55]

Serving with Jesus in the office of World Teacher is the Ascended Master Kuthumi, who presides over the Cathedral of Nature at Kashmir. In his focus at Shigatse he plays upon his majestic organ—keyed to the grand organ in the City Foursquare —chords that magnetize the harmony of the Great Central Sun Magnet. These chords repolarize the four lower bodies of mankind to the blueprint of their divine plan, thereby healing body, mind and soul of the impositions of mortal density.

In his embodiments as Pythagoras, Balthazar (one of the three wise men), Saint Francis of Assisi and Shah Jahan (ruler of the Mogul Empire in India and builder of the Taj Mahal), Kuthumi contributed the momentum of his adoration of the Christ to bringing forth the illumination, peace, beauty and love exemplified in the second person of the Trinity. In his final embodiment as Koot Hoomi Lal Singh, he assisted El Morya in anchoring the knowledge of the Great White Brotherhood into the Western consciousness through the Theosophical Society.

After his ascension in the latter part of the nineteenth

century, Kuthumi served as Chohan of the Second Ray. (He was replaced as Chohan by Lord Lanto in 1958.) In 1956 Kuthumi was appointed to assist the Master Jesus in the office of World Teacher during the crucial period of transition before the golden age.

Fount of Purity: The Holy Spirit

What? Know ye not that your body is the temple of the Holy Ghost which is in you, which ye have of God, and ye are not your own?[56]

The responsibility of the office of Maha Chohan ("Great Lord") is given to the one most qualified to represent the flame of the Holy Spirit on behalf of the evolutions of a planet. Maintaining the focus of the Great Central Sun Magnet, the Maha Chohan serves as the instrument of God to infuse the nature kingdom with the sacred fire breath (prana), the quintessence of the Father-Mother principle necessary to sustain life in the four lower bodies of a planet and its embodied evolutions.

The one presently holding this office for the earth was embodied as the blind poet Homer. In his retreat in Ceylon he enshrines the flame of the Holy Spirit (white) and the comfort flame (white tinged with pink, with gold at its base).

The Holy Spirit is the Comforter of whom Jesus spoke to his disciples: "But when the Comforter is come, whom I will send unto you from the Father, even the Spirit of Truth, which proceedeth from the Father, he shall testify of me.... It is expedient for you that I go away: for if I go not away, the Comforter will not come unto you; but if I depart, I will send him unto you."[57]

The ritual of the return whereby the son reunites with the Father in the ascension (or the electron with the proton) is necessary in order for the light of Alpha and Omega to be released in form. When the fusion of the first and second persons of the Trinity is accomplished, the power of the Spirit of God is released through the third person. Until this ritual is completed, the Spirit is not forthcoming: "If I go not away, the Comforter will not come unto you."

In the ritual of baptism, it is the twin flames of the Holy Spirit, the essence of the Father-Mother God, that infuses the supplicant with the energies required for the fulfillment of the individual divine plan of Christ-attainment in the world of form. This fire of the Holy Spirit is communicative of the highest good from the Center of Being to the periphery. It sets the matrix for the whole man to be made whole.

The office of Maha Chohan oversees the Chohans of the Seven Rays, the seven sons of the Holy Spirit. The seven color rays focused by the Chohans merge in the intensity of the dazzling white light of the Holy Spirit, represented by the white dove and the cloven tongues of fire—the twin-ray action of the Spirit Most Holy of the Father-Mother God. The activity of this office is therefore not confined to any one of the rays but reigns supreme over all. Through the prism of the consciousness of the Holy Spirit, all can find their specific ray of service, which leads to mastery on all the rays and to the attainment of the Christ consciousness.

Fount of Love: The World Mother

> *And there appeared a great wonder in heaven; a woman clothed with the sun, and the moon under her feet, and upon her head a crown of twelve stars.*[58]

Omega—Mother of eternal cycles, ensouling the feminine ray throughout cosmos, enshrining the Motherhood of God!

Mater of Macrocosmic wonder, how beautiful thy virgin consciousness! How delightful thy Divine Manchild! How sacred thy crystal fire mist adorning the Father of eternal being! Thy strength is the structure of the universe, the fragility of a robin's egg in spring, the might of an ocean wave, of summer rain and thunder echoing in the hills.

Every soul, every heart flame descending into Matter is wrapped in the swaddling garments of thy love. As thou, O Mother, art the instrument of the Father's love, our four lower bodies, which thou hast made, complement his Spirit who dwelleth in us. Fashioned of the dust, our destiny is thine. Mingling with the elements, we merge with Spirit and transcend time. Nestled in the heart of earth, we know the comfort of life. Whatever our awareness, you teach us to know him, the only begotten Son who is our reality made clear. In the stars above and below the firmament, we see his face appear. But most of all, within our hearts—fashioned of thine own—we see him there a perfect rose.

All who embody in feminine form and all Ascended Lady Masters keep the flame on behalf of the World Mother. The fires of her heart are theirs, and they carry coals of her love to warm the hearths of children, angels and elementals.

The highest representative of the masculine ray of God on earth is he who holds the office of Lord of the World, who must have attained the fullness of the Buddhic enlightenment on the path of initiation. The highest representative of the feminine ray on earth is she who attains to the office of Mother of the World, or the World Mother.

The one selected by the Lords of Karma and the Lord of the World as the representative of the World Mother to the earth wears the crown of the World Mother—a crown of twelve stars—and holds her scepter of authority, keeping the flame of the immaculate concept on behalf of all evolving upon the earth.

The office of Mother of the Flame is held by an unascended member of hierarchy, selected from among the most highly evolved women devotees of the World Mother. She holds a life tenure unless removed for failure or incompetence.

In this age, the flame and the womb—the cosmic fire and matrix—of the World Mother are undergoing tremendous opposition from the forces of evil that have arrayed themselves against the feminine aspect of God who bears the Divine Manchild, the image most holy of his offspring.

Jesus revealed to John the travail of the woman that would come in the last days before the coming of the kingdom of God upon earth. In the twelfth chapter of the Revelation of John is a description of the archetypal pattern of the Divine Mother and the Christ Child.

Every woman bears the burden of this office. And every son and daughter of God is the remnant of her seed, who must fight the dragon of the carnal mind[59] that makes war against the Christ.

> *And there appeared a great wonder in heaven; a woman clothed with the sun, and the moon under her feet, and upon her head a crown of twelve stars:*
>
> *And she being with child cried, travailing in birth, and pained to be delivered.*
>
> *And there appeared another wonder in heaven; and behold a great red dragon, having seven heads and ten horns, and seven crowns upon his heads.*
>
> *And his tail drew the third part of the stars of heaven, and did cast them to the earth: and the dragon stood before the woman which was ready to be delivered, for to devour her child as soon as it was born.*
>
> *And she brought forth a man child, who was to rule all nations with a rod of iron: and her child was*

caught up unto God, and to his throne.

And the woman fled into the wilderness, where she hath a place prepared of God, that they should feed her there a thousand two hundred and threescore days.

And there was war in heaven: Michael and his angels fought against the dragon; and the dragon fought and his angels,

And prevailed not; neither was their place found any more in heaven.

And the great dragon was cast out, that old serpent, called the Devil, and Satan, which deceiveth the whole world: he was cast out into the earth, and his angels were cast out with him. . . .

And when the dragon saw that he was cast unto the earth, he persecuted the woman which brought forth the man child.

And to the woman were given two wings of a great eagle, that she might fly into the wilderness, into her place, where she is nourished for a time, and times, and half a time, from the face of the serpent.

And the serpent cast out of his mouth water as a flood after the woman, that he might cause her to be carried away of the flood.

And the earth helped the woman, and the earth opened her mouth, and swallowed up the flood which the dragon cast out of his mouth.

And the dragon was wroth with the woman, and went to make war with the remnant of her seed, which keep the commandments of God, and have the testimony of Jesus Christ.[60]

Fount of Authority: Gods and Goddesses

I have said, Ye are gods; and all of you are children of the most High.[61]

The authority for the 144,000 virtues that blossom from the twelve godly attributes is ensouled by Cosmic Beings who have devoted themselves to the externalization of these virtues in the planes of Spirit and Matter.

All of God's children, having been given the gift of free will, have the opportunity to consecrate their energies to the ray and to the flame of their calling and election. They then have the opportunity to magnify an aspect of the spark until it becomes first a whirlwind, then a miniature sun, and finally an orb of cosmic dimension—a veritable lodestone of virtue, a fount of authority from which all who hunger and thirst after righteousness may drink and be filled.

Archangel Michael expounds upon this mystery: "I AM an Archangel, and I deal with the passions and feelings of Gods and men. When I speak of 'Gods,' I trust you will understand that there is but one LORD. 'Hear, O Israel: The LORD our God is one LORD!'[62] remains the fiat of the ages.

"But there are many sons and daughters who have begun to exhibit that self-mastery and cosmic control which lead to higher initiation and engagement in the eternal track of universal certitude. They have become, as it were, Gods in their own domain. These, too, must be reckoned with—these Cosmic Beings, Ascended Masters, angels, Archangels and Mighty Elohim—for they have become cocreators with him by virtue of the godlike qualities they have externalized.

"Finite man seldom thinks on such as these—servant Sons who have risen in the cosmic peerage to adorn the heavens with his expanding love. And this is the meaning of the statement 'Ye are Gods!'[63] cited by Jesus, who had the courage to preach the cosmic truth that every manifestation of God has the opportunity of becoming godlike, even as the Father is in them and they are in him.

"The faith of mortals is usually centered on this one or that one among their contemporaries, for whom they have changing esteem or contempt. What a pity! For all men are becoming, all men are evolving—even when the forward movement can only be measured in inches. Let men learn, then, to have faith in the potential of their own evolvement, and let them accord the same to others. For the arc of God stretches across the heavens and reaches the life of each individual according to his capacity to receive."[64]

As it is written in the Book of Psalms, so the LORD pronounces the authority of those who have magnetized a solar momentum of light's virtue: "I have said, Ye are gods; and all of you are children of the Most High."[65]

Being awarded the title of God or Goddess is a sacred trust, a cosmic honor and a universal responsibility. It means that through invocation of the sacred fire in the white fire core of the flame, a son of God has drawn to his aura a light of solar magnitude enabling him to merge with that flame in the heart of the Great Central Sun and still retain his immortal identity.

And so a God is born in the flame of eternal being. Thus the Almighty honors a portion of himself. Can we do aught else—we who, following in their cosmic footsteps, are beckoned to come up higher because they have risen?

These Cosmic Beings, so dedicated to the fulfillment of the Christ in all, extend to embodied souls the waters of eternal life flowing from their fountains of living flame. Vendors of the Spirit, they cry, "Ho, every one that thirsteth, come ye to the waters, and he that hath no money; come ye, buy, and eat; yea, come, buy wine and milk without money and without price."[66]

Fount of Opportunity: The Lords of Karma

Be not deceived; God is not mocked: for whatsoever a man soweth, that shall he also reap.[67]

In addition to the offices we have discussed, there are several hierarchical positions held by groups of Ascended Masters. Some of these are almost of the nature of ad hoc committees—committees set up to meet a particular need and dissolved as that need is fulfilled. Others are of a permanent nature; among these are the Darjeeling and Indian Councils of the Great White Brotherhood, and the Council of the Royal Teton. But the most important to the evolutions of earth is the Karmic Board.

The Karmic Board is appointed as the Supreme Court of Opportunity. The open portal to unity with God, which the eight-member board guards on behalf of the evolutions of this solar system, provides the means for mankind's liberation from the web of their own karma.

Out of his great mercy, God has anointed these beings to act as Mediators between the perfection of the Law and the imperfection of those who have departed from the state of grace. The Karmic Board serves, then, at the level of the Christ Self of mankind, daily weighing the balance of mankind's use of energy Above and below.

Just as the Supreme Court of the United States rules upon the constitutionality of the laws enacted by the legislative branch of the federal government, so the Karmic Board upholds through its rulings and dispensations those laws that are inherent within the framework of Cosmic Law. Receiving petitions and appeals from both ascended and unascended beings, this august body carefully considers each case placed before it in the light of world need and individual karma.

So merciful are the judgments of these Lords of Life that

their decisions often give the impression of an absence of justice to those who do not have access to the total record. Perhaps the actions of a particular man deserve no mercy at all, in the eyes of his peers. But the Lords of Karma, who check the records of his past lives, may find mitigating circumstances—grave injustices practiced against him by individuals and society—that cause them to grant him a renewed opportunity to find Christ rather than mete out a burden of karmic return that he could not carry. At a later date when he is strengthened in Christ, he must by Cosmic Law bear the full weight of his karma. Thus opportunity, the keynote of life, is reflected in the judgments of the Lords of Karma.

Kuan Yin, who occupies the position of Goddess of Mercy on the Karmic Board, relates an instance when the Goddess of Liberty pled for mercy on behalf of one soul: "I recall a case of a very young man who is presently in physical embodiment who mercilessly lashed his own brother in a previous embodiment with a whip—until he maimed him to such a degree that the child could never walk again. According to the great Cosmic Law it was decreed that this young man should enter life without limbs. The Goddess of Liberty herself stood and addressed the entire Board and pleaded for this young man as though he were her own son. And so he was born with limbs that were useless. Although he did not have the power, he was not deformed in appearance. I cite this example to you as touching upon the magnanimity of spiritual beings, which is little recognized by mankind."[68]

Whenever the Karmic Board issues an edict, the directors of the elements immediately translate and enact it throughout the natural order. For there exists between the Lords of Karma and the elemental kingdom a network of instantaneous communication whereby the Divine Will is implemented.

Changes in climatic conditions (as well as storm, flood,

fire, tornado and cataclysm) are brought about as the result of man's misuse of the creative power of the Holy Spirit. Through these periodic disturbances in nature, when Atlas shrugs off human discord, the balance of the four elements is restored and the four lower bodies of the planet are purified and realigned.

The Lords of Karma always decide in favor of the expansion of the Christ Flame in the individual and the world. Only after mankind fail repeatedly over a prolonged period to take advantage of spiritual opportunity do these Lords take stern measures to rebuke a recalcitrant lifestream or an entire generation.

This was the case when the continents of Lemuria and Atlantis sank. For cataclysm is the means whereby the evil patterns inherent within a decadent civilization are broken. Then hierarchy may begin anew to build a godly society where the children of the light can be given the true teachings of the Christ and the Law.

Fount of Freedom:
The Fourteen Ascended Masters
Who Govern the Destiny of America

> *Stand fast therefore in the liberty wherewith Christ hath made us free, and be not entangled again with the yoke of bondage.*[69]

The Fourteen Ascended Masters Who Govern the Destiny of America are great beings of light from the God Star Sirius, which is the seat of God-government in this galaxy. These Masters have been appointed by God to direct the course of the United States of America and to assist in the establishment of God-government in America.

For, as the Spirit of Freedom in these Fourteen Ascended

Masters says, "the victory of America is not the victory of a nation. It is the victory of the Twelve Hierarchies of the Sun in the twelve tribes of Israel who have come forth from every nation to dip into the flame, and who shall return to every nation to ignite the flame. They shall be unto all people the carriers of the fires of freedom.

"Let the runners in the race then hear the cry of the Fourteen Ascended Masters. Ours is a cry for freedom throughout the land of Terra. Ours is a cry for the Divine Mother. Ours is a cry of liberation for the souls of humanity."[70]

More than fifty thousand years ago, in a fertile country where the Sahara Desert now is, Saint Germain worked with fourteen Ascended Masters who guided the government and culture. The Messenger Guy Ballard, under the pen name Godfre Ray King, recorded the story of this civilization in his book *Unveiled Mysteries.*

Saint Germain ruled this civilization with supreme justice and wisdom. The majority of his subjects retained full, conscious use of God's wisdom and power. They possessed abilities that today would seem superhuman or miraculous. This civilization was filled with great peace, happiness and prosperity. The empire reached a height of beauty, symmetry and perfection unexceeded in the physical octave. For hundreds of years, this perfection was maintained without army or navy of any kind.

Two of the Ascended Masters serving with Saint Germain worked on each of the seven rays. Under these fourteen Ascended Masters were fourteen lesser Masters, who formed the heads of seven departments controlling the activities of science, industry and art.

Saint Germain showed Guy Ballard the record of the decline of that civilization. The beginning of the end came when a portion of the people became more interested in the temporary pleasures of the senses than in the larger creative plan of the Great God Self. Those governing realized they must withdraw and let the people learn through hard experience that all their happiness and good had come from adoration of the God within—and that they must again adore and serve the light if they were to be happy.

A cosmic council instructed the ruler that he must leave his empire and his people. The king and his children withdrew seven days later. A foreign prince arrived the next day and took over without opposition. Two thousand years later, as a result of the discord and selfishness of the once-great people who had lived there, most of the empire had become barren land.[71]

How can America and all nations avoid the same fate? The Fourteen Ascended Masters Who Govern the Destiny of America tell us:

"We place before you the challenge, the challenge that you know, yet it must be so stated. It must be so written. And you must be so notified by the Cosmic Council that you have full awareness of that which Saint Germain himself has referred to as 'the realm of the possible.'[72]

"If we are to direct the course of this nation as we were appointed by God to do, then we must have in place those individuals who have attunement with the Mind of God, who are humble and will obey the inner calling and the direction.

"At this date on planet earth we find entrenched in all nations, midst all peoples and, sadly, in the houses of worship and in organized religion those archdeceivers and fallen ones, the godless in whom there is no spark of life, for they have long ago extinguished it by their denial of the living God.

"Those who direct and make decisions in positions of power in every nation neglect to do and to be what to the people is obvious. This must cease! ...

"Thus we call upon you who have built the lifeline to the

Presence, who have strengthened your crystal cord, who have access to great beings of light through the call: Do not let the sun go down each day without imploring the Cosmic Virgin, your own blessed Mother, Mary, to let the right hand of her Son Jesus Christ descend upon those who utter the words of the defense of life and freedom and yet have betrayed every people who have stood for that freedom in this and all centuries....

"How are we to direct the course of this nation or any nation when you the people of light have allowed these fallen ones to remain in positions of power?[73]

"Saint Germain has said, 'Enough is enough! I have sponsored a nation. I have sponsored a people of God. And they have gone their ways and they have allowed themselves to be divided and they have not moved together in one fiery spirit to challenge the godless who take from them my dispensation of the age of Aquarius. Go, then, ye Fourteen Ascended Masters. Tell them! Tell them that they must galvanize a people, not according to political alliances but according to the alliance of Almighty God!'...

"Call upon the LORD, your Mighty I AM Presence, and he will descend into your temple with thunder and lightning and the rushing of a mighty wind! Call upon the Lord, your Holy Christ Self, and he will descend into your temple and you will be shining like that Son of God and your words will carry the authority of your personal Christhood.

"Do not deal, therefore, with this Evil by means of your human consciousness but always pray. Always seek the cosmic honor flame. Always be hid with Christ in God.[74]

"Call on the law of forgiveness daily for those things you know of and those things you know not of in yourself that may be an offense to your God or to your neighbor. Therefore each day receive forgiveness, absolution, and be one with the heart of Christ and therefore have the full protection of Archangel Michael. Be honest with your God. Be honest with yourself. Be honest with your Messenger! And come clean of 'all these things' and move forward with courage and no longer as cowards, slinking back into your old garments.

"We are determined to turn this nation around!"[75]

The Fourteen Ascended Masters caution us not to let down our guard: "Many things can change. And when they change for the worse and not for the better, that may mean a swift and sudden descent, a descent of energy, a descent of consciousness.

"Simply because things seem to be in a lull, do not believe it. Things can change quickly, and you may find yourselves much unprepared. See that you are as alert as any great patriot of old has been—alert as the watchman on the wall. Yes, you be that watchman. For I tell you it is necessary, for the nations are asleep. Those who plot evil and destruction, they do not sleep. The devil does not sleep. The fallen angels do not sleep.

"Now is not the hour to slouch. Now is not the hour to say, 'I have done my part. I will retire. I will go golfing. I will not be where I must be in that moment when the fire of the fallen ones is unleashed.'"[76]

The Fourteen Ascended Masters offer us their assistance, if we will only invoke it: "Do not treat us as though we were from distant stars and relatives who come now and then to visit! We are here! We will help you in answer to your call!

"Remember, when we hear those fiats so fiercely given, we respond. We call for reinforcements. And *you* have the victory. And the fallen ones are totally defeated. They have no power! They have no power! They have no power over you!

"Wherefore, call upon the Lord! Rise in his dominion! And remember that the Archangels do battle for you. Never enter in to a direct confrontation with aliens or fallen ones but turn them over in your decrees to the hosts of the LORD. This is the formula, beloved. It works.

"I ask you for the sake of all evolutions of this planet, make the formulas of the Great White Brotherhood work in your life every single day!"[77]

Fount of the Golden Age: Saint Germain

> *And the seventh angel sounded; and there were great voices in heaven, saying, The kingdoms of this world are become the kingdoms of our Lord, and of his Christ; and he shall reign for ever and ever.*[78]

Jewel in the heart of the lotused founts of hierarchy, central star in the crown of the LORD's rejoicing, keystone in the holy arch—"Saint Germain" is the new name that is written in the white stone, Saint Germain is the flame of the new order of the ages.

Holding the title of God of Freedom to this system of worlds, Saint Germain has stood for centuries as the defender of individual and world freedom.

On Atlantis he served in the Order of Lord Zadkiel as high priest in the Temple of Purification. Midst marble halls glistening white, surrounded by ancient pines whose branches blended with the winds of the Holy Spirit, his invocations sustained a pillar of fire, a fountain of violet singing flame that magnetized the great and the small who came from near and far to be set free from every binding condition of body, soul and mind.

Here gathered nature spirits and angel devas in praise of one whose love was ever the source of regenerative hope and joyous freedom to outpicture in the nature kingdom the geometric forms of Truth and Freedom, Mercy and Justice.

Prior to the sinking of Atlantis, while Noah was yet building his ark and warning the people of the great flood to come, Saint Germain, accompanied by a few faithful priests, transported the flame of freedom from the Temple of Purification to a place of safety in the Carpathian foothills in Transylvania. Here they carried on the sacred ritual of expanding the fires of freedom, even while mankind's karma was being exacted by divine decree.

In succeeding embodiments, under the guidance of his master and teacher, the Great Divine Director, Saint Germain and his followers rediscovered the flame and continued to guard the shrine. Later the Great Divine Director, assisted by his disciple, established a retreat at the site of the flame and founded the House of Rakoczy. This same flame, brilliant in its transmutative radiance like the color of cattleya orchids, has been focused in the etheric retreat of Archangel Zadkiel and Holy Amethyst above the island of Cuba since the early days of Atlantis.

As a child, when embodied as the prophet Samuel (meaning "his name is God"), Saint Germain heard the voice of God and responded, "Speak, Lord; for thy servant heareth." It is recorded that "Samuel grew, and the Lord was with him, and did let none of his words fall to the ground. And all Israel from Dan even to Beer-sheba knew that Samuel was established to be a prophet of the Lord."[79] Anointer of kings, oracle of the people, confidant of Saul and David, Samuel one day would be held affectionately in the hearts of a people sworn to a mighty union as "Uncle Sam."

Having assisted in laying the spiritual foundations of Israel, Saint Germain invoked the Christ Flame for the Christian dispensation when he was embodied as Joseph, protector of Jesus and Mary. Always close at hand when he was needed, he ever lent his strong arm in defense of mother and child.

At the turn of the fourth century, this holy brother laid down his life for Amphibalus, another devout Christian, and became the first martyr of England, later canonized as Saint Alban. As Merlin, "the wise old man," he assisted King Arthur (El Morya) in framing the holy order of the Knights of the Round Table and in establishing the quest for the Holy Grail, the cup from which our Lord drank at the Last Supper.[80]

When Saint Germain was embodied as Roger Bacon (c. 1220–1292), he authored *Opus Majus* and other well-known treatises on physics, chemistry and mathematics.

In the fifteenth century, Destiny smiled again upon the Son of Freedom. An arc from the flame in the retreat above Cuba leaped into the heart of the young man now embodied in the little town of Genoa as the relatively unknown sailor Christopher Columbus (1451–1506). Fate had sent out a line, and despite all obstacles, the captain of the *Santa Maria* was drawn to the shores of a new world.

In his embodiment as Christopher (meaning "lightbearer") Columbus, Saint Germain charted a path of freedom that millions were destined to follow. No wonder! For, sponsored by the Archangel and Archeia of the seventh ray at their retreat, he had practiced the sacred science of alchemy for centuries, both between and during his many embodiments. Thus, for Christopher Columbus, the New World was home port. Appropriately, angels of the sacred fire were on the island of San Salvador to welcome the three ships on that triumphant October 12 in 1492.

As Francis Bacon (1561–1626), Saint Germain was the *fils naturel* of Queen Elizabeth I and Lord Leicester, thus the rightful heir to the throne of England. He oversaw the translation of the King James version of the Bible and wrote *Novum Organum* and the Shakespearean plays, which contain in code many of the sacred mysteries of the Brotherhood, as well as the story of his life. After completing the work he had set out to do in that embodiment, he made his exit with his usual good humor by attending his own funeral in 1626. (The body in the coffin was not that of Francis Bacon.)

On May 1, 1684, Saint Germain accepted his immortal freedom, which he had espoused and won over a period of thousands of years by making (he says without exaggeration) two million right decisions. Thus Francis Bacon, hero of letters who through his writings has lived on in the hearts of millions, is truly immortal.

Saint Germain ascended from the Rakoczy Mansion in Transylvania, where he had been practicing spiritual alchemy since his departure from the world scene in 1626. The Ascended Master Saint Germain entered the Great Silence (nirvana). There his beloved twin flame Portia, whose name he had inscribed in *The Merchant of Venice,* had long been awaiting his return. (Portia is known as the Goddess of Justice or the Goddess of Opportunity, since justice is love's opportunity to right all wrong and balance life's energies.)

Not long thereafter, the beloved Sanctus Germanus ("Holy Brother") entered the cosmic service of freedom. He was given the dispensation by the Lords of Karma to function in the world of form as an Ascended Being, taking on the appearance of a physical body at will. Thus throughout the courts of eighteenth-century Europe he was known as Le Comte de Saint Germain.[81]

From 1710 to 1822, he appeared, disappeared and reappeared in and out of royal circles with his outstanding quality of realism in an age that was closing in upon itself by the weight of its own hypocrisy. Voltaire aptly described him in a letter to Frederick II of Prussia as "a man who never dies, and who knows everything." The archives of France contain evidence that English, Dutch and Prussian statesmen of his time regarded the count as an authority in many fields. He was hated by some, loved and held in awe by others. Yet historians have not understood Saint Germain's real mission: the carrying of the torch of freedom for the age.

His personal accomplishments as Le Comte de Saint Germain seem overwhelming by the standards of human achievement. He spoke French, German, English, Italian, Spanish, Portuguese and Russian, in addition to classical Greek, Latin, Sanskrit, Chinese and Arabic. He composed, improvised, accompanied on the piano without music and played the violin "like an orchestra." His compositions are in the British Museum and the library of the Castle of Raudnitz in Bohemia.

The count painted in oils with colors of gemlike brilliance that he himself discovered. He maintained an alchemical laboratory; he was an adept in precipitating and perfecting gems, transmuting base metals into gold, and discovering herbs and elixirs to prolong life and maintain health. To intimates he displayed powers bordering on the incomprehensible.

Many of his demonstrations of mastery are described in the diaries of Mme d'Adhémar, who knew him for at least half a century. She records Saint Germain's visits to her and to the courts of Louis XV and Louis XVI, noting his glowing countenance and appearance of a man in his early forties throughout the period. She mentions a personal conversation with the count in 1789 in which he appeared "with the same countenance as in 1760, while mine was covered with furrows and marks of decrepitude." In that conversation he predicted the Revolution of 1789, the fall of the House of Bourbon and the course of modern French history.

More important than the Master's spectacular feats, however, was the use to which he put his talents. As one of his friends said, "He was, perhaps, one of the greatest philosophers who ever lived. . . . His heart was concerned only with the happiness of others."

Saint Germain was an intimate of Louis XV, who gave him a suite at the Royal Chateau at Chambord. Introducing the science of modern diplomacy, Saint Germain carried out many secret diplomatic missions for the king to the courts of Europe. Had his counsels been heeded by Louis XVI, they would have prevented the French Revolution and saved the lives of many who were sacrificed at the guillotine.

Having failed to prevent the French Revolution, Saint Germain sought to establish a United States of Europe under Napoleon Bonaparte. But neither the crown, the nobility nor Le Petit Caporal caught the vision of the master plan. Reflecting upon this experience, the Master says:

"Long ago, individuals at the court of France thought to deceive me. They considered me to be a charlatan, but I fear that I have outlived them and their usefulness. For many of them who dwelled in positions of grandeur in the outer world of form are presently engaged in sweeping the streets of some of these larger cities. Thus the Law, coming full circle, has exacted from them the very demands that they placed upon those whom they thought to be inferior in their time."[82]

"Having failed in securing the attention of the court of France and others of the crowned heads of Europe, I turned myself to the perfectionment of mankind at large. And I recognized that there were many who, hungering and thirsting after righteousness, would indeed be filled with the concept of a perfect union that would inspire them to take dominion over the New World and create a union among the sovereign states.

"Thus the United States was born as a child of my heart, and the American Revolution was the means of bringing freedom in all of its glory into manifestation from the East unto the West."[83]

The United States has indeed prospered with the assistance of this Master. Ever behind the scenes to see that liberty should not perish from the earth, he broke the deadlock and inspired the early American patriots to sign the Declaration of Independence. It was he who shouted from the balcony of Independence Hall, "Sign that document!" He stood by General Washington through the long winter at Valley Forge. When it came time to dedicate a new nation, conceived in liberty, he assisted in the framing of the Constitution.

In the early 1930s Saint Germain contacted his "general in the field," the soul of George Washington reembodied as Guy Ballard, whom he trained as a Messenger for hierarchy. Under the pen name of Godfre Ray King was released the foundation of Saint Germain's instruction for the New Age in *Unveiled Mysteries, The Magic Presence* and *The "I AM" Discourses.*

During this period the Goddess of Justice and other Cosmic Beings came forth from the Great Silence to assist Saint Germain in bringing the teachings of the sacred fire to mankind to pave the way for the golden age. During the same period the Master undertook our training as Messengers. Subsequently we were called by El Morya, Chief of the Darjeeling Council, to establish The Summit Lighthouse as another open door for the release of Ascended Master instruction to mankind.

While serving in the world of form as Le Comte de Saint Germain, the Master assumed the office of Chohan of the Seventh Ray, which had been held by Kuan Yin, the Goddess of Mercy, for the previous two-thousand-year period.

Today, Saint Germain maintains a focus in the golden etheric city over the Sahara Desert, where he brought a great civilization to its height seventy thousand years ago. He is also the hierarch of the etheric retreat over the Rakoczy Mansion in Transylvania and of the Cave of Symbols, his focus in America. His electronic pattern is the Maltese cross; his fragrance, that of violets.

On May 1, 1954, Saint Germain and his twin flame,

Portia, were crowned the directors of the two-thousand-year cycle we are now entering, known as the seventh dispensation, which comes under the activities of the seventh ray. During this era mankind will be given the opportunity of mastering himself and his environment through the correct knowledge of the laws of true freedom and justice; the science of alchemy, of precipitation and transmutation; and the rituals of invocation to the sacred fire that can bring in an age of enlightenment and peace such as the world has never known.

Of Saint Germain it has been said by another Ascended Brother that no sooner is an idea conceived in the Mind of God than it is received in the heart of Saint Germain, so sweet is his rapport with Alpha and Omega and the Great Maxim Light. The blessed name of Saint Germain is known throughout cosmos. Down the grand highways of the Great Central Sun Galaxy and in the City of the Sun, this beloved Son of God is cherished by angels, Gods and Elohim.

O mankind, knowest thou not how privileged thou art to entertain one so loved in the courts of heaven—this holy one, this advocate of thy Christed being, sworn to defend the freedom of thy heart's desire! And thou who knowest not the name Sanctus Germanus, penned in the hearts of men with living flame: Be thou not forgetful to entertain strangers, for thereby some have entertained *this* angel unawares![84]

The Matrix Is the Key

"WHAT CHILD IS THIS? WHO IS this Holy One? Who is this dedicated son who has the sense of the invisible bond of hierarchy?

"Let such a one grasp the meaning of the 'thread of contact,' as Morya calls it. For this bond of hierarchy, this thread of contact, denotes the fragility of the divine experience when man is yet identified with and wedded to mortal form and consciousness."[85]

Having examined the structure of the atom, the universe and hierarchy, we see that man is like a hydrogen atom, one electron going forth from the nucleus of the I AM Presence. This electron is the human Monad, a son of flame coming forth from the Center of Being to release the full energy potential of the Christ in the world of form.

Hydrogen atoms travel in pairs, because the single electron in their shell, having either a plus or a minus spin, seeks its other half—its atomic counterpart, its twin flame. Infused with the fire breath of God, man becomes a living soul. In like manner, the combination of a hydrogen molecule with an oxygen atom—the essence of the Holy Spirit at this level of God's Self-awareness—becomes water, the basic ingredient of life.

What, then, is the difference between man (who himself is about two-thirds water) and the hydrogen atom when that atom gains dimension in combination with oxygen? Is man indeed a hydrogen atom having no conscious awareness in the world of form before the Spirit of God moves upon the gaseous nature of his soul? Is man patterned after the hydrogen atom? Or is the hydrogen atom patterned after man? Which, then, came first?

All life at every level of awareness is a combination of the four primary forces: earth, air, fire and water. Upon our planetary home, scientists have isolated many of the 144 elements—flame-virtues condensed as Matter, forming the platform for man's spiritual evolution from the form to the formless.

We asked the Masters, "Can the code of the elements and their magnificent combination in man and in nature be deciphered?" And they answered: "The law of the matrix governs the manifestation of man's being. The matrix is the key to his individualization in form. We can give you the law, but you must look within to discover its scientific application."

Looking within, we see that the physical body of man is the H_2O molecule in combination with many other atoms and molecules locked in a pattern or matrix. Without the pattern that the Father-Mother God has impressed upon the creation, the elements would go their separate ways. Witness what occurs when the Creator withdraws his matrix: death or dissolution. But governed by the matrix, they cling together as an organized whole, a unit of expression endowed by the Spirit with the Christ consciousness, nobly enshrined as a temple of the living God.

To better understand this key, let us examine the inner meaning of the word *matrix*. The first letter, *m*, intones the sacred name of the Mother principle, who energizes the matrix of that which comes forth from the formless into form. The cosmic womb is the matrix for all creation, which holds the manifold designs of the Creator's consciousness.

The second letter, *a,* stands for *atom,* meaning "*A*lpha *t*o *Om*ega." The atom is the nexus of contact whereby Spirit becomes Matter and Matter becomes Spirit, that point at which the Father-Mother God brings forth the creative energies of the Christ.

The third letter, *t,* is the symbol of the light of the Christ that comes forth from the heart of the atom in nuclear transformations. It is the symbol of man. It is Spirit perpendicular to Matter. It is also the design of the center of the universal sphere where our universe, as a cross section of God's consciousness, manifests the Spirit that infuses it with life.

The last three letters of *matrix* stand for the "*r*ay of the *I* in a*ct*ion."

In the word *matrix,* then, is the key that man will one day use to unlock the secrets of creation as it comes forth scientifically from the Mind of God. *Matrix:* the Mother aspect holding the matrix of the atom of the Christ, which oscillates between Alpha and Omega with the speed of light—the Christ coming forth as the ray of the I AM in action.

"What is man, that thou art mindful of him?"[86] Man is the most beautiful matrix that God could ever imagine, the matrix that was fashioned after his own image and likeness. Let each reader ask himself, "Who AM I that God is mindful of me?" He would do well to listen to the answer of the soul:

"I AM the whole-eye spirit in manifestation. I have come forth from the great center of Being. That point of light which is my identity, whom God called I AM, is a replica of the Great Central Sun, a whirling galaxy of energy unlimited, potential unrestrained.

"God has sent me forth from the Hub of Life to do his will in form. And because I AM a flaming spark of his identity, aligned with the matrix of his will, all power in heaven and earth is given unto me.[87] I AM free in the Ovoid of God's Mind. I whirl with the speed of light around the core of Being. I AM known because I know who I AM.

"God's laws are the foundation of my existence. His holy science is my reason for being; it is the essence of my life. My joy is in the discovery and application of God's laws; for I am endowed with the full mastery of the Christ, if I will but make his mastery my own.

"I am destined to become a cocreator with God once I have completed my round and returned to the Hub of Being. Therefore shall I use God's energies and the free will he has entrusted to my care to expand his universe, to bring forth beauty and culture, the children of his love, and every floral offering that I lay at the altar of my God.

"For has he not said unto us: 'My sons and daughters, it is not necessary for you to split the atom in order to release its power. You need only invoke in my name the power of the Holy Spirit to release the energies of the Logos locked in the heart of the nucleus. I AM your Father-Mother God. Unto you it is given to have and to hold the secrets of the universe.

"'Have you forgotten that right within your four lower bodies the matrix of your own I AM Presence and Causal Body is duplicated millions of times in every atom of your being? That flaming potential is yours to command in the name of the Almighty One.

"'For the song of the atoms is the song of my heart: I...AM, I...AM, I...AM. Their flames are droplets of Alpha and Omega, crystals of the diamond-shining Mind of God, ready and waiting to expand according to the matrix of your command. If you will only use that crystal fire mist in keeping with the law of love, standing in this place in time, you will unlock the mysteries of the universe.

" 'The sacred fire will adjust all resistance to my perfection through the action of atomic/karmic law. By the fire of the atom, you can heal worlds within and worlds without. Whether in your body, in the world body, in the blessed earth, or in the solar system, my love will mend the flaws—if you will but invoke the light that is locked within the heart of the atom by which I have endowed you with form and consciousness and life.

" 'There is no limit to the transformations that are possible unto you by the power of my Holy Spirit, now alive and brilliant, awaiting your command in every cell of your being. You are a God in the making, the most magnificent ideation of my heart, endowed with the love, wisdom and power of the creative flame.

" 'You can enter into the heart of any atom and feel at home, for it is a replica of that Great Hub from whence you came. Even while in the dimension of time and space, seemingly separated from the center of my Being by the orbit of the electrons and the cycles of their revolutions, you are nevertheless intimately one with the Father-Mother principle when you live in the heart of the atom.

" 'By the law of congruency you can control your environment and you can transcend the reaches of cosmos. By mentally simulating the atomic pattern and then becoming that pattern by the adjustment of your consciousness, you can walk through a garden wall, enter into the heart of a flower or journey to the depths of the sea. You can become all things, know all things and energize star clusters and systems of worlds without end.

" 'I AM thy God. Thou art in me, and I AM in thee. We are one through that point of contact, the "Alpha to Omega," formless form. When you understand the love of my voice, the Word that went forth in the beginning and echoes still within the chamber of the atom, you will experience a million miracles and in so doing bless the entire sphere of your consciousness.

" 'Then shall I hear prayers of men rising in the words of the Christ:

" ' "I cannot fail, because I AM thyself in action
      everywhere.
I ride with thee upon the mantle of the clouds.
I walk with thee upon the waves and crests of
      water's abundance.
I move with thee in the undulations of thy currents,
Passing over the thousands of hills composing
      earth's crust.
I AM alive with thee in each bush, flower and
      blade of grass.
All Nature sings in thee and me, for we are one.
I AM alive in the hearts of the downtrodden,
Raising them up.
I AM the Law exacting the truth of being
In the hearts of the proud,
Debasing the human creation therein and
Spurring the search for thy reality.
I AM all things of bliss
To all people of peace.
I AM the full facility of divine grace,
The spirit of holiness,
Releasing all hearts from bondage into unity.[88]" ' "

Notes

Introduction

1. John 10:9, 14, 27–29.

Chapter 1 · The Highest Yoga

Opening quotation: John 10:30.

1. Chananda, December 29, 1979.
2. Bhagavad Gita 8:3, in Swami Prabhavananda and Christopher Isherwood, trans., *The Song of God: Bhagavad-Gita* (New York: New American Library, 1972), p. 74.
3. Matt. 11:29–30.
4. For the story of Jesus' travels in the East, including translations of ancient texts, see Elizabeth Clare Prophet, *The Lost Years of Jesus* (Corwin Springs, Mont.: Summit University Press, 1987).
5. See Elizabeth Clare Prophet with Erin L. Prophet, *Reincarnation: The Missing Link in Christianity* (Corwin Springs, Mont.: Summit University Press, 1997).
6. Patanjali, Yoga Sutras 3:38, 51, in Swami Prabhavananda and Christopher Isherwood, trans., *How to Know God* (Hollywood, Calif.: Vedanta Press, 1981), pp. 188, 194.
7. Mark 4:1–11.
8. For an explanation of the Cosmic Clock, see Elizabeth Clare

Prophet, *The Great White Brotherhood in the Culture, History and Religion of America* (Corwin Springs, Mont.: Summit University Press, 1987), pp. 173–206.

9. Swami Nikhilananda, *Hinduism: Its Meaning for the Liberation of the Spirit* (London: Allen & Unwin, 1958), p. 121.

10. Ibid., pp. 124–25.

11. Ibid., pp. 125–26.

12. Ibid., pp. 126–27.

13. Juan Mascaro, trans., *The Bhagavad Gita* (New York: Penguin Books, 1962), p. 64.

14. Nikhilananda, *Hinduism,* pp. 109, 116.

15. Padma Sambhava, "God Is Just: All Will Receive Their Just Reward," *Pearls of Wisdom,* vol. 38, no. 36, August 20, 1995.

16. Mascaro, op. cit., pp. 115–16.

17. Swami Nikhilananda, trans., *The Upanishads,* 4th ed. (New York: Ramakrishna-Vivekananda Center, 1977), vol. 1, p. 143.

18. John 15:16.

19. Leto, April 15, 1976.

20. Alain Daniélou, *Yoga: Mastering the Secrets of Matter and the Universe* (Rochester, Vt.: Inner Traditions International, 1991), p. 31.

21. Patanjali, Yoga Sutra 2:47, in Prabhavananda and Isherwood, *How to Know God,* p. 161.

22. Patanjali, Yoga Sutra 2:49–50, in Prabhavananda and Isherwood, *How to Know God,* p. 162.

23. Patanjali, Yoga Sutra 1:39, in Prabhavananda and Isherwood, *How to Know God,* p. 76.

24. Patanjali, Yoga Sutra 1:41, in Prabhavananda and Isherwood, *How to Know God,* p. 79.

25. Shankara, quoted in Prabhavananda and Isherwood, *How to Know God,* p. 93.

26. See Daniel 3.

27. *Agni Yoga,* 5th ed. rev. (New York: Agni Yoga Society, 1980), pp. 100–102.

28. Deut. 4:24; Heb. 12:29.

29. The Hindus meditate upon Mother as the Goddess Kundalini, describing her as the white light, or the coiled serpent, that rises from the base of the spine to the crown, activating levels

of spiritual consciousness in each of the chakras through which the light passes along the way.

Some whose desire to raise the Kundalini fire is inordinate resort unwisely to a haphazard use of various forms of yoga or even illegal drugs. The raising of the Kundalini under the Ascended Masters' tutelage is not a sudden burst of fire, but a gentle rising of strength and consciousness.

The key to unlocking this energy of the Kundalini is adoration of the Mother Principle. The rosary is a safe and effective method of raising the Mother light by the fervent heat of love and adoration, without a violent eruption of energy. Mother Mary has given us the following Hail Mary for the New Age:

> Hail, Mary, full of grace.
> The Lord is with thee.
> Blessed art thou among women
> and blessed is the fruit of thy womb, Jesus.
> Holy Mary, Mother of God,
> Pray for us, sons and daughters of God,
> Now and at the hour of our victory
> Over sin, disease and death.

The cleansing of the aura and chakras with the violet flame also enables the Kundalini to rise gradually without danger. Saint Germain is the sponsoring master for the raising of the Kundalini energy.

30. *Heart* (New York: Agni Yoga Society, 1944), p. 244.

31. Ramakrishna, quoted in Prabhavananda and Isherwood, *How to Know God,* p. 158.

32. Bhagavad Gita 4:11, in Prabhavananda and Isherwood, *The Song of God,* p. 51.

33. Cyclopea, "The Personal Path of Christhood," *Pearls of Wisdom,* vol. 25, no. 40, October 3, 1982.

34. Rom. 8:17.

35. Djwal Kul, "The Sacred Fire Breath," *Pearls of Wisdom,* vol. 17, no. 42, October 20, 1974; also published in Kuthumi and Djwal Kul, *The Human Aura* (Corwin Springs, Mont.: Summit University Press, 1996), pp. 199–217.

36. Saint John Chrysostom, quoted in Prabhavananda and Isher-

wood, *How to Know God,* pp. 63–64.

37. *Prayers, Meditations, Dynamic Decrees for the Coming Revolution in Higher Consciousness* (Corwin Springs, Mont.: Summit University Press, 1984).

38. *Kuan Yin's Crystal Rosary: Devotions to the Divine Mother East and West* is a New Age ritual of hymns, prayers, and ancient Chinese mantras that invoke the merciful presence of Kuan Yin, Bodhisattva of Compassion, and of Mary, mother of Jesus. Includes a booklet and three audiocassettes that you may offer singly or in sequence. (Available from Summit University Press.)

39. Lanto, "The Essence of Higher Consciousness," in Mark L. Prophet and Elizabeth Clare Prophet, *Understanding Yourself,* revised ed. (Corwin Springs, Mont.: Summit University Press, 1999), pp. 23–24.

40. Job 3:25.

41. 1 Cor. 15:42–45. Lanto, "The Essence of Higher Consciousness," pp. 24–25.

42. Matt. 17:10–13.

43. Phil. 3:14.

44. El Morya, "Message to America on the Mission of Jesus Christ," *Pearls of Wisdom,* vol. 27, no. 47, September 23, 1984.

45. Prov. 14:12.

46. Saint Germain, "Dare to Do!" *Pearls of Wisdom,* vol. 5, no. 29, July 20, 1962; also published in Mark L. Prophet and Elizabeth Clare Prophet, *Saint Germain On Alchemy* (Corwin Springs, Mont.: Summit University Press, 1993), pp. 24–31.

47. Gen. 37:3.

48. The Great Divine Director, "Leadership, Take an Uncompromising Stand for Righteousness!" *Pearls of Wisdom,* vol. 11, no. 36, September 8, 1968.

49. Ps. 23:4.

50. 1 Cor. 9:26.

51. Rev. 6:10. The Great Divine Director, "Grids," *Pearls of Wisdom,* vol. 8, no. 9, February 28, 1965; also published in Mark L. Prophet, *The Soulless One: Cloning a Counterfeit Creation* (Corwin Springs, Mont.: Summit University Press, 1981), pp. 45–56.

52. See Saint Germain, "Methods of Transfer," *Pearls of Wisdom,* vol. 5, no. 32, August 10, 1962; also published in Mark L. Prophet and Elizabeth Clare Prophet, *Alchemy,* pp. 49–62; see also pp. 277–84.

53. Lord Maitreya, "Love of the Person and the Law of the Word: God and My Right," *Pearls of Wisdom,* vol. 23, no. 51, December 21, 1980.

54. Gautama Buddha, "Have Mercy!" *Pearls of Wisdom,* vol. 35, no. 20, May 17, 1992.

55. Matt. 4:7.

56. Archangel Michael, "A Divine Mediatorship," *Pearls of Wisdom,* vol. 25, no. 45, November 7, 1982.

57. Exod. 3:13–14.

58. Archangel Zadkiel, April 5, 1968.

59. 1 Cor. 15:31; 3:13.

60. Eph. 5:26.

61. Luke 3:16.

62. Job 22:28.

63. Johnny Mercer and Harold Arlen, "Ac-cent-tchu-ate the Positive," from *Here Come the Waves,* 1944.

64. Matt. 13:24–30.

65. See Acts 2:1–4; Matt. 3:11. Lanto, "The Essence of Higher Consciousness," pp. 10–11, 22.

66. Matt. 12:43–45.

67. 1 John 3:3.

68. God Harmony, "The Initiation of Our Chelas in the Flame of God Harmony: The Scientific Method for a Greater Area of Self-Mastery," *Pearls of Wisdom,* vol. 23, no. 24, June 15, 1980.

69. The three Gods of the Hindu Trinity: Brahma, the Creator; Vishnu, the Preserver; and Shiva, the Destroyer.

70. 1 Cor. 3:19.

71. Serapis Bey, "The Triangle within the Circle," *Pearls of Wisdom,* vol. 10, no. 15, April 9, 1967; also published in *Dossier on the Ascension* (Corwin Springs, Mont.: Summit University Press, 1978), pp. 19–26.

Chapter 2 · The Ascension

Opening quotation: Gen. 5:24.

1. Serapis Bey, "The Reality of the Inner Walk with God," *Pearls of Wisdom*, vol. 10, no. 13, March 26, 1967; also published in *Dossier*, pp. 1–8.
2. 2 Kings 2:11. The Great Divine Director, "Identity," *Pearls of Wisdom*, vol. 8, no. 11, March 14, 1965; also published in Prophet, *Soulless One*, pp. 63–70.
3. John 4:32.
4. Saint Germain, "The Crucible of Being," *Pearls of Wisdom*, vol. 5, no. 34, August 24, 1962; also published in Mark L. Prophet and Elizabeth Clare Prophet, *Alchemy*, pp. 73–99.
5. Acts 1:11.
6. Acts 9:1–19. Rev. 1:1–2, 9–10.
7. Serapis Bey, "The Destiny of Every Man," *Pearls of Wisdom*, vol. 10, no. 31, July 30, 1967; also published in *Dossier*, pp. 171–79.
8. The Maha Chohan, "The High Rope," *Pearls of Wisdom*, vol. 37, no. 15, April 10, 1994.
9. Matt. 11:30.
10. John 1:9.
11. John the Beloved, April 12, 1974.
12. Serapis Bey, "Memory and Residual Magnetism," *Pearls of Wisdom*, vol. 10, no. 22, May 28, 1967; also published in *Dossier*, pp. 83–91.
13. Luke 7:12–16. Luke 8:49–56. John 11:1–44.
14. Gautama Buddha, "The Resurrection May Not Be Postponed," *Pearls of Wisdom*, vol. 33, no. 2, January 14, 1990.
15. Acts 1:11.
16. Gautama Buddha, "The Resurrection May Not Be Postponed."
17. John 3:8.
18. Serapis Bey, "The Great Electronic Fire Rings: Seraphic Meditations I," *Pearls of Wisdom*, vol. 10, no. 25, June 18, 1967; also published in *Dossier*, pp. 115–23.
19. John the Beloved, April 12, 1974.
20. Matt. 22:37–39. John 21:22.

21. 1 John 2:2. 2 Pet. 1:17; Mark 1:11.
22. The Great Divine Director, "Brotherhood," *Pearls of Wisdom,* vol. 8, no. 4, January 22, 1965, and "Identity," *Pearls of Wisdom,* vol. 8, no. 11, March 14, 1965; also published in Prophet, *Soulless One,* pp. 11–16, 63–70.
23. Acts 16:31.
24. Serapis Bey, "The Divine Right of Every Man," *Pearls of Wisdom,* vol. 10, no. 19, May 7, 1967; also published in *Dossier,* pp. 55–63.
25. Jude 14; Gen. 5:24.
26. John 8:58.
27. Heb. 10:7, 9. Exod. 3:14.
28. Serapis Bey, "Memory and Residual Magnetism."
29. Jer. 13:23. Matt. 6:27.
30. Saint Germain, "Intermediate Cosmo-Science, Part I," in *Keepers of the Flame Lesson* 13.
31. Ibid.
32. John 14:12.
33. 1 Cor. 15:26.
34. Serapis Bey, "The Great Deathless Solar Body," *Pearls of Wisdom,* vol. 10, no. 29, July 6, 1967; also published in *Dossier,* pp. 151–59.
35. Rev. 1:1–2, 9–10.
36. Acts 8:26–40.
37. 2 Kings 2:11.
38. Ezek. 1:16.
39. Serapis Bey, "The Destiny of Every Man."
40. Serapis Bey, July 3, 1967.
41. John 1:5.
42. Rev. 6:16. Matt. 10:26. Ps. 136.
43. Lord Maitreya, "The Initiatic Process: 'The Light of God I See,'" *Pearls of Wisdom,* vol. 10, no. 10, March 5, 1967.
44. Serapis Bey, "The Banner of Humility," *Pearls of Wisdom,* vol. 10, no. 16, April 16, 1967; also published in *Dossier,* pp. 27–34.
45. Gal. 6:7.
46. Serapis Bey, July 3, 1967.
47. Serapis Bey, "Purification of the Memory," *Pearls of Wisdom,*

vol. 10, no. 17, April 23, 1967; also published in *Dossier,* pp. 35–43.

48. Sanat Kumara, "In My Name, Cast Out Devils," *Pearls of Wisdom,* vol. 22, no. 37, September 16, 1979.
49. Archangel Michael, "A Divine Mediatorship," *Pearls of Wisdom,* vol. 25, no. 45, November 7, 1982.
50. 2 Cor. 3:17.
51. 1 Cor. 15:54–55.
52. John 14:2–3.
53. Serapis Bey, July 3, 1967.
54. Gen. 13:18.
55. Rev. 4:6; 15:2; 22:1.
56. Serapis Bey, "The Destiny of Every Man."
57. Luke 15:11–32. Serapis Bey, "The Great Electronic Fire Rings: Seraphic Meditations I."

Chapter 3 · Ascended and Unascended Masters

Opening quotation: 1 Cor. 15: 40.
1. 2 Pet. 2:19.
2. "A Letter from Beloved Djwal Kul," in *Keepers of the Flame Lesson* 23.
3. Lady Master Leto, "On Visiting the Sacred Retreats," in *Keepers of the Flame Lesson* 7.
4. Serapis Bey, "Initiation from the Emerald Sphere," *Pearls of Wisdom,* vol. 27, no. 56, November 25, 1984.
5. John 10:30.
6. Saint Germain, "Verity," in *Keepers of the Flame Lesson* 19.
7. Lanello, "In the Spirit of the Great White Brotherhood," *Pearls of Wisdom,* vol. 31, no. 86, December 24, 1988.
8. Matt. 12:37.
9. Saint Germain, "Intermediate Cosmo-Science, Part II," in *Keepers of the Flame Lesson* 14.
10. Kuan Yin, "Brothers and Sisters of Mercy unto the Children of Addiction," in Mark L. Prophet and Elizabeth Clare Prophet, *Kuan Yin Opens the Door to the Golden Age* (Corwin Springs, Mont.: Summit University Press, 1984), Book II, pp. *125–32.*

11. Kuan Yin, "The Quality of Mercy for the Regeneration of the Youth of the World," in Mark L. Prophet and Elizabeth Clare Prophet, *Kuan Yin,* Book II, pp. *120–21.*

12. Helena Roerich, *Foundations of Buddhism* (New York: Agni Yoga Society, 1971), pp. 141–42.

13. Kuan Yin, "The Heart's Capacity for Love," *Pearls of Wisdom,* vol. 31, no. 61, September 18, 1988.

14. Saint Germain, "The Individual Path," *Pearls of Wisdom,* vol. 31, no. 50, August 13, 1988.

15. Bhikshu Sangharakshita, *The Three Jewels: An Introduction to Buddhism* (1967; reprint, London: Windhorse Publications, 1977), pp. 170–71.

16. Lord Maitreya, "Fearless Compassion and the Eternal Flame of Hope," *Pearls of Wisdom,* vol. 33, no. 1, January 7, 1990.

17. Ibid.

18. A tail gunner (World War II aviation slang).

19. Matt. 11:30.

20. Lord Lanto, July 4, 1967.

21. Jesus, February 18, 1973.

22. Lady Master Venus, February 4, 1962.

23. Goddess of Purity, November 4, 1966.

24. 2 Kings 2:11. Luke 1:17.

25. Matt. 14:1–12; 17:1–13.

26. John 3:30. Matt. 3:3.

27. Matt 3:3; 11:9–10. "A Letter from Beloved Chananda," in *Keepers of the Flame Lesson* 21.

28. Matt. 11:14; 17:10–13.

29. 1 Kings 18:17–40.

30. 1 Kings 17:14.

31. 1 Kings 19:19–21.

32. For the account of the ascension of Elijah and the transfer of his mantle to Elisha, see 2 Kings 2:1–15.

33. Matt. 11:11.

34. Jesus, "The Opening of the Temple Doors VII," *Pearls of Wisdom,* vol. 16, no. 16, April 22, 1973.

35. This occurred on January 1, 1956.

36. Saint Germain, "Intermediate Cosmo-Science, Part I."

37. Ps. 16:9–10.

38. 1 Cor. 13:12.
39. Matt. 5:48.
40. Saint Germain, "Intermediate Cosmo-Science, Part II."
41. Jude 14.
42. Gen. 5:24.
43. Saint Germain, "Intermediate Cosmo-Science, Part I."
44. Jer. 31:33–34.
45. Isa. 30:20–21.
46. El Morya, November 3, 1966.
47. Titus 1:15.
48. James 3:17.
49. John 14:12.
50. Saint Germain, "Intermediate Cosmo-Science, Part II."

Chapter 4 · Hierarchy

Opening quotation: Ps. 8:3–6, 9.
1. Serapis Bey, "The Great Electronic Fire Rings: Seraphic Meditations I."
2. Merriam-Webster's Collegiate Dictionary, 10th ed., s.v. "logos."
3. John 1:1.
4. 2 Cor. 3:18.
5. Saint Germain, "The Rigors of Initiation Can Be Invoked from the Hand of the Great Initiator," *Pearls of Wisdom,* vol. 14, no. 7, February 14, 1971.
6. Heb. 11:1.
7. 1 Cor. 12:4–12, 14.
8. Gen. 4:26.
9. Surya, "The Arhat—A Repository of God's Good," *Pearls of Wisdom,* vol. 13, no. 32, August 9, 1970.
10. John 6:56. 1 Cor. 11:24.
11. Rev. 22:13.
12. Gen. 1:3.
13. John 3:3, 5.
14. Alpha, "A Replica of the Crystal Atom," *Pearls of Wisdom,* vol. 25, no. 51, December 19, 1982.

15. John 1:14.
16. 1 Cor. 15:36.
17. See note 21 below.
18. Matt. 12:31–32.
19. Acts 1:9. This demonstration of the ascension by Jesus was not his actual ascension. See chapter 2, pp. 90–91.
20. Ps. 8:1.
21. The Ritual of Creation is accomplished as the energies of God descend from Spirit to Matter over the clockwise or positive spiral passing through the planes of fire, air, water and earth. This is the Alpha cycle of materialization or precipitation; it is the going-out or evolutionary process that is a masculine activity of the sacred fire.

     The Ritual of Preservation, the sustaining of form in Matter and in Spirit, is accomplished via the clockwise figure-eight pattern (moving in a clockwise direction from the point of origin on the twelve o'clock line) as energy flows through the planes of fire, water, air and earth. This is a masculine activity of the sacred fire, used to seal energy in a given matrix.

     The Ritual of Disintegration is accomplished as the energies of God return from Matter to Spirit over the counterclockwise spiral for the purposes of canceling unworthy creations through the planes of earth, water, air and fire. This is the Omega cycle of disintegration or dematerialization. It is the involutionary or negative spiral used to free energy of the imperfect patterns of the human consciousness. This pattern is also used in the "going-within" cycle that is the feminine activity of the sacred fire.

     The Ritual of Sublimation, the spiritualization or ascension of form and consciousness, is accomplished via the counterclockwise figure-eight pattern (moving in a counterclockwise direction from the point of origin on the twelve o'clock line) as energy flows through the planes of earth, air, water and fire. This action of sublimation ("to make sublime, to refine") is used to immortalize or make permanent the works of God and man.
22. The Great Divine Director, "Identity."
23. Luke 15:11–32.

24. John 16:24.
25. Matt. 4:6.
26. Gen. 4:9.
27. El Morya, "Individual Responsibility," *Pearls of Wisdom,* vol. 13, no. 31, August 2, 1970.
28. Matt. 25:23.
29. The names the Knight Commander Saint Germain has given to a few members of the Keepers of the Flame Fraternity in the knighting ceremony are the keys to their mission and service upon earth. Each name contains the blueprint of the divine plan that this soul is required to fulfill before she ascends.

    This is not the new name she will receive after her ascension, but the name written upon the chalice that holds her Christ consciousness. It is the name assigned at birth by the Lords of Karma for the service to be rendered in that embodiment. Sometimes this name remains the same for several embodiments; sometimes it is heard by the parents when they name the child. If this is so, the name given in the knighting ceremony will be the same as the given name.
30. Rev. 2:17.
31. El Morya, "Individual Responsibility."
32. Ps. 8:3–4.
33. John 6:51, 53–54, 66–68.
34. Job 38:1, 4, 7.
35. Matt. 25:14–30.
36. Rev. 21:6–7.
37. Gen. 2:18.
38. Matt. 25:21.
39. John 14:2.
40. Gen. 3:24.
41. Alpha, December 29, 1963.
42. Rev. 19:4.
43. Rev. 7:17.
44. Rev. 4:8.
45. Isa. 41:17–18, 20.
46. Heb. 1:6–9.
47. Heb. 10:9.
48. Heb. 2:9.

49. Rev. 5:13.
50. Ps. 36:9.
51. Dan. 7:9.
52. John 10:30.
53. Luke 22:42.
54. Gen. 22:17.
55. Jesus, April 18, 1965.
56. 1 Cor. 6:19.
57. John 15:26; 16:7.
58. Rev. 12:1.
59. Rom. 8:7.
60. Rev. 12: 1–9, 13–17.
61. Ps. 82:6.
62. Deut. 6:4.
63. John 10:31–38.
64. Archangel Michael, "The Leap of the God Flame," *Pearls of Wisdom,* vol. 14, no. 12, March 21, 1971.
65. Ps. 82:6.
66. Isa. 55:1.
67. Gal. 6:7.
68. Kuan Yin, April 12, 1963.
69. Gal. 5:1.
70. The Spirit of Freedom in the Fourteen Ascended Masters Who Govern the Destiny of America, November 22, 1975.
71. Godfre Ray King, *Unveiled Mysteries,* 3rd ed. (Chicago: Saint Germain Press, 1939), pp. 39–61.
72. Saint Germain, September 4, 1983.
73. For the history of the fallen ones and their corruption of the people of light on earth, see Elizabeth Clare Prophet, *Fallen Angels and the Origins of Evil* (Corwin Springs, Mont.: Summit University Press, 2000). Spiritual solutions to the problems posed by the presence of the fallen ones on earth are outlined on pages 343–56.
74. Col. 3:3.
75. The Fourteen Ascended Masters Who Govern the Destiny of America, "The Alliance of Almighty God," *Pearls of Wisdom,* vol. 34, no. 19, May 12, 1991.
76. The Fourteen Ascended Masters Who Govern the Destiny of

America, July 1, 1996.

77. Ibid.

78. Rev. 11:15.

79. 1 Sam. 3:1–20.

80. The Holy Grail was carried by boat to the British Isles by Mary, the mother of Jesus, assisted by Joseph of Arimathea and several others who made the pilgrimage with her. They established focuses at Lourdes and Fátima, which would later be used for her visitations. The cup, traditionally associated with the town of Glastonbury, became the focal point for the spread of Christianity during the period of British colonization.

81. For an account of this remarkable personage based on the letters and accounts of the day, see Isabel Cooper-Oakley, *The Count of Saint Germain* (Blauvelt, N.Y.: Rudolf Steiner Pub., 1970).

82. Saint Germain, October 29, 1966.

83. Saint Germain, November 4, 1966.

84. Heb. 13:2.

85. Serapis Bey, "Step by Step the Way Is Won," *Pearls of Wisdom,* vol. 10, no. 20, May 14, 1967; also published in *Dossier,* pp. 65–73.

86. Ps. 8:4.

87. Matt. 28:18.

88. *Watch With Me, Jesus' Vigil of the Hours* (Corwin Springs, Mont.: Summit University Press, 1987), p. 17.

Glossary

Terms set in italics are defined elsewhere in the glossary.

Adept. An initiate of the *Great White Brotherhood* of a high degree of attainment, especially in the control of *Matter*, physical forces, nature spirits and bodily functions; fully the alchemist undergoing advanced initiations of the *sacred fire* on the path of the *ascension*.

Akashic records. The impressions of all that has ever transpired in the physical universe, recorded in the etheric substance and dimension known by the Sanskrit term *akasha*. These records can be read by those with developed *soul* faculties.

Alchemical marriage. The soul's permanent bonding to the *Holy Christ Self*, in preparation for the permanent fusing to the *I AM Presence* in the ritual of the *ascension*. See also *Soul; Secret chamber of the heart*.

All-Seeing Eye of God. See *Cyclopea*.

Alpha and Omega. The divine wholeness of the Father-Mother God affirmed as "the beginning and the ending" by the Lord *Christ* in Revelation (Rev. 1:8, 11; 21:6; 22:13). Ascended *twin flames* of the *Cosmic Christ* consciousness who hold the balance of the masculine-feminine polarity of the Godhead in the *Great Central Sun* of cosmos. Thus through the *Universal Christ* (the *Word* incarnate), the Father is the origin and the Mother is the fulfillment of the cycles of God's consciousness expressed throughout the *Spirit-Matter* creation. See also *Mother.*

Ancient of Days. See *Sanat Kumara.*

Angel. A divine spirit, a herald or messenger sent by God to deliver his *Word* to his children. A ministering spirit sent forth to tend the heirs of *Christ*—to comfort, protect, guide, strengthen, teach, counsel and warn. The fallen angels, also called the dark ones, are those angels who followed Lucifer in the Great Rebellion, whose consciousness therefore "fell" to lower levels of vibration. They were "cast out into the earth" by Archangel Michael (Rev. 12:7–12)—constrained by the karma of their disobedience to God and his Christ to take on and evolve through dense physical bodies. Here they walk about, sowing seeds of unrest and rebellion among men and nations.

Antahkarana. The web of life. The net of *light* spanning *Spirit* and *Matter,* connecting and sensitizing the whole of creation within itself and to the heart of God.

Archangel. The highest rank in the orders of *angels.* Each of the *seven rays* has a presiding Archangel who, with his divine complement or Archeia, embodies the God consciousness of the ray and directs the bands of angels serving in their command on that ray. The Archangels and Archeiai of the rays and the locations of their *retreats* are as follows:

First ray, blue, Archangel Michael and Faith, Banff, near Lake Louise, Alberta, Canada.

Second ray, yellow, Archangel Jophiel and Christine, south of the Great Wall near Lanchow, north central China.

Third ray, petal pink, deep rose and ruby, Archangel Chamuel and Charity, St. Louis, Missouri, U.S.A.

Fourth ray, white and mother-of-pearl, Archangel Gabriel and Hope, between Sacramento and Mount Shasta, California, U.S.A.

Fifth ray, green, Archangel Raphael and Mary, Fátima, Portugal.

Sixth ray, purple and gold with ruby flecks, Archangel Uriel and

Aurora, Tatra Mountains, south of Cracow, Poland.

Seventh ray, violet and purple, Archangel Zadkiel and Holy Amethyst, Cuba.

Archeia (pl. **Archeiai**). Divine complement and *twin flame* of an *Archangel.*

Ascended Master. One who, through *Christ* and the putting on of that Mind which was in Christ Jesus (Phil. 2:5), has mastered time and space and in the process gained the mastery of the self in the *four lower bodies* and the four quadrants of *Matter,* in the *chakras* and the balanced *threefold flame.* An Ascended Master has also transmuted at least 51 percent of his karma, fulfilled his divine plan, and taken the initiations of the ruby ray unto the ritual of the *ascension*—acceleration by the *sacred fire* into the Presence of the I AM THAT I AM (the *I AM Presence*). Ascended Masters inhabit the planes of *Spirit*—the kingdom of God (God's consciousness)—and they may teach unascended souls in an *etheric temple* or in the cities on the *etheric plane* (the kingdom of heaven).

Ascension. The ritual whereby the *soul* reunites with the *Spirit* of the living God, the *I AM Presence.* The ascension is the culmination of the soul's God-victorious sojourn in time and space. It is the process whereby the soul, having balanced her karma and fulfilled her divine plan, merges first with the Christ consciousness and then with the living Presence of the I AM THAT I AM. Once the ascension has taken place, the soul—the corruptible aspect of being—becomes the incorruptible one, a permanent atom in the Body of God. See also *Alchemical marriage.*

Aspirant. One who aspires; specifically, one who aspires to reunion with God through the ritual of the *ascension.* One who aspires to overcome the conditions and limitations of time and space to fulfill the cycles of karma and one's reason for being through the sacred labor.

Astral plane. A frequency of time and space beyond the physical, yet below the mental, corresponding to the *emotional body* of man and the collective unconscious of the race; the repository of mankind's thoughts and feelings, conscious and unconscious. Because the astral plane has been muddied by impure human thought and feeling, the term "astral" is often used in a negative context to refer to that which is impure or psychic.

Astrea. Feminine Elohim of the fourth ray, the ray of purity, who works to cut *souls* free from the *astral plane* and the projections of the dark forces. See also *Elohim; Seven rays.*

Atman. The spark of the divine within, identical with *Brahman;* the ultimate essence of the universe as well as the essence of the individual.

AUM. See *OM.*

Avatar. The incarnation of the *Word.* The avatar of an age is the *Christ,* the incarnation of the Son of God. The *Manus* may designate numerous Christed ones—those endued with an extraordinary *light*—to go forth as world teachers and wayshowers. The Christed ones demonstrate in a given epoch the law of the *Logos,* stepped down through the Manu(s) and the avatar(s) until it is made flesh through their own word and work—to be ultimately victorious in its fulfillment in all souls of light sent forth to conquer time and space in that era.

Bodhisattva. (Sanskrit, 'a being of *bodhi* or enlightenment.') A being destined for enlightenment, or one whose energy and power is directed toward enlightenment. A Bodhisattva is destined to become a *Buddha* but has forgone the bliss of *nirvana* with a vow to save all children of God on earth. An Ascended Master or an unascended master may be a Bodhisattva.

Brahman. Ultimate Reality; the Absolute.

Buddha. (From Sanskrit *budh* 'awake, know, perceive.') "The enlightened one." Buddha denotes an office in the spiritual *hierarchy* of worlds that is attained by passing certain initiations of the *sacred fire,* including those of the *seven rays* of the Holy Spirit and of the five secret *rays,* the raising of the feminine ray (sacred fire of the *Kundalini*) and the "mastery of the seven in the seven multiplied by the power of the ten."

Gautama attained the enlightenment of the Buddha twenty-five centuries ago, a path he had pursued through many previous embodiments culminating in his forty-nine-day meditation under the Bo tree. Hence he is called Gautama, the Buddha. He holds the office of *Lord of the World*, sustaining, by his *Causal Body* and *threefold flame*, the divine spark and consciousness in the evolutions of earth approaching the path of personal Christhood. His aura of love/wisdom ensouling the planet issues from his incomparable devotion to the Divine *Mother*. He is the hierarch of Shamballa, the original *retreat* of *Sanat Kumara* now on the *etheric plane* over the Gobi Desert.

Lord Maitreya, the *Cosmic Christ*, has also passed the initiations of the Buddha. He is the long-awaited Coming Buddha who has come to the fore to teach all who have departed from the way of the Great *Guru*, Sanat Kumara, from whose lineage both he and Gautama descended. In the history of the planet, there have been numerous Buddhas who have served the evolutions of mankind through the steps and stages of the path of the *Bodhisattva*. In the East Jesus is referred to as the Buddha Issa. He is the World Saviour by the love/wisdom of the Godhead.

Caduceus. The Kundalini. See *Sacred fire*.

Causal Body. Seven concentric spheres of *light* surrounding the *I AM Presence*. The spheres of the Causal Body contain the records of the virtuous acts we have performed to the glory of God and the blessing of man through our many incarnations on earth. See also *Chart of Your Divine Self*; color illustration facing page 44.

Central Sun. A vortex of energy, physical or spiritual, central to systems of worlds that it thrusts from, or gathers unto, itself by the Central Sun Magnet. Whether in the *microcosm* or the *Macrocosm*, the Central Sun is the principal energy source, vortex, or nexus of energy interchange in atoms, cells, man (the heart center), amidst plant life and the core of the earth. The Great Central Sun is the center of cosmos; the point of integration of the *Spirit-Matter* cosmos; the point of origin of all physical-spiritual creation; the nucleus, or white fire core, of the *Cosmic Egg*. (The God Star, Sirius, is the focus of the Great Central Sun in our sector of the galaxy.) The Sun behind the sun is the spiritual Cause behind the physical effect we see as our own physical sun and all other stars and star systems, seen or unseen, including the Great Central Sun.

Chakra. (Sanskrit, 'wheel, disc, circle.') Center of *light* anchored in the *etheric body* and governing the flow of energy to the *four lower bodies* of man. There are seven major chakras corresponding to the *seven rays*, five minor chakras corresponding to the five secret rays, and a total of 144 light centers in the body of man.

Chart of Your Divine Self. (See color illustration facing page 44.) There are three figures represented in the Chart. The upper figure is the *I AM Presence,* the I AM THAT I AM, the individualization of God's presence for every son and daughter of the Most High. The Divine Monad consists of the I AM Presence surrounded by the spheres (color rings) of *light* that make up the body of First Cause, or *Causal Body.*

The middle figure in the Chart is the Mediator between God and man, called the *Holy Christ Self,* the *Real Self* or the *Christ* consciousness. It has also been referred to as the Higher Mental Body or one's Higher Consciousness. This Inner Teacher overshadows the lower self, which consists of the *soul* evolving through the four planes of *Matter* using the vehicles of the *four lower bodies*—the *etheric* (memory) *body,* the *mental body,* the *emotional* (desire) *body,* and the *physical body*—to balance karma and fulfill the divine plan.

The three figures of the Chart correspond to the Trinity of Father, who always includes the *Mother* (the upper figure), Son (the middle figure) and Holy Spirit (the lower figure). The latter is the intended temple of the Holy Spirit, whose *sacred fire* is indicated in the enfolding *violet flame.* The lower figure corresponds to you as a disciple on the *Path.*

The lower figure is surrounded by a *tube of light,* which is projected from the heart of the I AM Presence in answer to your call. It is a cylinder of white light that sustains a forcefield of protection twenty-four hours a day, so long as you guard it in harmony. The *threefold flame* of life is the divine spark sent from the I AM Presence as the gift of life, consciousness and free will. It is sealed in the *secret chamber of the heart* that through the love, wisdom and power of the Godhead anchored therein the *soul* may fulfill her reason for being in the physical plane. Also called the Christ Flame and the Liberty Flame, or fleur-de-lis, it is the spark of a man's divinity, his potential for Christhood.

The silver cord (or *crystal cord*) is the stream of life, or *lifestream,* that descends from the heart of the I AM Presence to the Holy Christ Self to nourish and sustain (through the *chakras*) the soul and its vehicles of expression in time and space. It is over this 'umbilical cord' that the energy of the Presence flows, entering the being of man at the crown and giving impetus for the pulsation of the threefold flame as well as the physical heartbeat.

When a round of the soul's incarnation in Matter-form is finished, the I AM Presence withdraws the silver cord (Eccles. 12:6), whereupon the threefold flame returns to the level of the Christ, and the soul clothed in the etheric garment gravitates to the highest level of her attainment, where she is schooled between embodiments until her final incarnation when the Great Law decrees she shall go out no more.

The dove of the Holy Spirit descending from the heart of the Father is shown just above the head of the Christ. When the son of man puts on and becomes the Christ consciousness as Jesus did, he merges with the Holy Christ Self. The Holy Spirit is upon him and the words of the Father, the beloved I AM Presence, are spoken: "This is my beloved Son, in whom I AM well pleased" (Matt. 3:17).

Chela. (Hindi *celā* from Sanskrit *ceṭa* 'slave,' i.e., 'servant.') In India, a disciple of a religious teacher or *guru.* A term used generally to refer to a student of the *Ascended Masters* and their teachings. Specifically, a student of more than ordinary self-discipline and devotion initiated by an Ascended Master and serving the cause of the *Great White Brotherhood.*

Chohan. (Tibetan, 'lord' or 'master'; a chief.) Each of the seven *rays* has a Chohan who focuses the *Christ* consciousness of the ray.

Having ensouled and demonstrated the law of the ray throughout numerous incarnations, and having taken initiations both before and after the *ascension,* the candidate is appointed to the office of Chohan by the Maha Chohan (the "Great Lord"), who is himself the representative of the Holy Spirit on all the rays. The names of the Chohans of the Rays (each one an *Ascended Master* representing one of the seven rays to earth's evolutions) and the locations of their physical/etheric focuses are as follows:

First ray, El Morya, Retreat of God's Will, Darjeeling, India

Second ray, Lanto, Royal Teton Retreat, Grand Teton, Jackson Hole, Wyoming, U.S.A.

Third ray, Paul the Venetian, Château de Liberté, southern France, with a focus of the *threefold flame* at the Washington Monument, Washington, D.C., U.S.A.

Fourth ray, Serapis Bey, the Ascension Temple and Retreat at Luxor, Egypt

Fifth ray, Hilarion (the apostle Paul), Temple of Truth, Crete

Sixth ray, Nada, Arabian Retreat, Saudi Arabia

Seventh ray, Saint Germain, Royal Teton Retreat, Grand Teton, Wyoming, U.S.A.; Cave of Symbols, Table Mountain, Wyoming, U.S.A. Saint Germain also works out of the Great Divine Director's focuses—the Cave of Light in India and the Rakoczy Mansion in Transylvania, where Saint Germain presides as hierarch.

Christ. (From the Greek *Christos* 'anointed.') Messiah (Hebrew, Aramaic 'anointed'); 'Christed one,' one fully endued and infilled—anointed—by the *light* (the Son) of God. The *Word,* the *Logos,* the Second Person of the Trinity. In the Hindu Trinity of Brahma, Vishnu and Shiva, the term "Christ" corresponds to or is the incarnation of Vishnu, the Preserver; Avatāra, God-man, Dispeller of Darkness, *Guru.*

The term "Christ" or "Christed one" also denotes an office in *hierarchy* held by those who have attained self-mastery on the *seven rays* and the seven *chakras* of the Holy Spirit. Christ-mastery includes the balancing of the *threefold flame*—the divine attributes of power, wisdom and love—for the harmonization of consciousness and the implementation of the mastery of the seven rays in the chakras and in the *four lower bodies* through the Mother Flame (the raised *Kundalini*).

At the hour designated for the *ascension,* the *soul* thus anointed raises the spiral of the threefold flame from beneath the feet through the entire form for the transmutation of every atom and cell of her being, consciousness and world. The saturation and acceleration of the *four lower bodies* and the soul by this transfiguring light of the Christ Flame take place in part during the initiation of the *transfiguration,* increasing through the resurrection and gaining full intensity in the ritual of the ascension.

Christ Self. The individualized focus of "the only begotten of the Father, full of grace and Truth." The *Universal Christ* individualized as the true identity of the *soul;* the *Real Self* of every man, woman and child, to which the soul must rise. The Christ Self is the Mediator between a man and his God. He is a man's own personal teacher, master and prophet.

Color rays. See *Seven rays.*

Cosmic Being. (1) An *Ascended Master* who has attained cosmic consciousness and ensouls the *light*/energy/consciousness of many worlds and systems of worlds across the galaxies to the Sun behind the *Great Central Sun.* (2) A being of God who has never descended below the level of the *Christ,* has never taken physical embodiment, and has never made human karma.

Cosmic Christ. An office in *hierarchy* currently held by Lord Maitreya under Gautama *Buddha,* the *Lord of the World.* Also used as a synonym for *Universal Christ.*

Cosmic Clock. The science of charting the cycles of the *soul's* karma and initiations on the twelve lines of the Clock under the *Twelve Hierarchies of the Sun.* Taught by Mother Mary to Mark and Elizabeth Prophet for sons and daughters of God returning to the Law of the One and to their point of origin beyond the worlds of form and lesser causation.

Cosmic Egg. The spiritual-material universe, including a seemingly endless chain of galaxies, star systems, worlds known and unknown, whose center, or white fire core, is called the *Great Central Sun*. The Cosmic Egg has both a spiritual and a material center. Although we may discover and observe the Cosmic Egg from the standpoint of our physical senses and perspective, all of the dimensions of *Spirit* can also be known and experienced within the Cosmic Egg. For the God who created the Cosmic Egg and holds it in the hollow of his hand is also the God Flame expanding hour by hour within his very own sons and daughters. The Cosmic Egg represents the bounds of man's habitation in this cosmic cycle. Yet, as God is everywhere throughout and beyond the Cosmic Egg, so by his Spirit within us we daily awaken to new dimensions of being, soul-satisfied in conformity with his likeness.

Cosmic Law. The Law that governs mathematically, yet with the spontaneity of Mercy's flame, all manifestation throughout the cosmos in the planes of *Spirit* and *Matter*.

Crystal cord. The stream of God's *light,* life and consciousness that nourishes and sustains the *soul* and her *four lower bodies.* Also called the silver cord (Eccles. 12:6). See also *Chart of Your Divine Self;* color illustration facing page 44.

Cyclopea. Masculine Elohim of the fifth ray, also known as the All-Seeing Eye of God or as the Great Silent Watcher. See also *Elohim; Seven rays.*

Deathless solar body. See *Seamless garment.*

Decree. A dynamic form of spoken prayer used by students of the *Ascended Masters* to direct God's *light* into individual and world conditions. The decree may be short or long and is usually marked by a formal preamble and a closing or acceptance. It is the authoritative *Word* of God spoken in man in the name of the *I AM Presence* and the living *Christ* to bring about constructive change on earth through the will of God. The decree is the birthright of the sons and daughters of God, the "Command ye me" of Isaiah 45:11, the original fiat of the Creator: "Let there be light: and there was light" (Gen. 1:3). It is written in the Book of Job, "Thou shalt decree a thing, and it shall be established unto thee: and the light shall shine upon thy ways" (Job 22:28).

Dictation. A message from an *Ascended Master,* an *Archangel* or another advanced spiritual being delivered through the agency of the Holy Spirit by a *Messenger* of the *Great White Brotherhood.*

Divine Monad. See *Chart of Your Divine Self; I AM Presence.*

Electronic Presence. A duplicate of the *I AM Presence* of an Ascended Master.

Elohim. (Hebrew; plural of *Eloah,* 'God.') The name of God used in the first verse of the Bible: "In the beginning God created the heaven and the earth." The Seven Mighty Elohim and their feminine counterparts are the builders of form. They are the "seven spirits of God" named in Revelation 4:5 and the "morning stars" that sang together in the beginning, as the LORD revealed them to Job (Job 38:7). In the order of *hierarchy,* the Elohim and *Cosmic Beings* carry the greatest concentration, the highest vibration of *light* that we can comprehend in our present state of evolution. Serving directly under the Elohim are the four beings of the elements (the *Four Cosmic Forces*), who have dominion over the elementals—the gnomes, salamanders, sylphs and undines.

    Following are the names of the Seven Elohim and their divine complements, the ray they serve on and the location of their etheric *retreat:*

First ray, Hercules and Amazonia, Half Dome, Sierra Nevada, Yosemite National Park, California, U.S.A.

Second ray, Apollo and Lumina, western Lower Saxony, Germany

Third ray, Heros and Amora, Lake Winnipeg, Manitoba, Canada

Fourth ray, Purity and *Astrea,* near Gulf of Archangel, southeast arm of White Sea, Russia

Fifth ray, *Cyclopea* and Virginia, Altai Range where China, Siberia and Mongolia meet, near Tabun Bogdo

Sixth ray, Peace and Aloha, Hawaiian Islands

Seventh ray, Arcturus and Victoria, near Luanda, Angola, Africa

Emotional body. One of the *four lower bodies* of man, corresponding to the water element and the third quadrant of *Matter;* the vehicle of the desires and feelings of God made manifest in the being of man. Also called the astral body, the desire body or the feeling body.

Entity. A conglomerate of misqualified energy or disembodied individuals who have chosen to embody evil. Entities that are focuses of sinister forces may attack disembodied as well as embodied individuals.

Etheric body. One of the *four lower bodies* of man, corresponding to the fire element and the first quadrant of *Matter;* called the envelope of the *soul,* holding the blueprint of the divine plan and the image of *Christ*-perfection to be outpictured in the world of form. Also called the memory body.

Etheric octave or etheric plane. The highest plane in the dimension of *Matter;* a plane that is as concrete and real as the physical plane (and even more so) but is experienced through the senses of the *soul* in a dimension and a consciousness beyond physical awareness. This is the plane on which the *akashic records* of mankind's entire evolution register individually and collectively. It is the world of *Ascended Masters* and their *retreats,* etheric cities of *light* where *souls* of a higher order of evolution abide between embodiments. It is the plane of reality.

The lower *etheric plane,* which overlaps the astral/mental/ physical belts, is contaminated by these lower worlds occupied by the false hierarchy and the mass consciousness it controls.

Etheric temple. See *Retreat.*

Fallen angels. See *Angels.*

Father-Mother God. See *Alpha and Omega.*

Four Cosmic Forces. The four beasts seen by Saint John and other seers as the lion, the calf (or ox), the man and the flying eagle (Rev. 4:6–8). They serve directly under the Elohim and govern all of the Matter cosmos. They are transformers of the Infinite Light unto souls evolving in the finite. See also *Elohim*.

Four lower bodies. Four sheaths of four distinct frequencies that surround the *soul* (the physical, emotional, mental and etheric bodies), providing vehicles for the soul in her journey through time and space. The etheric sheath, highest in vibration, is the gateway to the three higher bodies: the *Christ Self*, the *I AM Presence* and the *Causal Body*. See also *Physical body*; *Emotional body*; *Mental body*; *Etheric body*.

Great Central Sun. See *Central Sun*.

Great Hub. See *Central Sun*.

Great White Brotherhood. A spiritual order of Western saints and Eastern adepts who have reunited with the *Spirit* of the living God; the heavenly hosts. They have transcended the cycles of karma and rebirth and ascended (accelerated) into that higher reality which is the eternal abode of the soul. The *Ascended Masters* of the Great White Brotherhood, united for the highest purposes of the brotherhood of man under the Fatherhood of God, have risen in every age from every culture and religion to inspire creative achievement in education, the arts and sciences, God-government and the abundant life through the economies of the nations. The word "white" refers not to race but to the aura (halo) of white *light* surrounding their forms. The Brotherhood also includes in its ranks certain unascended *chelas* of the Ascended Masters.

Guru. (Sanskrit.) A personal religious teacher and spiritual guide; one of high attainment. A guru may be unascended or ascended.

Hierarchy. The universal chain of individualized God-free beings fulfilling the attributes and aspects of God's infinite Selfhood. Included in the cosmic hierarchical scheme are *Solar Logoi, Elohim,* Sons and Daughters of God, ascended and unascended masters with their circles of *chelas, Cosmic Beings,* the *Twelve*

Hierarchies of the Sun, Archangels and *angels* of the *sacred fire,* children of the *light,* nature spirits (called elementals) and *twin flames* of the *Alpha/Omega* polarity sponsoring planetary and galactic systems.

This universal order of the Father's own Self-expression is the means whereby God in the *Great Central Sun* steps down the Presence and power of his universal being/consciousness in order that succeeding evolutions in time and space, from the least unto the greatest, might come to know the wonder of his love. The level of one's spiritual/physical attainment—measured by one's balanced self-awareness "hid with *Christ* in God" and demonstrating his Law, by his love, in the *Spirit/Matter* cosmos—is the criterion establishing one's placement on this ladder of life called hierarchy.

Higher Mental Body. See *Chart of Your Divine Self.*

Higher Self. The *I AM Presence;* the *Christ Self;* the exalted aspect of selfhood. Used in contrast to the term "lower self," or "little self," which indicates the *soul* that went forth from and may elect by free will to return to the Divine Whole through the realization of the oneness of the self in God. Higher consciousness.

Holy Christ Self. See *Christ Self.*

Human monad. The entire forcefield of self; the interconnecting spheres of influences—hereditary, environmental, karmic—which make up that self-awareness which identifies itself as human. The reference point of lesser- or non-awareness out of which all mankind must evolve to the realization of the *Real Self* as the *Christ Self.*

I AM Presence. The I AM THAT I AM (Exod. 3:13–15); the individualized Presence of God focused for each individual *soul.* The God-identity of the individual; the Divine Monad; the individual Source. The origin of the soul focused in the planes of *Spirit* just above the physical form; the personification of the God Flame for the individual. See also *Chart of Your Divine Self;* color illustration facing page 44.

I AM THAT I AM. See *I AM Presence.*

Kali Yuga. (Sanskrit.) Term in Hindu mystic philosophy for the last and worst of the four yugas (world ages), characterized by strife, discord and moral deterioration.

Karmic Board. See *Lords of Karma.*

Keepers of the Flame Fraternity. Founded in 1961 by Saint Germain, an organization of *Ascended Masters* and their *chelas* who vow to keep the flame of life on earth and to support the activities of the *Great White Brotherhood* in the establishment of their community and mystery school and in the dissemination of their teachings. Keepers of the Flame receive graded lessons in *Cosmic Law* dictated by the *Ascended Masters* to their *Messengers* Mark and Elizabeth Prophet.

Kundalini. See *Sacred fire.*

Lifestream. The stream of life that comes forth from the one Source, from the *I AM Presence* in the planes of *Spirit,* and descends to the planes of *Matter* where it manifests as the *threefold flame* anchored in the heart *chakra* for the sustainment of the *soul* in Matter and the nourishment of the *four lower bodies.* Used to denote souls evolving as individual "lifestreams" and hence synonymous with the term "individual." Denotes the ongoing nature of the individual through cycles of individualization.

Light. The energy of God; the potential of the *Christ.* As the personification of *Spirit,* the term "light" can be used synonymously with the terms "God" and "Christ." As the essence of Spirit, it is synonymous with *"sacred fire."* It is the emanation of the *Great Central Sun* and the individualized *I AM Presence*—and the Source of all life.

Logos. (Greek, 'word, speech, reason.') The divine wisdom manifest in the creation. According to ancient Greek philosophy, the Logos is the controlling principle in the universe. The Book of John identifies the *Word,* or Logos, with Jesus Christ: "And the Word was made flesh, and dwelt among us" (John 1:14). Hence, Jesus Christ is seen as the embodiment of divine reason, the Word Incarnate.

Lord of the World. *Sanat Kumara* held the office of Lord of the World (referred to as "God of the earth" in Rev. 11:4) for tens of thousands of years. Gautama Buddha recently succeeded Sanat Kumara and now holds this office. His is the highest governing office of the spiritual *hierarchy* for the planet—and yet Lord Gautama is truly the most humble among the *Ascended Masters.* At inner levels, he sustains the *threefold flame,* the divine spark, for those *lifestreams* who have lost the direct contact with their *I AM Presence* and who have made so much negative karma as to be unable to magnetize sufficient *light* from the Godhead to sustain their *soul's* physical incarnation on earth. Through a filigree thread of light connecting his heart with the hearts of all God's children, Lord Gautama nourishes the flickering flame of life that ought to burn upon the altar of each heart with a greater magnitude of love, wisdom and power, fed by each one's own *Christ* consciousness.

Lords of Karma. The Ascended Beings who comprise the Karmic Board. Their names and the *rays* that they represent on the board are as follows: first ray, the Great Divine Director; second ray, the Goddess of Liberty; third ray, the Ascended Lady Master Nada; fourth ray, the *Elohim Cyclopea;* fifth ray, Pallas Athena, Goddess of Truth; sixth ray, Portia, Goddess of Justice; seventh ray, Kuan Yin, Goddess of Mercy. The Buddha Vairochana also sits on the Karmic Board.

   The Lords of Karma dispense justice to this system of worlds, adjudicating karma, mercy and judgment on behalf of every *lifestream.* All *souls* must pass before the Karmic Board before and after each incarnation on earth, receiving their assignment and karmic allotment for each lifetime beforehand and the review of their performance at its conclusion. Through the Keeper of the Scrolls and the recording *angels,* the Lords of Karma have access to the complete records of every lifestream's incarnations on earth. They determine who shall embody, as well as when and where. They assign souls to families and communities, measuring out the weights of karma that must be balanced as the "jot and tittle" of the Law. The Karmic Board, acting in consonance with the individual *I AM Presence* and *Christ Self*, determines when the soul has earned the right to be free from the wheel of karma and the round of rebirth.

The Lords of Karma meet at the Royal Teton Retreat twice yearly, at winter and summer solstice, to review petitions from unascended mankind and to grant dispensations for their assistance.

Macrocosm. (Greek, 'great world.') The larger cosmos; the entire warp and woof of creation, which we call the *Cosmic Egg*. Also used to contrast man as the microcosm ('little world') against the backdrop of the larger world in which he lives. See also *Microcosm*.

Mantra. A mystical formula or invocation; a word or formula, often in Sanskrit, to be recited or sung for the purpose of intensifying the action of the *Spirit* of God in man. A form of prayer consisting of a word or a group of words that is chanted over and over again to magnetize a particular aspect of the Deity or of a being who has actualized that aspect of the Deity. See also *Decree*.

Manu. (Sanskrit.) The progenitor and lawgiver of the evolutions of God on earth. The Manu and his divine complement are *twin flames* assigned by the *Father-Mother God* to sponsor and ensoul the Christic image for a certain evolution or lifewave known as a root race—*souls* who embody as a group and have a unique archetypal pattern, divine plan and mission to fulfill on earth.

According to esoteric tradition, there are seven primary aggregations of souls—that is, the first to the seventh root races. The first three root races lived in purity and innocence upon earth in three golden ages before the fall of Adam and Eve. Through obedience to *Cosmic Law* and total identification with the *Real Self*, these three root races won their immortal freedom and ascended from earth.

It was during the time of the fourth root race, on the continent of Lemuria, that the allegorical Fall took place under the influence of the fallen *angels* known as Serpents (because they used the serpentine spinal energies to beguile the soul, or female principle in mankind, as a means to their end of lowering the masculine potential, thereby emasculating the Sons of God). The fourth, fifth and sixth root races (the latter soul group not having entirely descended into physical incarnation) remain in embodiment on earth today. Lord Himalaya and his beloved are the Manus for the fourth root race, Vaivasvata Manu and his consort are the Manus for the fifth root race, and the God and Goddess Meru are the Manus for the sixth root race. The seventh root race is destined to incarnate on the continent of South America in the Aquarian age under their Manus, the Great Divine Director and his divine complement.

Manvantara. (Sanskrit, from *manv,* used in compounds for *manu,* + *antara,* 'interval, period of time.') In Hinduism, the period or age of a *Manu,* consisting of 4,320,000 solar years; one of the fourteen intervals that constitute a *kalpa* (Sanskrit), a period of time covering a cosmic cycle from the origination to the destruction of a world system. In Hindu cosmology, the universe is continually evolving through periodic cycles of creation and dissolution. Creation is said to occur during the outbreath of the God of Creation, Brahma; dissolution occurs during his inbreath.

Mater. (Latin, 'mother.') See *Matter; Mother.*

Matter. The feminine (negative) polarity of the Godhead, of which the masculine (positive) polarity is Spirit. Matter acts as a chalice for the kingdom of God and is the abiding place of evolving *souls* who identify with their Lord, their *Holy Christ Self.* Matter is distinguished from matter (lowercase m)—the substance of the earth earthy, of the realms of maya, which blocks rather than radiates divine *light* and the Spirit of the *I AM THAT I AM.* See also *Mother; Spirit.*

Mental body. One of the *four lower bodies* of man, corresponding to the air element and the second quadrant of *Matter;* the body that is intended to be the vehicle, or vessel, for the Mind of God or the *Christ* Mind. "Let this [Universal] Mind be in you, which was also in Christ Jesus" (Phil. 2:5). Until quickened, this body remains the vehicle for the carnal mind, often called the lower mental body in contrast to the Higher Mental Body, a synonym for the *Christ Self* or *Christ* consciousness.

Messenger. Evangelist. One who goes before the *angels* bearing to the people of earth the good news of the gospel of Jesus Christ and, at the appointed time, the Everlasting Gospel. The Messengers of the *Great White Brotherhood* are anointed by the *hierarchy* as their apostles ("one sent on a mission"). They deliver through the *dictations* (prophecies) of the *Ascended Masters* the testimony and lost teachings of Jesus Christ in the power of the Holy Spirit to the seed of *Christ,* the lost sheep of the house of Israel, and to every nation. A Messenger is one who is trained by an Ascended Master to receive by various methods the words, concepts, teachings and messages of the Great White Brotherhood; one who delivers the law, the prophecies, and the dispensations of God for a people and an age.

Microcosm. (Greek, 'small world.') (1) The world of the individual, his *four lower bodies,* his aura, and the forcefield of his karma. (2) The planet. See also *Macrocosm.*

Mother. "Divine Mother," "Universal Mother" and "Cosmic Virgin" are alternate terms for the feminine polarity of the Godhead, the manifestation of God as Mother. *Matter* is the feminine polarity of *Spirit,* and the term is used interchangeably with Mater (Latin, 'mother'). In this context, the entire material cosmos becomes the womb of creation into which Spirit projects the energies of life. Matter, then, is the womb of the Cosmic Virgin, who, as the other half of the Divine Whole, also exists in Spirit as the spiritual polarity of God.

Nirvana. The goal of life according to Hindu and Buddhist philosophy: the state of liberation from the wheel of rebirth through the extinction of desire.

OM (AUM). The Word; the sound symbol for ultimate Reality.

Omega. See *Alpha and Omega.*

Path. The strait gate and narrow way that leadeth unto life (Matt. 7:14). The path of initiation whereby the disciple who pursues the *Christ* consciousness overcomes step by step the limitations of selfhood in time and space and attains reunion with Reality through the ritual of the *ascension.*

Pearls of Wisdom. Weekly letters of instruction dictated by the *Ascended Masters* to their *Messengers* Mark L. Prophet and Elizabeth Clare Prophet for students of the sacred mysteries throughout the world. *Pearls of Wisdom* have been published by *The Summit Lighthouse* continuously since 1958. They contain both fundamental and advanced teachings on *Cosmic Law* with a practical application of spiritual truths to personal and planetary problems.

Physical body. The most dense of the *four lower bodies* of man, corresponding to the earth element and the fourth quadrant of *Matter.* The physical body is the vehicle for the *soul's* sojourn on earth and the focus for the crystallization in form of the energies of the *etheric, mental* and *emotional bodies.*

Rays. Beams of *light* or other radiant energy. The light emanations of the Godhead that, when invoked in the name of God or in the name of the *Christ,* burst forth as a flame in the world of the individual. Rays may be projected by the God consciousness of ascended or unascended beings through the *chakras* and the third eye as a concentration of energy taking on numerous God-qualities, such as love, truth, wisdom, healing and so on. Through the misuse of God's energy, practitioners of black magic project rays having negative qualities, such as death rays, sleep rays, hypnotic rays, disease rays, psychotronic rays, the evil eye and so on. See also *Seven rays.*

Real Self. The *Christ Self;* the *I AM Presence;* immortal *Spirit* that is the animating principle of all manifestation. See also *Chart of Your Divine Self.*

Reembodiment. The rebirth of a *soul* in a new human body. The soul continues to return to the physical plane in a new body temple until she balances her karma, attains self-mastery, overcomes the cycles of time and space, and finally reunites with the *I AM Presence* through the ritual of the *ascension.*

Retreat. A focus of the *Great White Brotherhood,* usually on the *etheric plane* where the *Ascended Masters* preside. Retreats anchor one or more flames of the Godhead as well as the momentum of the Masters' service and attainment for the balance of *light* in the *four lower bodies* of a planet and its evolutions. Retreats serve many functions for the councils of the *hierarchy* ministering to the lifewaves of earth. Some retreats are open to unascended mankind, whose *souls* may journey to these focuses in their *etheric body* between their incarnations on earth and in their finer bodies during sleep or *samadhi.*

Root race. See *Manu.*

Sacred fire. The Kundalini fire that lies as the coiled serpent in the base-of-the-spine *chakra* and rises through spiritual purity and self-mastery to the crown chakra, quickening the spiritual centers on the way. God, *light,* life, energy, the *I AM THAT I AM.* "Our God is a consuming fire" (Heb. 12:29). The sacred fire is the precipitation of the Holy Ghost for the baptism of souls, for purification, for alchemy and transmutation, and for the realization of the *ascension,* the sacred ritual whereby the *soul* returns to the One.

Samadhi. Deep spiritual meditation; absorption in God; the many stages of union with God.

Sanat Kumara. (From the Sanskrit, 'always a youth.') Great *Guru* of the seed of *Christ* throughout cosmos; hierarch of Venus; the Ancient of Days spoken of in Daniel 7. Long ago he came to earth in her darkest hour when all light had gone out in her evolutions, for there was not a single individual on the planet who gave adoration to the God Presence. Sanat Kumara and the band of 144,000 souls of light who accompanied him volunteered to keep the flame of life on behalf of earth's people. This they vowed to do until the children of God would respond to the love of God and turn once again to serve their Mighty *I AM Presence.* Sanat Kumara's retreat, Shamballa, was established on an island in the Gobi Sea, now the Gobi Desert. The first to respond to his flame was Gautama *Buddha*, followed by Lord Maitreya and Jesus. See also *Lord of the World.*

Seamless garment. Body of *light* beginning in the heart of the *I AM Presence* and descending around the *crystal cord* to envelop the individual in the vital currents of the *ascension* as he invokes the holy energies of the Father for the return home to God. Also known as the deathless solar body.

Secret chamber of the heart. The sanctuary of meditation behind the heart *chakra,* the place to which the *souls* of lightbearers withdraw. It is the nucleus of life where the individual stands face to face with the inner *Guru,* the beloved *Holy Christ Self,* and receives the soul testings that precede the alchemical union with that Holy Christ Self—the marriage of the soul to the Lamb.

Seed Atom. The focus of the Divine *Mother* (the feminine ray of the Godhead) that anchors the energies of *Spirit* in *Matter* at the base-of-the-spine *chakra.* See also *Sacred fire.*

Seven rays. The *light* emanations of the Godhead; the seven *rays* of the white light that emerge through the prism of the *Christ* consciousness.

Siddhis. Spiritual powers such as levitation, stopping the heartbeat, clairvoyance, clairaudience, materialization and bilocation. The cultivation of siddhis for their own sake is often cautioned against by spiritual teachers.

Solar Logoi. *Cosmic Beings* who transmit the *light* emanations of the Godhead flowing from *Alpha and Omega* in the *Great Central Sun* to the planetary systems. Also called Solar Lords.

Soul. God is a *Spirit,* and the soul is the living potential of God. The soul's demand for free will and her separation from God resulted in the descent of this potential into the lowly estate of the flesh. Sown in dishonor, the soul is destined to be raised in honor to the fullness of that God-estate which is the one Spirit of all life. The soul can be lost; Spirit can never die.

The soul remains a fallen potential that must be imbued

with the reality of Spirit, purified through prayer and supplication, and returned to the glory from which it descended and to the unity of the Whole. This rejoining of soul to Spirit is the *alchemical marriage* that determines the destiny of the self and makes it one with immortal Truth. When this ritual is fulfilled, the highest Self is enthroned as the Lord of Life and the potential of God, realized in man, is found to be the All-in-all.

Spirit. The masculine polarity of the Godhead; the coordinate of *Matter;* God as Father, who of necessity includes within the polarity of himself God as *Mother* and hence is known as the *Father-Mother God.* The plane of the *I AM Presence,* of perfection; the dwelling place of the *Ascended Masters* in the kingdom of God. (When lowercased, as in "spirits," the term is synonymous with discarnates, or astral *entities;* "spirit," singular and lowercased, is used interchangeably with soul.)

Spoken Word. The *Word* of the LORD God released in the original fiats of Creation. The release of the energies of the Word, or the *Logos,* through the throat *chakra* by the Sons of God in confirmation of that lost Word. It is written, "By thy words thou shalt be justified, and by thy words thou shalt be condemned" (Matt. 12:37). Today disciples use the power of the Word in *decrees,* affirmations, prayers and *mantras* to draw the essence of the *sacred fire* from the *I AM Presence,* the *Christ Self* and *Cosmic Beings* to channel God's *light* into matrices of transmutation and transformation for constructive change in the planes of *Matter.*

The Summit Lighthouse. An outer organization of the *Great White Brotherhood* founded by Mark L. Prophet in 1958 in Washington, D.C., under the direction of the *Ascended Master* El Morya, Chief of the Darjeeling Council, for the purpose of publishing and disseminating the teachings of the Ascended Masters.

Threefold flame. The flame of the *Christ,* the spark of life that burns within the *secret chamber of the heart* (a secondary *chakra* behind the heart). The sacred trinity of power, wisdom and love that is the manifestation of the *sacred fire.* See also *Chart of Your Divine Self;* color illustration facing page 44.

Transfiguration. An initiation on the path of the *ascension* that takes place when the initiate has attained a certain balance and expansion of the *threefold flame*. Jesus' transfiguration is described in Matthew 17:1–8.

Tube of light. The white *light* that descends from the heart of the *I AM Presence* in answer to the call of man as a shield of protection for his *four lower bodies* and his *soul* evolution. See also *Chart of Your Divine Self*; color illustration facing page 44.

Twelve Hierarchies of the Sun. Twelve mandalas of *Cosmic Beings* ensouling twelve facets of God's consciousness, who hold the pattern of that frequency for the entire cosmos. They are identified by the names of the signs of the zodiac, as they focus their energies through these constellations. Also called the twelve solar hierarchies. See also *Cosmic Clock*.

Twin flame. The *soul's* masculine or feminine counterpart conceived out of the same white fire body, the fiery ovoid of the *I AM Presence*.

Unascended master. One who has overcome all limitations of *Matter* yet chooses to remain in time and space to focus the consciousness of God for lesser evolutions. See also *Bodhisattva*.

Universal Christ. The Mediator between the planes of *Spirit* and the planes of *Matter*. Personified as the *Christ Self*, he is the Mediator between the Spirit of God and the *soul* of man. The Universal Christ sustains the nexus of (the figure-eight flow of) consciousness through which the energies of the Father (Spirit) pass to his children for the crystallization (*Christ*-realization) of the God Flame by their soul's strivings in the cosmic womb (matrix) of the *Mother* (Matter).

Violet flame. Seventh-ray aspect of the Holy Spirit. The *sacred fire* that transmutes the cause, effect, record and memory of sin, or negative karma. Also called the flame of transmutation, of freedom and of forgiveness. See also *Decree; Chart of Your Divine Self*; color illustration facing page 44.

Word. The Word is the *Logos*: it is the power of God and the realization of that power incarnate in and as the Christ. The energies of the Word are released by devotees of the Logos in the ritual of the science of the *spoken Word*. It is through the Word that the *Father-Mother God* communicates with mankind. The Christ is the personification of the Word. See also *Christ; Decree.*

World Teacher. Office in *hierarchy* held by those Ascended Beings whose attainment qualifies them to represent the universal and personal *Christ* to unascended mankind. The office of World Teacher, formerly held by Maitreya, was passed to Jesus and his disciple Saint Francis (Kuthumi) on January 1, 1956, when the mantle of *Lord of the World* was transferred from *Sanat Kumara* to Gautama *Buddha* and the office of *Cosmic Christ* and Planetary Buddha (formerly held by Gautama) was simultaneously filled by Lord Maitreya. Serving under Lord Maitreya, Jesus and Kuthumi are responsible in this cycle for setting forth the teachings leading to individual self-mastery and the *Christ* consciousness. They sponsor all *souls* seeking union with God, tutoring them in the fundamental laws governing the cause-effect sequences of their own karma and teaching them how to come to grips with the day-to-day challenges of their individual dharma, the duty to fulfill the Christ potential through the sacred labor.

Note from the Editor

I am so grateful to have worked on this volume of the Climb the Highest Mountain series, the Everlasting Gospel for the age of Aquarius.

Mark L. Prophet and Elizabeth Clare Prophet were and are twentieth-century prophets and true masters, interpreting God's mysteries in a way that all of us can understand. My years working with them were among the happiest of my life, and certainly some of the most productive.

It was they who explained to me the path to the ascension and told me that I can make it if I try. Walking in the footsteps of the Masters as explained in this book, you too can make it if you try!

As the Master El Morya says, "The trek upward is worth the inconvenience."

Annice Booth

Other Titles from
SUMMIT UNIVERSITY ⚬ PRESS®

Summit University Press books
are available at fine bookstores worldwide.

For More Information

Summit University Press books are available at
fine bookstores worldwide, including Barnes & Noble,
B. Dalton Bookseller, Borders, Hastings, Waldenbooks
and your favorite on-line bookstore.

If you would like a free catalog of Summit University
Press books, please contact Summit University Press,
PO Box 5000, Corwin Springs, MT 59030-5000 USA.
Telephone: 1-800-245-5445 (406-848-9500 outside the U.S.A.)
Fax: 1-800-221-8307 (406-848-9555 outside the U.S.A.)
Web site: www.summituniversitypress.com
E-mail: info@summituniversitypress.com

Mark L. Prophet and Elizabeth Clare Prophet are pioneers of modern spirituality. They are the authors of several best-selling books, such as *The Lost Years of Jesus,* *The Lost Teachings of Jesus, Saint Germain On Alchemy* and *Understanding Yourself.* Their books have been translated into twenty languages and are available in more than thirty countries.

The Prophets have also conducted seminars and workshops worldwide. Mark passed on in 1973 and Elizabeth has carried on their work.

Mrs. Prophet has been featured on NBC's "Ancient Prophecies" and has talked about her work on "Donahue," "Larry King Live!" "Nightline," "Sonya Live" and "CNN & Company."